D. H. LAWRENCE

SONS AND LOVERS

OUR BOOKS ON LITERATURE

D. H. Lawrence

SONS AND LOVERS

[Book includes Biography of Author, Textual Interpretations and Study Questions]

Aditya Nandwani
B.A. English (Hons) , Delhi University;
M.A. (English), IGNOU; Print Journalism (English) YMCA

ANMOL PUBLICATIONS PVT. LTD.
NEW DELHI - 110 002 (INDIA)

ANMOL PUBLICATIONS PVT. LTD.

H.O.: 4374/4B, Ansari Road, Darya Ganj,
New Delhi-110 002 (India)
Ph.: 23278000, 23261597

B.O.: No. 1015, Ist Main Road, BSK IIIrd Stage
IIIrd Phase, IIIrd Block
Bangalore - 560 085 (India)
Visit us at: www.anmolpublications.com

Sons and Lovers

First Published, 2009

PRINTED IN INDIA

Printed at Mehra Offset Press, Delhi.

Contents

Preface

D. H. Lawrence, criticized, censored and dismissed in his lifetime, now stands as one of the major imaginative novelists of the early twentieth-century.

David Herbert Richards Lawrence (11 September 1885 – 2 March 1930) was an English writer of the 20th century, whose prolific and diverse output included novels, short stories, poems, plays, essays, travel books, paintings, translations, literary criticism, and personal letters. His collected works represent an extended reflection upon the dehumanizing effects of modernity and industrialization. In them, Lawrence confronts issues relating to emotional health and vitality, spontaneity, sexuality, and human instinct.

Clear, vivid and convincing, introduction to the life and works of D. H. Lawrence, sets the reader firmly in the context of his times and outlines his life and intellectual background, and their effect on his writing, looks in detail at Lawrence's work, Sons and Lovers, examines Lawrence as a literary critic and covers important people and places in Lawrence's life and their effect on him.

The following book presents a critical approach to Lawrence Sons and Lovers useful for students of both graduate and postgraduate level. We thus look forward to your response and wish that book proves to be a useful study aid.

Author

Chapter 1

Introduction

Sons and Lovers is one of the landmark novels of the twentieth century. When it appeared in 1913, it was immediately recognized as the first great modern restatement of the oedipal drama, and it is now widely considered the major work of D. H. Lawrence's early period. This intensely autobiographical novel recounts the story of Paul Morel, a young artist growing to manhood in a British working-class family rife with conflict. The author's vivid evocation of the all-consuming nature of possessive love and sexual attraction makes this one of his most powerful novels.

For the critic Kate Millet, "Sons and Lovers is a great novel because it has the ring of something written from deeply felt experience. The past remembered, it conveys more of Lawrence's own knowledge of life than anything else he wrote. His other novels appear somehow artificial beside it."

As a twentieth century novelist, essayist, and poet, David Herbert Lawrence brought the subjects of sex, psychology, and religion to the forefront of literature. One of the most widely read novels of the twentieth century, Sons and Lovers, which Lawrence wrote in 1913, produces a sense of Bildungsroman1, where the novelist re-creates his own personal experiences through the protagonist in. Lawrence uses Paul Morel, the protagonist in Sons and Lovers, for this form of fiction. With his mother of critical importance, Lawrence uses Freud's Oedipus complex, creating many analyses for critics. Alfred Booth Kuttner states the Oedipus complex as: "the struggle of a man to emancipate himself from his maternal allegiance and to transfer his affections to a woman who stands outside the family circle". Paul's compromising situations with Miram Leivers and Clara Dawes, as well as the death of his mother, display the Oedipus complex throughout Sons and Lovers. At an adolescent age, Paul's oedipal love towards his mother is compromised by a young lady named Miram Leivers.

This profound situation puts Paul to the emotional test of Oedipal versus physical love. As Kuttner goes on to state: "Paul's admiration for his mother know no bounds; her presence is always absorbing. Often at the sight of her, 'his heart contracts with love'". Paul's maternal relationship defines the Oedipus complex. Miram pulls Paul away from his mother, while Paul's mother, Gertrude, sees Miram as a threat to her son. Paul, even though Miram is around, still will not commit totally to her because of the strong ties between mother and son. Paul says to his mother, "I'll never marry while I've got you – I won't...".

Lawrence wrote frequently of Paul's love belonging to his mother and only his mother. Though Miram Leivers could not truly find Paul's heart, another woman named Clara Dawes provides more stress on Paul's maternal relationship. Although Paul loved Clara, he still kept his attraction toward his mother. "Everything he does is for her, the flowers he picks as well as the prizes he wins at school. His mother is his intimate and his confidant".

Clara tried desperately to win Paul over, but her social sophistication was too much for him. Paul tells his mother: "I don't want to belong to the well-to-do middle class. I like my common people the best. I belong to the common people". Clara shows frustration with Paul because of his maternal devotion. Again Lawrence displays the Oedipus complex through Paul to his mother, "And I shall never meet the right woman as long as you live".

Paul's oedipal love would be tested once more by him dealing with the death of his mother. Paul, though, was tough enough in handling this dilemma. R.P. Draper recognizes the loss of Paul's mother as: Their special, private, intimate grief over the impossible dream, and the magnificence of the woman, and the devotional quality of Paul's love, render the deathbed scenes poignant and innocent.

The verification of Kuttner's statement is seen as Lawrence has Paul react to her death in this manner: "my love – my love – oh, my love! My love – oh, my love!". Lawrence also writes of Paul's continuing love for his mother: "Looking at her, he felt he could never, never let her go. No!". Kuttner Implies: "But death has not freed Paul from his mother. It has completed his allegiance to her. For death has merely removed the last earthly obstacle to their ideal union".

The love that Paul feels towards his mother would never die. He loves her just as much when she died as he did when she was still alive. Paul continues life having a maternal devotion that no other woman would ever be able to fill. Throughout the novel, Paul is seen as one who lives for his mother. Mark Spilka explains: "For if Paul has failed in his three loves, he has drawn from them the necessary strength to live". Sons and Lovers were written with Lawrence almost defining the Oedipus complex through Paul. With this in mind, Kuttner gives this insight about the novel: Sons and Lovers possess this double quality to a high degree. It ranks high, very high as a piece of literature and at the same time embodies a theory which it illustrates and exemplifies with a completeness that is nothing less than astonishing. Psychologists of today still accept the Oedipus complex as a viable explanation for the love and fascination that male children display towards their mothers.

Lawrence successfully created an educational novel as well as an easily readable and interesting novel. Literary critics tend to speculate that Sons and Lovers were written by Lawrence as somewhat of an autobiography centreing Paul's life around his own. Whether or not this is true will never be determined, though it will continue to remain a favourite topic for critical analysis for years to come.

Chapter 2

D. H. Lawrence: Biography

David Herbert Richards Lawrence (11 September, 1885 – 2 March, 1930) was a very important and controversial English writer of the 20th century, whose prolific and diverse output included novels, short stories, poems, plays, essays, travel books, paintings, translations, literary criticism, and personal letters. His collected works represent an extended reflection upon the dehumanizing effects of modernity and industrialization. In them, Lawrence confronts issues relating to emotional health and vitality, spontaneity, sexuality, and instinctive behaviour.

Lawrence's unsettling opinions earned him many enemies and he endured hardships, official persecution, censorship, and misrepresentation of his creative work throughout the second half of his life, much of which he spent in a voluntary exile he called his "savage pilgrimage." At the time of his death, his public reputation was that of a pornographer who had wasted his considerable talents. E. M. Forster, in an obituary notice, challenged this widely held view, describing him as "the greatest imaginative novelist of our generation."

Later, the influential Cambridge critic F. R. Leavis championed both his artistic integrity and his moral seriousness, placing much of Lawrence's fiction within the canonical "great tradition" of the English novel. He is now generally valued as a visionary thinker and a significant representative of modernism in English literature, although some feminists object to the attitudes toward women and sexuality found in his works.

LIFE

Early Life (1885-1912)

The fourth child of Arthur John Lawrence, a barely literate miner, and Lydia, née Beardsall, a former schoolmistress, David Herbert Richards Lawrence was born on September 11, 1885, and spent his formative years in the coal mining town of Eastwood, Nottinghamshire, United Kingdom. His birthplace, in Eastwood, 8a Victoria Street, is now a museum. His working class background and the tensions between his mismatched parents provided the raw material for a number of his early works and Lawrence would return to this locality, which he was to call "the country of my heart," as a setting for much of his fiction.

The young Lawrence attended Beauvale Board School from 1891 until 1898, becoming the first local pupil to win a County Council scholarship to Nottingham High School in nearby Nottingham. He left in 1901, working for three months as a junior clerk at Haywood's surgical appliances factory before a severe bout of pneumonia ended this career. Whilst convalescing he often visited Haggs Farm, the home of the Chambers family and began a friendship with Jessie Chambers.

An important aspect of this relationship with Jessie and other adolescent acquaintances was a shared love of books, an interest that lasted throughout Lawrence's life. In the years 1902 to 1906 Lawrence served as a pupil teacher at the British School, Eastwood. He went on to become a full-time student and received a teaching certificate from University College Nottingham in 1908. During these early years he was working on his first poems, some short stories, and a draft of a novel, *Laetitia* that was eventually to become *The White Peacock.* At the end of 1907 he won a short story competition in the *Nottingham Guardian*, the first time that he had gained any wider recognition for his literary talents.

In the autumn of 1908 the newly qualified Lawrence left his childhood home for London. Whilst teaching in Davidson Road School, Croydon he continued writing. Some of the early poetry, submitted by Jessie Chambers, came to the attention of Ford Maddox Huffier, editor of the influential *The English Review*. Huffier then commissioned the story *Odor of Chrysanthemums* which, when published in that magazine, encouraged Heinemann, a London publisher, to ask Lawrence for more work.

His career as a professional author now began in earnest, although he taught for a further year. Shortly after the final proofs of his first published novel *The White Peacock* appeared in 1910, Lawrence's mother died. She had been ill with cancer. The young man was devastated and he was to describe the next few months as his "sick year." It is clear that Lawrence had an extremely close relationship with his mother and his grief following her death became a major turning point in his life, just as the death of Mrs. Morel forms a major turning point in his autobiographical novel *Sons and Lovers*, a work that faithfully records much of the writer's provincial upbringing.

In 1911 Lawrence was introduced to Edward Garnett, a publisher's reader, who acted as a mentor, provided further encouragement, and became a valued friend. Throughout these months the young author revised *Paul Morel*, the first sketch of what was to become *Sons and Lovers*. In addition, a teaching colleague, Helen Corke, gave him access to her intimate diaries about an unhappy love affair, which formed the basis of *The Trespasser*, his second novel. In November 1911 pneumonia struck once again. After recovering his health Lawrence decided to abandon teaching in order to become a full time author. He also broke off an engagement to Louie Burrows, an old friend from his days in Nottingham and Eastwood.

Blithe Spirits (1912-1914)

In March 1912 the author met the free spirited woman with whom he was to share the rest of his life. She was six

The Rainbow (1915) was suppressed after an investigation into its alleged obscenity in 1915. Later, they were even accused of spying and signaling to German submarines off of the coast of Cornwall where they lived at Zennor. During this period he finished a sequel to *The Rainbow* that many regard as his masterpiece.

This radical new work, *Women in Love*, is a key text of European modernism. In it Lawrence explores the destructive features of contemporary civilization through the evolving relationships of four major characters as they reflect upon the value of the arts, politics, economics, sexual experience, friendship and marriage. This book is a bleak, bitter vision of humanity and proved impossible to publish in wartime conditions. It is now widely recognized as an English novel of great dramatic force and intellectual subtlety.

In late 1917, after constant harassment by the military authorities, Lawrence was forced to leave Cornwall at three days' notice under the terms of the Defence of the Realm Act (DORA). This persecution was later described in an autobiographical chapter of his Australian novel, *Kangaroo*, published in 1923. He spent some months in early 1918 in the small, beautiful rural village of Hermitage near Newbury in Berkshire. He then lived for just under a year (mid-1918 to early 1919) at Mountain Cottage, Middleton-by-Wirksworth, Derbyshire, where he wrote one of his most poetic short stories, *The Wintry Peacock*. Until 1919 he was compelled by poverty to shift from address to address and barely survived a severe attack of influenza.

The savage Pilgrimage Begins (1919-1922)

After the traumatic experience of the war years, Lawrence began what he termed his 'savage pilgrimage', a time of voluntary exile. He escaped from England at the earliest practical opportunity, to return only twice for brief visits, and with Frieda spent the remainder of his life travelling; settling down for only short periods. This wanderlust took him to Italy, years older than her new lover, married and with three youn children. Frieda Weekly *née* von Richthofen was then the wif of Lawrence's former modern languages professor fron Nottingham University, Ernest Weekly. Frieda was bored with her marriage and she had already had brief affairs with other lovers, including Otto Gross, a disciple of Freud. She now eloped with Lawrence to her parent's home in Metz, a garrison town in Germany near the disputed border with France.

Their stay here included Lawrence's first brush with militarism when he was arrested and accused of being a British spy, before being released following an intervention from Frieda's father. After this encounter Lawrence left for a small hamlet to the south of Munich where he was joined by Frieda for their "honeymoon," later memorialized in the series of love poems entitled *Look! We Have Come Through* (1917).

From Germany they walked southwards across the Alps to Italy, a journey that was recorded in the first of his brilliant travel books, a collection of linked essays entitled *Twilight in Italy* and the unfinished novel, *Mr Noon*. During his stay in Italy, Lawrence completed the final version of *Sons and Lovers* that, when published in 1913, was acknowledged to represent a vivid portrait of the realities of working class provincial life.

The couple returned to England in 1913 for a short visit. Lawrence now encountered and befriended John Middleton Murky, the critic, and the short story writer from New Zealand, Katherine Mansfield. Lawrence and Frieda soon went back to Italy, staying in a cottage in Fiascherino on the Gulf of Spezia. Here he started writing the first draft of a work of fiction that was to be transformed into two of his finest novels, *The Rainbow* and *Women in Love*. Eventually Frieda obtained her divorce. The couple returned to England at the outbreak of World War I and was married on the 13 July, 1914.

The Nightmare (1914-1919)

Frieda's German parentage and Lawrence's open contempt for militarism meant that they were viewed with suspicion in wartime England and lived in near destitution.

Ceylon (now called Sri Lanka), Australia, North America, and Mexico and after returning once more to Italy, southern France.

Lawrence abandoned England in November 1919 and headed south; first to the Abruzzi district in central Italy and then onwards to Capri and the Fontana Vecchia in Taormina, Sicily. From Sicily he made brief excursions to Sardinia, Monte Casino, Malta, Northern Italy, Austria and Southern Germany. Many of these places appeared in his writings. New novels included *The Lost Girl* (for which he won the James Tait Black Memorial Prize for fiction); *Aaron's rod* and the fragment entitled *Mr Noon* (the first part of which was published in the Phoenix anthology of his works, and the entirety in 1984). He experimented with shorter novels or novellas, such as *The Captain's Doll, The Fox* and *The Ladybird*. In addition, some of his short stories were issued in the collection *England, My England and Other Stories.*

During these years he produced a number of poems about the natural world in *Birds, Beasts and Flowers.* Lawrence is widely recognized as one of the finest travel writers in the English language and *Sea and Sardinia,* a book that describes a brief journey from Taormina undertaken in January 1921, is a vivid recreation of the life of the inhabitants of this part of the Mediterranean. Less well known is the brilliant memoir of Maurice Magnus, in which Lawrence recalls his visit to the monastery of Monte Casino. Other non-fiction books include two studies of Freudian psychoanalysis and *Movements in European History,* a school textbook that was published under a pseudonym, a reflection of his blighted reputation in England.

Seeking a New World (1922-1925)

In late February 1922 the Lawrence's left Europe behind with the intention of migrating to the United States. They sailed in an easterly direction, first to Ceylon and then on to Australia. A short residence in Darlington, Western Australia, which included an encounter with local writer Mollie Skinner, was followed by a brief stop in the small coastal town of Thirroul in New South Wales, during which Lawrence completed *Kangaroo,* a novel about local fringe politics that also revealed a lot about his wartime experiences in Cornwall.

Resuming their journey, Frieda and Lawrence finally arrived in the USA in September 1922. Here they encountered Mabel Dodge Luhan, a prominent socialite, and considered establishing a utopian community on what was then known as the 160-acre Kiowa Ranch near Taos, New Mexico. Lawrence and Frieda acquired the property, now called the D. H. Lawrence Ranch, in 1924 in exchange for the manuscript of *Sons and Lovers.* By all accounts Lawrence loved this ranch high up in the mountains, the only home that he ever owned. He stayed in New Mexico for two years, with extended visits to Lake Chapel and Oaxaca in Mexico.

Whilst in the New World, Lawrence rewrote and published his *Studies in Classic American Literature,* a set of critical essays begun in 1917, and later described by Edmund Wilson as "one of the few first-rate books that have ever been written on the subject." These provocative and original interpretations, with their insights into symbolism, New England Transcendentalism and the puritan sensibility, were a significant factor in the revival of the reputation of Herman Melville during the early 1920s. In addition, Lawrence completed a number of new fictional works, including *The Boy in the Bush, The Plumed Serpent, St Mawr, The Woman who Rode Away, The Princess* and assorted short stories. He also found time to produce some more travel writing, such as the collection of linked excursions that became *Mornings in Mexico.*

A brief voyage to England at the end of 1923 was a failure and he soon returned to Taos, convinced that his life as an author now lay in America. However, in March 1925 he suffered a near fatal attack of malaria and tuberculosis whilst on a third visit to Mexico. Although he eventually recovered, the diagnosis of his condition obliged him to return once again to Europe. He was dangerously ill and poor health limited his ability to travel for the remainder of his life.

Approaching Death (1925-1930)

Lawrence and Frieda made their home in a villa in Northern Italy, living near to Florence whilst he wrote *The Virgin and the Gipsy* and the various versions of *Lady Chatterley's Lover* (1928). This book, his last major novel, was initially published in private editions in Florence and Paris and reinforced his notoriety. Lawrence responded robustly to those who claimed to be offended, penning a large number of satirical poems, published under the title of *"Pansies"* and *"Nettles"*, as well as a tract on *Pornography and Obscenity.*

The return to Italy allowed Lawrence to renew some of his old friendships and during these years he was particularly close to Aldous Huxley, a loyal companion who was to edit the first collection of Lawrence's letters after his death, along with a generous memoir. With another friend, the artist Earl Brewster, Lawrence found the time to visit a number of local archaeological sites in April 1927. The resulting essays describing these visits to old tombs were written up and collected together as *Sketches of Etruscan Places,* a beautiful book that contrasts the lively past with Mussolini's fascism.

Lawrence continued to produce fiction, including short stories and *The Escaped Cock* (also published as *The Man Who Died*), an unorthodox reworking of the Christian belief of the resurrection that affirms the life of the body. During these final years Lawrence renewed a serious interest in oil painting. Official harassment persisted and an exhibition of some of these pictures at the Warren Gallery in London was raided by the British police in mid 1929 and a number of works were confiscated. Nine of the Lawrence oils have been on permanent display in the La Fonda Hotel in Taos since shortly after his death. They hang in a small office behind the hotel's front desk and are available for viewing.

He continued to write despite his physical frailty. In his last months he authored numerous poems, reviews, essays, and a robust defence of his last novel against those who sought to suppress it. His last significant work was a spirited reflection on the New Testament Book of Revelation, *Apocalypse*. After being discharged from a sanatorium he died at the Villa Roberson, Vance, France in 1930 at the age of 44 due to complications from Tuberculosis. Frieda returned to live on the ranch in Taos and later her third husband brought Lawrence's ashes to rest there in a small chapel set amidst the mountains of New Mexico.

Sexuality

Despite his marriage to Frieda, it was during the years in which *Women in Love* was being written that Lawrence developed a sexual relationship, in the town of Tregerthen, with a Cornish farmer by the name of William Henry Hocking. The affair, brief though it was, seems to indicate that Lawrence's fascination with themes of homosexuality, which he would explore further in *Women in Love* and *Aaron's rod* especially, related to his own, personal sexuality. Indeed, in a letter written during 1913, he writes, "I should like to know why nearly every man that approaches greatness tends to homosexuality, whether he admits it or not..." He is also quoted as saying, "I believe the nearest I've come to perfect love was with a young coal-miner when I was about sixteen."

Posthumous Reputation

The obituaries following Lawrence's death were, with the notable exception of E. M. Forster, unsympathetic, ill-informed or hostile. Fortunately there were those who articulated a more balanced recognition of the significance of this author's life and works. For example, his longtime friend Catherine Creswell summed up his life in a letter to the periodical *Time and Tide* published on 16 March 1930. In response to his mean-spirited critics she claimed:

In the face of formidable initial disadvantages and life-long delicacy, poverty that lasted for three quarters of his life and hostility that survives his death, he did nothing that he did not really want to do, and all that he most wanted to do he did. He went all over the world, he owned a ranch, he lived in the most beautiful corners of Europe, and met whom he wanted to meet and told them that they were wrong and he was right. He painted and made things, and sang, and rode. He wrote something like three dozen books, of which even the worst page dances with life that could be mistaken for no other man's, while the best are admitted, even by those who hate him, to be unsurpassed.

Without vices, with most human virtues, the husband of one wife, scrupulously honest, this estimable citizen yet managed to keep free from the shackles of civilization and the cant of literary cliques. He would have laughed lightly and cursed venomously in passing at the solemn owls — each one secretly chained by the leg — who now conduct his inquest. To do his work and lead his life in spite of them took some doing, but he did it, and long after they are forgotten, sensitive and innocent people — if any are left — will turn Lawrence's pages and will know from them what sort of a rare man Lawrence was.

A defence of Lawrence was also put forward by Aldous Huxley in his introduction to a collection of letters published in 1932. However, the most influential advocate of Lawrence's contribution to literature was the Cambridge literary critic F. R. Leavis who asserted that the author had made an important contribution to the tradition of English fiction. Leavis stressed that *The Rainbow, Women in Love,* and the short stories and tales were major works of art. Later, the Lady Chatterley Trial of 1960, and subsequent publication of the book, ensured Lawrence's popularity (and notoriety) with a wider public.

Some modern critics, including Lawrence biographer Brenda Maddox, have charged that Lawrence was over-prolific, and that his reputation was harmed by the amount of simply bad writing that he published; however, Lawrence made his living exclusively by his writing, and as a result wrote more commercial work than modernists such as Joyce or Woolf.

A number of feminist critics, notably Kate Millet, have questioned Lawrence's sexual politics, and this questioning has damaged his reputation in some quarters since then. On the other hand, Lawrence continues to find an audience for his artistic vision, and the ongoing publication of a new scholarly edition of his letters and writings has demonstrated the range of his achievement.

Also, in the classic film Easy Rider, Jack Nicholson's character makes a toast to Lawrence in the scene outside the jail house.

LIST OF LAWRENCE'S WRITINGS

Novels

- *The White Peacock* (1911), edited by Andrew Robertson, Cambridge University Press, 1983,
- *The Trespasser* (1912), edited by Elizabeth Mansfield, Cambridge University Press,1981,
- *Sons and Lovers* (1913), edited by Helen Baron and Carl Baron, Cambridge University Press, 1992,
- *The Rainbow* (1915), edited by Mark Kinkead-Weekes, Cambridge University Press, 1989,
- *Women in Love* (1920), edited by David Farmer, Lindeth Vasey and John Worthen, Cambridge University Press, 1987,
- *The Lost Girl* (1920), edited by John Worthen, Cambridge University Press, 1981,
- *Aaron's Rod* (1922) edited by Mara Kalnins, Cambridge University Press, 1988, *Kangaroo* (1923) edited by Bruce Steele, Cambridge University Press, 1994,
- *The Boy in the Bush* (1924), edited by Paul Eggert, Cambridge University Press,

- *The Plumed Serpent* (1926), edited by L.D. Clark, Cambridge University Press, *Lady Chatterley's Lover* (1928), edited by Michael Squires, Cambridge University
- *The Escaped Cock* (1929) (later re-published as *The Man Who Died*)
- *The Virgin and the Gypsy* (1930)

Short Stories

- *The Prussian Officer and Other Stories* (1914), edited by John Worthen, Cambridge University Press, 1983,
- *England, My England and Other Stories* (1922), edited by Bruce Steele, Cambridge University Press, 1990,
- *The Fox, The Captain's Doll, The Ladybird* (1923), edited by Dieter Mehl, Cambridge University Press, 1992,
- *St Mawr and other stories* (1925), edited by Brian Finney, Cambridge University Press, 1983,
- *The Woman who Rode Away and other stories* (1928) edited by Dieter Mehl and Christa Jansohn, Cambridge University Press, 1995,
- *The Virgin and the Gipsy and Other Stories* (1930), edited by Michael Herbert, Bethan Jones, Lindeth Vasey, Cambridge University Press, 2006 (forthcoming),
- *Love Among the Haystacks and other stories* (1930), edited by John Worthen, Cambridge University Press, 1987,
- *Collected Stories* (1994) - Everyman's Library, a comprehensive one volume edition that prints all sixty two of Lawrence's shorter fictions in chronological sequence
- *The Rocking-Horse Winner* (1926)
- *The Horse Dealer's Daughter* (1922)

Poetry

- *Love Poems and others* (1913)
- *Amores* (1916)
- *Look! We have come through!* (1917)
- *New Poems* (1918)
- *Bay: a book of poems* (1919)
- *Tortoises* (1921)
- *Birds, Beasts and Flowers* (1923)
- *The Collected Poems of D H Lawrence* (1928)
- *Pansies* (1929)
- *Nettles* (1930)
- *Last Poems* (1932)
- *Fire and other poems* (1940)
- *The Complete Poems of D H Lawrence* (1964), ed. Vivian de Sola Pinto and F. Warren Roberts

Plays

- *The Widowing of Mrs Holroyd* (1914)
- *Touch and Go* (1920)
- *David* (1926)
- *The Fight for Barbara* (1933)
- *A Collier's Friday Night* (1934)
- *The Married Man* (1940)
- *The Merry-go-round* (1941)
- *The Complete Plays of D H Lawrence* (1965)
- *The Plays*, edited by Hans-Wilhelm Schwarze and John Worthen, Cambridge University Press, 1999,

Non-fiction

- *Study of Thomas Hardy and other essays* (1914), edited by Bruce Steele, Cambridge University Press, 1985, Literary criticism and metaphysics

- *Movements in European History* (1921), edited by Philip Crumpton, Cambridge University Press, 1989, Originally published under the name of Lawrence H. Davison
- *Psychoanalysis and the Unconscious* and *Fantasia of the Unconscious* (1921/1922), edited by Bruce Steele, Cambridge University Press, 2004
- *Studies in Classic American Literature* (1923), edited by Ezra Greenspan, Lindeth Vasey and John Worthen, Cambridge University Press, 2003,
- *Reflections on the Death of a Porcupine and other essays* (1925), edited by Michael Herbert, Cambridge University Press, 1988,
- *A Propos of Lady Chatterley's Lover*(1929) - Lawrence wrote this pamphlet to explain his most notorious novel
- *Apocalypse and the writings on Revelation* (1931) edited by Mara Kalnins, Cambridge University Press, 1980,, His last book touching on primitive symbolism, paganism and pre-Christian religion
- *Phoenix: the posthumous papers of D H Lawrence* (1936)
- *Phoenix II: uncollected, unpublished and other prose works by D H Lawrence* (1968)
- *Introductions and Reviews*, edited by N. H. Reeve and John Worthen, Cambridge University Press, 2004,
- *Late Essays and Articles*, edited by James T. Boulton, Cambridge University Press, 2004,

Travel Books

- *Twilight in Italy and Other Essays* (1916), edited by Paul Eggert, Cambridge University Press, 1994,
- *Sea and Sardinia* (1921), edited by Mara Kalnins, Cambridge University Press, 1997,
- *Mornings in Mexico* (1927)
- *Sketches of Etruscan Places and other Italian essays* (1932), edited by Simonetta de Filippis, Cambridge University Press, 1992,

Works Translated by Lawrence

- Lev Isaakovich Shestov *All Things are Possible* (1920)
- Ivan Alekseyevich Bunin *The Gentleman from San Francisco* (1922), tr. with S. S. Koteliansky
- Giovanni Verga *Maestro-Don Gesualdo* (1923)
- Giovanni Verga *Little Novels of Sicily* (1925)
- Giovanni Verga *Cavalleria Rusticana and other stories* (1928)
- Antonio Francesco Grazzini *The Story of Doctor Manente* (1929)

Chapter 3

Introduction: Oedipus Complex

Description

In the Oedipus complex, a boy is fixated on his mother and competes with his father for maternal attention.

The opposite, the attraction of a girl to her father and rivalry with her mother, is sometimes called the Electra complex.

Sexual Awakening

At some point, the child realises that there is a difference between their mother and their father. Around the same time they realise that they are more alike to one than the other. Thus the child acquires gender.

The child may also form some kind of erotic attachment to the parent of the opposite sex. Whilst their understanding of the full sexual act may be questioned, some kind of primitive physical sensations are felt when they regard and think about the parent in question.

Jealousies

The primitive desire for the one parent may also awaken in the child a jealous motivation to exclude the other parent.

Transferring of affections may also occur as the child seeks to become independent and escape a perceived 'engulfing mother'.

A critical point of awakening is where the child realises that the mother has affections for others besides itself.

Primitive jealousies are not necessarily constrained to the child and both parents may join in the game, both in terms of competing with each other for the child's affections and also competing with the child for the affection of the other parent.

Note that opposition to parents may not necessarily be sexually based — this can also be a part of the struggle to assert one's identity and rebellion against parental control.

The Process of Transitioning

A critical aspect of the Oedipal stage is loosening of the ties to the mother of vulnerability, dependence and intimacy. This is a natural part of the child becoming more independent and is facilitated by the realization that the mother desires more than just the child.

The Oedipal move blocks the routes of sexual and identification love back to the mother. She becomes a separate object, removed from his ideal self. Thus she can be the subject of object love.

This separation and externalization of love allows a transition away from narcissism of earlier stages.

The father's role in this is much debated. In a number of accounts, such as Lacan's symbolic register, the child transitions their attentions from mother to father.

The father effectively says 'You must be like me — you may not be like the mother — you must wait to love her, as I do.' The child thus also learns to wait and share attention.

Separation

The boy thus returns to the mother as a separate individual. That separation may be emphasized with scorn and a sense of mastery over women. that can also be seen in the long separation of boys and girls in play and social relationships. This is a source of male denigration of women.

Women become separated reminders of lost and forbidden unity. Their unique attributes, from softness to general femininity are, in consequence, also lost and must be given up as a part of the distancing process. Women become thus both desired and feared. The symbolic phallus becomes a means of protection for the boy and the rituals of mastery used to cover up feelings of loss.

Separation leads to unavailability and hence the scarcity principle takes effect, increasing desire. Women thus create a tension in boys between a lost paradise and dangerous sirens.

Excessive separation leads to a sense of helplessness that can in turn lead to patterns of idealized control and self-sufficiency.

Whilst the boy becomes separated from the mother, it is a long time before he can be independent of her and hence must develop a working relationship that may reflect the tension of love and difference he feels.

The relationship thus may return to a closer mother-son tie, where the point of healthy distance is a dynamically negotiated position, such that comforting is available but is required only upon occasion.

What about the Girls?

Most writings about the Oedipal stage focus largely or exclusively on boys, who are seen to have a particular problem as they start with an attachment to the Mother that they have to relinquish both from the point of view of individual independence and especially as a result of the social incest taboo which forbids excessively-close in-family relationships.

The Electra complex, identified by Carl Jung, occurs where a triangle of mother-father-daughter plays out is not a part of traditional psychoanalysis. It is neither a direct mirror image of Oedipus, as the start position is female-female connection.

Jung suggested that when the girl discovers she lacks penis that her father possesses, she imagines she will gain one if he makes her pregnant, and so moves emotionally closer to him. She thus resents her mother who she believe castrated her.

The father symbolizes attractive power and a potentially hazardous male-female relationship is formed, with predictable jealousies and envy as the mother completes the triangle. The dangers of incestuous abuse add, and perhaps develop, the female position of siren temptation.

Girls, as well as boys, need to find independence and their separation from the mother is a matter of creating a separate femininity. This is not as strong a separation as boys and girls can sustain a closer female-female relationships with the mothers. This perhaps explains something of why relationships with others is a more important part of a female life than it is for a male.

The father does provide a haven from female-female jealousies, and so a healthy father-daughter relationship may be built, that also includes appropriate distance. As with mother-son, once the incest taboos are established, a uniquely satisfying opposite-sex relationship can be built, although secret desires for the father can result in the girl feeling some guilt about the relationship.

Discussion

There are three common threads in the Oedipus complex: The primacy of the desire for one-ness, the maternal embodiment of this and the necessity of paternal intervention.

Historical Oedipus

In the Greek play by Sophocles, Laius, king of Thebes, is told by an oracle that he would be killed by his son and so leaves Oedipus out on the mountainside to die. Oedipus is rescued by a shepherd and taken to the king of Corinth who raises him as a son.

Oedipus, in turn, is told by the Delphic oracle that he will kill his father and marry his mother. Horrified by this, he flees Corinth. At a crossroads he meets Laius, quarrels and kills him.

At Thebes, he correctly answers the sphinx's question and hence wins the hand of Jocasta, his real mother, with whom he had two sons and two daughters. When at last the truth comes out, Jocasta hangs herself and Oedipus, finding her, blinds himself with her golden brooch.

Electra was the daughter of Agamemnon who helped plan the murder of her mother.

Freud

Freud puts the Oedipal stage as occurring between 3-5 years. He considers it a stage where the child experiences an erotic attachment to one parent and hostility toward the other parent. The ensuing triangular tension is seen as being the root of most mental disorders.

Freud cites the incest taboo as at the root of many other prohibitions. He sees the struggle against this as a core part of this development period with transgressions in practice and fantasy.

'We cannot get away from the assumption that man's sense of guilt springs from the Oedipus complex and was acquired at the killing of the father by the brothers banned together'. (Freud, 1930)

Freud links the Oedipus complex with development the superego, which uses guilt to prevent continuation of incestuously oriented relationships.

Failure to get past this trigger point and into the symbolic order is considered to be a classic cause of lasting neurosis.

Lacan

For Lacan, the mother is characterized by 'lack' of a phallus. The pre-Oedipal child tries to make good the lack. But the mother desires the phallus that will cover over her division in language. The child then realises its own lack, or 'castration' and seeks to speak or use words such that it can stand in for that which is missing.

The child can hence either speak itself from the position of 'having the phallus' or lacking it. Having a penis, boys are more likely to take the former position. However, taking this position requires living up to the god-like status of having the phallus.

Note that Lacan considered that the Oedipal stage can be successfully navigated without the father, as long as cultural norms and prohibitions can be met, as it is these, rather than the father himself which facilitates the way through

Rose

Jacqueline Rose uses Lacan to show how sexual identity is acquired through the Oedipus crisis, rather than being something innate.

Klein

Melanie Klein, through her work with young children, saw oedipal conflict occurring much earlier than Freud and involving part-objects rather than whole parent-figures, and including infantile sadism. How early this starts has been questioned including a consideration that some version of the Oedipal stage occurring almost from the very beginning, at least in fantasy. She see emotional and sexual development occurring:

'...from early infancy onwards includes genital sensations and trends, which constitute the first stages of the inverted [desire toward the same-sex parent and aggression toward opposite sex one] and positive Oedipus complex.' (Klein, 1945)

She places the Oedipal complex as occurring in the paranoid-schizoid position, where the infant's world is largely split and relations are mainly to part-objects. Thus the Oedipal stage involves working through the paranoid-schizoid position to the depressive position.

As well as the classic early Oedipus complex, Klein also identifies the Oedipal situation which occurs throughout life.

She saw how children realises a sexual link between parents at an early age, but perceives it through the infantile experience, thus conceiving of feeding one another, devouring one another, or even exchanging bodily excretions.

Bion

Wilfred Bion placed the Oedipus complex even earlier than Klein, hypothesizing an innate oedipal preconception.

He related pairing to the Oedipal stage and the importance of the family group. Early group setting are familial or kinship and these are used as later templates for group activity, and early anxieties may reappear.

Other notes

A common experience in families is that the opposite gender relationships of mother-son and father-daughter are stronger than same-sex relationships, where there may be intra-gender rivalries, for example where the daughter continues to compete with the mother for the father's attention. In most cases, the incest taboo holds and this is a relatively harmless attachment.

Oedipus represents responsibility and guilt, in contrast to Narcissus, who represents self-involvement and denial of reality. Oedipus is an escape from early fantasy of omnipotence.

The gender polarity that Oedipus creates is echoed in modern feminist concerns and male confusion as rights issues erode instinctive positions.

Moving away from the mother, for the boy, is also a part of instilling the incest taboo.

Chapter 4

Introduction to the Times

MODERNIST LITERATURE

Modernism

Despite the widespread homophobia in the Modernist movement, several of its practitioners were homosexual, some of them wrote openly about homosexuality, and the groundwork was laid for the gay liberation movement.

A major cultural and artistic movement dominating the Western world from approximately 1890 to 1940, depending on the country, modernism is now recognized as one of the most creative periods in human history, worthy of being discussed alongside Periclean Athens and the European Renaissance. No art was left untouched, and most were transformed by this international movement.

The Characteristics of Modernism

It is generally agreed that the movement was cross-disciplinary, dominated by its own myth of discontinuity, fully urban and technological in nature, extremely self-conscious in its avant-garde and experimental facets, and characterized by both an elitist sensibility and an egotistical valuing of the self.

These last two features offended many at the time and others ever since, even more so than did its insistent questioning of received values and conventions, its revolutionary manifestos, and its outright rejection of the weight of conservative conventions and mores that had been gathering force in Europe since the Congress of Vienna in 1815.

Moreover, as with Classical Athens and Renaissance Europe, much of the dynamism of modernism came from a deep pessimism and a fascination with irrational forces. As early as 1891, Thomas Hardy had labeled the new cultural restiveness "the ache of modernism," a label that became more and more appropriate as modernism reached its heights during the 1920s.

Modernism in the Arts

In music, the pounding rhythms of Igor Stravinsky and the atonalities of Arnold Schoenberg displaced the swelling melodies of Pyotr Ilyich Tchaikovsky.

In painting, the cubism of Pablo Picasso and the abstractions of Wassily Kandinsky displaced the perspectives, representational, and impressionism of Gustave Courbet, Pierre Auguste Renoir, Hilaire-Germain-Edgar Degas, and Edouard Manet.

In sculpture, the polished forms of Constantin Brancusi and the emaciated figures of Alberto Giacometti displaced the public monumentalize and realism of works such as George Grey Barnard's Struggle of the Two Natures in Man (1888-1894) and Sir Edwin Landseer's Trafalgar Square lions (1858-1863).

In literature, the experimentalism of James Joyce, Gertrude Stein, and Ernest Hemingway, the temporal fragmentations of Joseph Conrad, Ford Madox Ford, and T. S. Eliot, the interiority of the characters of Virginia Woolf, Marcel Proust, and Thomas Mann emphatically displaced the chronologically organized, plot-driven, social novels of the nineteenth century.

Repudiating the Past

Whatever the actualities, modernism perceived itself as warring against continuity, tradition, and a sense of the past. In many ways, modernism styled itself as an arrogant repudiation of the past: Filippio Marinetti, the leading Italian futurist, for instance, proposed that museums be utterly destroyed so that the new century could escape the burden of the past.

These displacements, however, did not occur without battles of one kind or another. The premiere of Stravinsky's Rite of Spring in Paris in 1912 quite literally led to a riot in the theater.

Homophobia Among the Modernists

At first, modernism as a historical period does not appear friendly to either homosexuals or lesbians. After all, modernism is bounded by the 1895 London trial of Oscar Wilde, with one London newspaper reporting that Wilde had been "charged with one of the most heinous crimes that can be alleged against a man—a crime too horrible and too revolting to be spoken of even by man" and ended with homosexuals wearing pink triangles joining millions of others who had been marked for extermination in the Nazi death camps.

And although lesbian behaviour was not proscribed in numerous countries at this time, the obscenity trial of Radclyffe Hall's The Well of Loneliness in London in 1928 came as a public condemnation of lesbianism.

These actions, moreover, were not merely retrograde battles mounted by the old culture; modernism itself had an ugly subtext of sexism, homophobia, antisemitism, and at times, fascism. A number of modernist voices condemned homosexuals and lesbians.

Ezra Pound placed a coarse homophobic statement in the twelfth of his Cantos, and Wyndham Lewis savagely caricatured the homosexuality of the Bloomsbury Group in his novel The Apes of God (1930). Numerous painters and writers, among them Marinetti, Pablo Picasso, and Marcel Duchamp, were hostile to homosexuality.

Among the English, conflicts between the heterosexual and the homosexual worlds may best be seen in D. H. Lawrence's Women in Love (1922), especially in the nude wrestling scene between Rupert Birkin and Gerald Crich, mirroring Lawrence's own troubled sexuality.

Even in Virginia Woolf's novels, one finds unfavourable portraits of lesbians, especially Doris Kilman in Mrs. Dalloway (1925); however, the homoeroticism in the same novel makes a much more complex statement about human sexuality than the mere presence of Miss Kilman indicates.

Modernism and the Roots of Gay and Lesbian Liberation

Despite modernist homophobia, however, a number of events established the ground on which later twentieth-century gays and lesbians would begin to demand liberation. At first, these came in the form of books: Richard von Krafft-Ebing's Psychopathia Sexualis (1886), which openly discussed homosexuality, and Havelock Ellis's Sexual Inversion (1897), which was one of the first books to treat homosexuality as "neither a disease nor a crime."

In 1899, Magnus Hirschfeld founded Jahrbuch für sexuelle Zwischenstufen, a journal devoted to issues of human sexuality, and in 1911, he established the Institute for Sexual Science, described in Christopher Isherwood's Christopher and His Kind (1976), which remained the best-known centre for the study of sexuality until it was destroyed by Nazi troops May 6, 1933. During the twenty years of its existence, it and other groups worked in Germany to repeal the notorious Paragraph 175, which criminalized homosexual behaviour.

In 1921, Berlin hosted the First Congress of the World League for Sexual Science; this initial meeting was followed with meetings in Copenhagen (1928), London (1929), and Vienna (1930). In the Soviet Union, homosexuality was briefly decriminalized between 1917 and 1920 and not subjected to Stalinist repressions until 1934.

In 1924, the Society for Human Rights was founded in America, the first of several slight advances continuing until

Alfred Kinsey was assigned to teach a sex education class at Indiana University in 1937, research for which started Kinsey on his way to his monumental publications on human sexuality in 1948 and 1953.

Homosexual and Lesbian Modernist Writers

If one looks to modernist literature, one is struck more by the number of significant writers who were homosexual or lesbian than by the number of works addressing same-sex themes, depicting gay and lesbian characters, or exploring the relationships between these individuals and their societies.

In France, there were Colette, Jean Cocteau, André Gide, and Marcel Proust. In England, there were E. M. Forster, Lytton Strachey, Virginia Woolf, W. Somerset Maugham, Noël Coward, and a host of lesser writers such as E. F. Benson, Norman Douglas, Ronald Firbank, Hector Hugh Munro (Saki), and Frederick William Rolfe (Baron Corvo).

From America, came Gertrude Stein, Edna St. Vincent Millay, Amy Lowell, and Willa Cather, as well as Hart Crane. Elsewhere, Constantine Cavafy was boldly recording the urban gay man's world in his poems.

The homosexual and lesbian worlds of modernism also accomplished much outside fiction, drama, and poetry. Margaret Anderson founded The Little Review (1915-1917), one of the most forward-looking and experimental journals of the period, and in Paris, Sylvia Beach established perhaps the best-known bookstore of the period, Shakespeare and Company. Both women were instrumental in bringing James Joyce's Ulysses to readers.

Edward Carpenter edited Ioläus (1902), the first anthology of gay literature, one that stressed positive self-images, and other writers such as Hans Blucher in Germany and L. S. A. M. Romer in Holland brought balanced views of the homosexual to the attention of society in their The Role of the Erotic in Male Society (1917-1919) and Unknown People: The Physiological Development of the Sexes in Connection with Homosexuality (1904).

Homosexual and Lesbian Modernist Writing

Modernism saw a considerable outpouring of homosexual writing, especially in the short story and the novel, to a lesser extent in poetry, drama, and film. Although Radclyffe Hall's The Well of Loneliness (1928) achieved notoriety because of its pornography trial and the official destruction of its first edition, it was certainly not the only nor the best of the lesbian novels.

Among the others are Djuna Barnes's Ladies Almanack (1928) and Nightwood (1936), which depicts gay life in Paris and Berlin, Colette's many stories about the tomboyish Claudine, Vita Sackville-West's Challenge (1924), which fictionalized her affair with Violet Keppel, Gertrude Stein's Q. E. D., with its explicit lesbian relationship, and Virginia Woolf's Orlando (1928), which made perhaps the key statement on androgynyandrogyny through having Orlando metamorphose from an Elizabethan male into a neoclassical female.

Male novelists, though, were more recognized and more rewarded, two of them being honoured with the Nobel Prize for Literature.

Some, like W. Somerset Maugham, remained rigorously closeted, though his affair with Gerald Haxton and his inversion of one of his early homosexual affairs to a heterosexual affair in Of Human Bondage (1915) were well known.

Hector Hugh Munro, better known by his pen name "Saki," was equally guarded except in stories such as "Gabriel-Ernest" and "Quail Seed," and most of his readers would probably have been shocked had they known that his pen name refers to a cupbearer or beautiful boy and carries esoteric homoerotic connotations.

Even E. M. Forster, who in 1914 in Maurice, wrote one of the frankest and most romantic explorations of same-sex love, suppressed his work. His novel reached print only in 1971, the year following his death.

Others boldly, sometimes recklessly, pushed subject matter well into previously forbidden areas: Xavier Mayne (the pen name of Edward Irenaeus Prime-Stevenson) published Imre (1908), which chronicles Oswald's affair in Hungary with Imre, a cavalry officer.

Under the pen name "Sagitta," John Henry MacKay's Der Puppenjungen (1926) explored the milieu of boy prostitutes in Berlin and espoused an agenda of "equal freedom for all," topics also addressed by Aleister Crowley in White Stains (1898), a collection of poetry.

Near the end of the modernist period, George Santayana, an American better known as a philosopher, published The Last Puritan (1935), which treated a sailor in the Royal Navy caught up in a homosexual scandal aboard ship.

To these, however, must be added names indisputably central to modernist fiction: André Gide, Thomas Mann, and Marcel Proust.

Proust's A la recherche du temps perdu (1913-1927) depicts numerous homosexuals—Robert de Saint-Loup-en-Bray, Charles Morel, Prince Gilbert de Guermantes, Jupien, Legandin, Nissim Bernard, and of course, Baron de Charlus, one of the most memorable characters in the novel and yet one more fictionalization of Count Robert de Montesquiou (1855-1921), who had already appeared as Jean des Esseintes in Joris-Karl Huysmans's À rebours (1884) and as the peacock in Edmond Rostand's Chantecler (1910).

The title of Proust's fourth volume, Sodome et Gomorrhe (1922, translated as Cities of the Plain) foregrounded homosexuality firmly and openly, but readers expecting moral condemnation figured in the title's biblical allusion found more of Proust's attack on social snobbery and the affectations of Parisian society and were treated to an essay on the nature of homosexual love and ultimately, in the seventh volume, to the spectacle of Charlus chained to a bed in Jupien's male brothel, being whipped by a soldier.

The German author, Thomas Mann, offered an equally broad canvas liberally populated by gays, ranging from his now classic depiction of boy-man love in Death in Venice (1912) to male adolescent love in Tonio Kroger (1903) and The Magic Mountain (1924). His Doctor Faustus (1947) linked homosexuality to artistic creativity.

Mann's son, Klaus Mann, built his own literary career on tales of same-sex love, first with a collection of short stories, Before Life (1925), in which the lovers have little chance of success, and then with historical novels about three famous homosexuals: Alexander the Great (1930), Tchaikovsky (1935), and Ludwig II (1937).

Beside the works of Proust and Mann, Gide's Corydon (1924), a Socratic dialogue on sexuality, seems a slight accomplishment. Minor accomplishments can be seen in the other genres.

Mauritz Stiller, the Swedish director, created what is often called the first gay film with The Wings in 1916.

Gay and lesbian literature had indeed made major steps in subject matter, tone, and theme, in the years since Teleny; or, The Reverse of the Medal (1893) had defined suicide by the protagonist as appropriate closure.

Having been written and published between 1890 and 1940, however, does not necessarily mark a book as being "modernist." A book needs to partake of the modernist temper and ethos before it can be so marked.

But since most of the gay and lesbian fiction written during these fifty years is part of the modernist reaction against standards of both past and present and since any number of these works are also experimental in their handling of narrative, they can validly be considered a significant part of the modernist movement.

Conclusion

Modernism gradually saw authority begin to shift from religion, which considered homosexuality a sin, to psychology, which early saw homosexuality as an illness. Ironically, the arts and their cultures were moving in opposite directions.

The literature of modernism moved boldly, occasionally stridently, and at most times favourably toward serious treatment of homosexuals and homosexual cultures, striking out against sexual repressions in many forms while the cultures were preparing the way for suppression, even destruction, of the same individuals and subcultures.

Sponsor Message

The socially conscious, activist authors began to displace modernism as early as the 1930s, and in their agendas for reshaping civilization and making the world anew gays and lesbians and their literature were once more emphatically marginalized and, in some countries, silenced.

Chapter 5

D. H. Lawrence as a Writer

Lawrence and Homosexual Desire

Much of the bitterness of the war years, along with Lawrence's disenchantment with English narrow-mindedness, can be found in what is perhaps the novelist's greatest exploration of homosexual subject matter, *Women in Love* (1920).

Here Lawrence and Frieda are depicted as Rupert Birkin and Ursula Brangwen in a tale based partly on Lawrence's clamorous relationship with the writer Katherine Mansfield, her husband, the literary critic John Middleton-Murray (Gudrun and Gerald of the novel), and Lady Ottoline Morrell (Hermione Roddice).

It was during the composition of *Women in Love* that Lawrence, frustrated by his failure to forge a deeper bond with Murray, evidently had a sexual relationship with a Cornish farmer named William Henry Hocking in the town of Tregerthen.

The short-lived affair was the culmination of a long-standing struggle with homosexual feelings. "I would like to know why nearly every man that approaches greatness tends to homosexuality, whether he admits it or not," Lawrence wrote to a friend in 1913. Lawrence told another acquaintance, "I believe the nearest I've come to perfect love was with a coal-miner when I was about sixteen."

Yet Lawrence's inability to intensify his relationships with either Murray or Hocking generated his most forthright fictional examinations of homosexual desire, an intense five-year absorption in the subject that included not only *Women in Love* and *Aaron's Rod* (1922) but the treatise "Goats and Compasses" (1917) and the self-suppressed Prologue to *Women In Love*.

Lawrence destroyed "Goats and Compasses," and though no pages survive, both Ottoline Morrell and Lawrence's friend Cecil Gray read it and found it to be shrilly dogmatic. Its argument remains unknown, although the essay's title suggests a struggle between panlike homoerotics and scientific rationalism.

Lawrence spent the last part of his short life traveling with Frieda to Italy, America, and Mexico, the last the setting for *The Plumed Serpent* (1926). In addition to his fiction, Lawrence published several volumes of poetry, critical essays, and travel narratives.

Lawrence's last novel, *Lady Chatterley's Lover* (1928), won him his greatest fame but was not published in an unexpurgated English edition until after a ground-breaking censorship trial in 1961. Always frail in health, Lawrence died of tuberculosis in 1930 in Vence, France, while traveling with Frieda in the company of Aldous and Maria Huxley.

Lawrence was a twentieth-century maverick in his open and formally adventurous discussion of all sexual issues and especially homosexuality. Perhaps no other major modernist author was so continually absorbed in the subject of homosexual desire, a theme that continually informs Lawrence's work, beginning with the swimming idyll sequence of his first novel, *The White Peacock* (1911), and continuing with the initiation ritual in *The Plumed Serpent*, Lawrence's penultimate novel.

Throughout the fiction, poetry, and even plays (his 1926 *David* in part depicted the story of the Biblical David's friendship with Jonathan), Lawrence explored homosexual love in both male and female relations.

The Rainbow, for example, includes a character of obvious lesbian inclinations, Winifred Inger, and her emotional hold on Ursula Brangwen, and the novella *The Fox* explores the intimate friendship between two women as it is shattered by a male intruder to their farm.

Like Forster and Gide, Lawrence was fascinated by the mystique of sexual relations with working-class men; unlike them, however, he expounded this fascination from the perspective of the working-class artist.

Deeply suspicious of the effects of industrialization—he had himself witnessed it destroy the English landscape and the vestiges of communal culture—Lawrence grew to love primitive civilizations and all he imagined they offered in the way of expansive love.

Although he proselytized on behalf of the unconscious, Lawrence repudiated psychoanalysis's attempt at thoroughly calibrating human sexuality and criticized Freud's project as fomenting mere "sex in the head." Psychoanalysis, he believed, robbed modern man of the dark, mythic power inherent in true eros.

This belief in the mythopoetic value of the darkly erotic led him to stress nonverbal zed expressions of homoerotic feeling, often with a violent, primitivism undercurrent. The much-anthologized story "The Prussian Officer" (1914), for example, portrays the masochistic yearning of an officer for the youthful soldier under his command in a tightly wrought narrative containing virtually no dialogue and ending with a dual death in an eerily peaceful forest.

Homosexual Desire in Lawrence's Writings

Lawrence's writing dealing with homosexuality poses unusual problems, for the novelist was highly conflicted in his attitude toward homosexual desire and was, in many ways, a social conservative of a markedly puritan temperament.

Many readers, moreover, have been troubled by Lawrence's glorification of what has been characterized as his misogynistic "cult of the phallus," as well as by the fascistic implications of his philosophy of "blood consciousness." Others have found Lawrence's often febrile, repetitive prose style to be an obstacle to a full appreciation of his work.

In addition, Lawrence's fictional endorsement of homosexual desire is generally represented as existing in conflict with either a fearful sexual domination by women or a repellently effete homosexual coterie. Thus Gudrun and the memorably malevolent bisexual German artist Loerke in *Women in Love* come to represent a deadly alliance that defeats Gerald in his unrealised love for Birkin.

Lawrence's own experiences with homosexual men were acrimonious; he once claimed that Bloomsbury homosexuals such as the painter Duncan Grant and the economist John Maynard Keynes made him "mad with misery and hostility and rage."

Lawrence, Whitman, and Carpenter

Still, Lawrence's torment over his own homosexual inclinations give his work an extraordinary, unsentimental force that is lacking in the fiction of more inwardly resolved writers of the day and that renders much of the period's homosexual writing restrained by comparison. In rejecting homosexual aestheticism for a more masculine credo and a devotion to savage nature, Lawrence is close in spirit to the English and American writers Edward Carpenter and Walt Whitman.

A great admirer of the American poet, Lawrence claimed to find in Whitman's *Calamus* poems "one of the clues to a real solution—a new adjustment. I believe in what he calls 'manly love', the real implicit reliance of one man on another... only it must be deeper, more ultimate than emotion and personality, cool separateness and yet the ultimate reliance."

Women in Love

Women in Love, a masterpiece of modernist fiction, is the novelist's most daring exploration of homosexuality through

Rupert in the chapter "Man to Man"—real devotion between men is stymied by a failure of nerve.

Nonetheless, the tragedy of Gerald's death is undercut by *Women in Love*'s extraordinary concluding endorsement of bisexuality. "You can't have two kinds of love," Ursula insists to Birkin after Gerald's body has been buried, as she dismisses Birkin's ideas as "an obstinacy, a theory, a perversity." Rupert's response and *Women in Love*'s final sentence is a refusal to accept a delimited heterosexual arrangement: "I don't believe that."

Aaron's Rod

In affirming same-sex friendship, Lawrence typically contrasted his all-male idylls with effete homosexual men, while portraying women as upholders of suffocating marital convention. In Aaron's Rod, a coal miner leaves his fatuous wife, takes up the flute, and travels to Italy to join the free-spirited Rawdon Lily.

There he encounters a group of vacationing English exiles, whose homosexuality is implied in their doting interest in the working-class Aaron as well as in their social cattiness. (Wilde's friend Reggie Turner appears in the biting portrait of Algy Constable, "flapping his eyelids like some crazy owl.") The novel concludes with Rawdon beseeching Aaron to submit to the demands of his own soul.

Homosexual Themes in Later Works

Lawrence returned to homosexual themes in episodes in later works, among them the "Nightmare" chapter of Kangaroo (1923), as well in several short stories. His tales "The Blind Man" (1924) and "Jimmy and the Desperate Woman" (1928) both powerfully recast the familiar Lawrentian scenario in which homoerotic affection threatens—yet also complements—an unsatisfying marital relationship.

Conclusion

Lawrence's genius consists in his emphasis on the barely articulated, unconscious dynamics of homoerotic relations as its hero Birkin's search for a bisexual ethic as a v transcending what Lawrence considered a crisis in E culture. The twin poles of Birkin's agonized e consciousness and his search for "two kinds of love," we to the novel's heightened sense of cultural fragmentation, Women in Love an exceptional tensile strength and apocal magnitude.

In the novel's preface, Lawrence claimed the catastro of the Great War required that men form a bond lest "n life" be "strangled unborn within them." This statement is more poetic expression of what the novel itself makes implic and the Prologue rendered emphatic: Heterosexual marriag must acknowledge man's need to have the love of another ma or else all will suffer a spiritual death.

Excised from the final text by Lawrence himself, the Prologue reveals in great detail Rupert Birkin's struggle against overwhelming homosexual longings. It was not published until 1965 and was not included in an edition of *Women in Love* until 1987.

Hocking himself is probably twice alluded to in the Prologue in the description of the "strange Cornish type of man, with dark eyes likes holes in his head" who powerfully attracts Birkin as well as in the minor character of William Hosken.

The Rupert of the Prologue is torn not only betweer females and males, but between "two classes of men," th "white-skinned, keen limbed men with eyes like blue-flashin ice and hair like crystals of winter sunshine" and "men wit dark eyes that one can enter and plunge into, bathe in as i liquid darkness." Although Rupert wants to "cast out thes desires," he senses that a "man can no more slay a living desi in him" than "he can prevent his body from feeling heat ar cold."

Despite the potential for true passion and tenderne between men—glimpsed in the famous wrestling sequence the novel's "Gladiatorial" chapter and in Gerald's nursing they move in a state of crisis, flux, and cathartic confrontation. His willingness to transcend the conventions of the nineteenth-century novel, subverting what he once characterized as the "old, stable ego," and, in turn, the stable sexual self, enabled him at his best to depict the experimental excitement of same-sex relations.

Alone among writers of the period, he brought to the theme of homosexuality a genuine working-class perspective. A self-proclaimed enemy of the hyperarticulated sexuality of forward-thinking individuals, he was, paradoxically, himself the great novelist of the painfully unsayable. It was a gift that rendered Lawrence exceptionally adept at apprehending the "unspeakable" promptings of same-sex desire.

A ferociously brilliant artist, he remains one of the most forcefully imaginative, complicated, and least understood navigators of homosexual consciousness in the twentieth century.

Chapter 6

Plot Overview

In the rolling hills and coal-pitted fields of central England, known as the British Midlands, live the Morels, a poor mining family. The family has just moved down in the world from the nearby village of Bestwood to the Bottoms, a complex of working-class row houses.

Gertrude Morel is a small, stern woman, pregnant with her third child, Paul, the protagonist of this novel. The Morels' other children are William and Annie. But unlike his siblings, Paul is not wanted by his mother. The poverty-stricken household cannot easily handle another hungry mouth to feed. Walter Morel, Paul's father, is a hard-working coal miner with a lively spirit and a severe drinking problem.

Mr. and Mrs. Morel were initially attracted to each other because they were so different. He is working-class, sensual, nonintellectual, and fairly irresponsible. His wife is middle-class, pious, intellectual, and eminently reliable. The passion that held them together in the first glowing months of their marriage cannot survive their social and moral differences.

When Paul is born, Mrs. Morel is determined to make him feel loved, to compensate for his unwanted conception. Paul is a feeble, oversensitive child, who seems to be living proof of the shattered love of his mismatched parents.

William, the eldest son, is the favourite of the family. He's a great athlete, student, worker, and companion. He lands a good job in London and gets caught up in the exciting urban life. He becomes engaged to Louisa Lily Denys Western ("Gyp"), a young woman who is beautiful but not bright.

Meanwhile, Paul gets an office job at Jordan's artificial limb factory in Nottingham. The shop girls, particularly the hunchbacked Fanny, adore this shy, sweet boy who offers them encouragement and kindness. He has also become serious about landscape painting.

On a holiday visit to the farm of family friends, Paul meets his first sweetheart, Miriam Leivers. At first, Miriam means far less to Paul than do the other members of the Leivers family, whom he visits frequently.

In the city, William works endlessly to support his fiancee's extravagant whims. He resents Gyp's frivolity and stupidity but is sexually enthralled by her. She satisfies his passion, without loosening his mother's hold on his heart and mind. The conflict between William's attraction to Gyp and his devotion to Mrs. Morel eventually undermines his health. He dies of pneumonia in his cold, lonely London flat (apartment).

Now all Mrs. Morel's passions and aspirations pour into Paul. As he becomes the centre of his mother's universe, he truly begins to live.

The Leivers become like a second family to Paul. Soon, the daughter Miriam grows closest to the sensitive, artistic youth. The two share long, idyllic walks through the countryside, talking and reading to each other. Paul helps Miriam overcome her many physical fears, such as climbing fences and letting the barnyard chickens eat out of her hand. He teaches her French and algebra, opening up a new, exciting world. Miriam appeals to Paul's own growing mysticism and creativity and loves nurturing Paul's artistic growth. They experience an intense relationship but don't know how to express it physically.

As Paul grows into manhood, he finds his abstract, spiritual relationship with Miriam unsatisfactory. Mrs. Morel, however, is jealous of Miriam's influence over Paul. She fears

Miriam will suck the life and energy out of him with her dreamy mysticism. Paul, in turn, becomes frustrated by Miriam's otherworldliness. He eventually realises he wants to have a sexual relationship with her, but can't get up the courage to make a pass at her. He knows how much she fears sex. Confused and frustrated, Paul starts to hate Miriam and treat her cruelly.

At the Leivers farm, Paul meets Clara Dawes, a political and social activist who has left her unfaithful husband. As the relationship between Miriam and Paul becomes more hopeless, his affinity for the older, sensuous Clara develops. Clara suggests to Paul that Miriam might actually want him as a man and helps him find the courage to approach Miriam as a lover.

Finally Paul and Miriam make love. The act dissatisfies both of them. Miriam acts as if making love is an unenjoyable sacrifice she endures for Paul's benefit only. Paul can't stand feeling that his wanting Miriam as a woman hurts her. He finally follows his mother's advice and ends his affair with Miriam. In hope of finding an outlet for his intense sexual passions, he turns to Clara.

Paul and Clara have an affair. She satisfies his sensuality without breaking his attachment to his mother. But Clara, like Miriam, wants to make their relationship permanent, or at least stable. This is impossible because of Paul's devotion to Mrs. Morel.

Paul comes to befriend Clara's husband, Baxter, who has not hidden his hatred for Paul and even thrashed him for having an affair with his wife. While Baxter is in the hospital, Paul visits him, then helps place the broken man in a convalescent home. Meanwhile, Paul's mother is dying of stomach cancer.

Neither Paul nor his sister Annie can bear to see their mother in pain. Paul finally gives her an overdose of morphine to end her suffering. After his mother's death, Paul feels that life isn't worth living. His relationship with Clara has disintegrated, and he decides to renounce her. Clara, believing she will never get close to Paul, goes back to Baxter.

Paul remains in deep despair over his mother's death. He can't do anything but mourn and think about dying. Eventually, his will to live wins out. Paul heads toward the blazing lights of Nottingham and a new life.

Setting

Sons and Lovers is set in the British Midlands at the turn of the twentieth century. This is a region in central England that is highly industrialized. Factories, coal pits, and ugly row houses are abundant. Yet, Robin Hood's Sherwood Forest is close by the busy industrial city of Nottingham, where Paul works, and the river Trent swirls its way from the city through the wide-open country hills and vales. Sons and Lovers constantly contrasts the sensuous, natural environment with that of the cold, drab monuments of industrial town and city life.

Paul grows up in the vicinity of Bestwood, a mining village within an hour's train ride of Nottingham, a large, factory-lined city. Bestwood, which is based on Lawrence's birthplace of Eastwood, is a conglomerate of company-owned miners' dwellings. The homes are ugly and impractical; the adjacent areas, dirty and crowded. The town is surrounded by coal pits, lush green valleys, and old farms, such as Willey Farm, where Paul spends a great deal of time.

In Sons and Lovers, natural landscapes are the true home of human sexuality. Most of the lovemaking scenes take place out-of-doors, near rivers, in forests, by the sea. Nature represents life's beauty and fertility. Flower imagery abounds in this novel. You'll see how Lawrence uses flowers as both spiritual and sexual symbols.

The industrial cityscapes in Sons and Lovers serve to show us how modern technological life ravages people, depriving them of their dignity, sense of beauty, and natural drives. You'll notice this particularly in the Jordan factory scenes and at Clara's home, where she's a "slave" to the cottage-industry of lace-making. Her job is quite similar to ones in the computer industry, where people are often paid minimum wages to make various computer parts at home.

At the same time, town life means human community, with its ongoing survivalist drive. You'll see at the end of the novel that Paul walks away from the dark, uninhabited country fields and toward the bright city lights. Some readers see this act as Paul's walking away from death and toward life. Consider this interpretation in light of Lawrence's comparison of city and country. Is it consistent to identify the city with life and the country with death?

Style

Lawrence uses a combination of realistic description and poetic images to create the world of Sons and Lovers. Realism is a style of writing that attempts to describe in a true-to-life manner concrete, everyday events. Poetic narrative, on the other hand, serves to lift life out of its normality, making it seem supernatural or symbolic of universal themes outside ordinary daily experience. Poetic narrative achieves this feat by using word comparisons, metaphors and similes, many adjectives, or elaborate and rhythmical language, rather than everyday speech.

The realism in Sons and Lovers is strongest in the first half of the novel, where the narrator describes the Morel family's day-to-day existence. Mr. Morel hammers away at work, and the children help him along with his tasks. Mrs. Morel goes out marketing and comes home with a load of domestic treasures. The narrator also uses realistic detail to great effect when he presents the miners dividing their weekly pay in the Morel home. The men's gestures are carefully described in almost photographic detail. The realism of Sons and Lovers gives you an accurate picture of working-class life at the turn of the century. You come to know, almost as if you were there, the pains and joys of their hard lives.

Lawrence's poetry comes to the forefront in his descriptions of nature, where, for example, vivid sunsets and blazing rosebushes stand out against darkening skies. The poetic portions of Sons and Lovers seem to make the common lives of its characters miraculous and heroic.

Many times Lawrence uses a pattern that starts in realism, expands into lyrical poetic narrative, and then puts you back on your feet with a return to realism. You'll notice this particularly in the scenes between Paul and his women- his mother, Miriam, and Clara. He'll start them off on a normal walk or conversation and then heighten the language to give you a sense of their souls' communion. The poetic style serves the purpose of evoking an emotional response in the reader rather than advancing the plot's action. As you read Sons and Lovers, try to discover where the different styles are used and what each of them offers. How do they enhance each other and create what's unique about the novel as a whole?

Lawrence also uses dialect to accurately convey his working-class characters' conversations. The Midlands dialect is quite different from standard English and you may have some difficulty understanding its slang terms, as well as its contractions of words. The dialect often drops beginning consonants of words and employs the old-fashioned "thee" and "thou" for "you." To Lawrence, this sort of language was more warm and intense than standard English. Walter Morel speaks in dialect, emphasizing his social background and his sensuality. Gertrude Morel, on the other hand, speaks the standard English of the educated middle class. You'll notice that Paul speaks both "languages," as well as French, which he teaches Miriam. Paul uses dialect for sensuous love with the sexually uninhibited Clara and for flirtation with Beatrice. He reserves proper English for Miriam and his prim mother.

Point of View

Sons and Lovers is told from the point of view of an omniscient, or all-knowing, narrator. Most of the time, the narrator tells you more about the characters than they themselves know. This helps you accept and understand actions that might otherwise seem arbitrary or unmotivated.

Since this book is highly autobiographical, many readers identify the narrator with Lawrence, who seems to be looking back and trying to come to terms with his own youthful problems and feelings through the character of Paul Morel. The narrator's subjectivity about Paul shows through. At times he sympathizes with Paul, and at other times he condemns him. You may find the other characters judged in a similar way. Some readers find the narrator's changing opinion indicative of Lawrence's own confusion over his various past relationships. Others feel that the narrator is simply reflecting how people naturally change their perspective depending on the circumstances.

At times, the narrator seems to step aside and allow the characters to speak for themselves in passages of dialogue. You may feel closer to them when the narrator doesn't guide your view of their motivations. But don't forget that the narrator is choosing the speech and actions to be revealed, in order to influence your reactions.

Sometimes, instead of stepping aside, the narrator seems almost to take over a character, even if the result is at odds with that character's personality. For instance, when Gertrude Morel is locked out of her house in Chapter 1, she seems mystically transported by her experience with the daylilies. But isn't she really "out of character"? Some would say that the narrator (or author?) has stepped into her shoes in such a totally subjective way that he reveals his own artistic and spiritual nature rather than Gertrude's. Others might feel this is the only way to depict a character's hidden inner feelings.

Structure

Sons and Lovers has fifteen episodic chapters, divided into Parts One and Two. Part One deals with the Morel family home life, emphasizing social and historical influences. Paul, the protagonist, is not yet the main focus of the novel. The core of Part One is the story of Mr. and Mrs. Morel's failed marriage and the promise of son William's success in life. Part One ends with the death of William and Mrs. Morel's new hope in her younger son, Paul.

Part Two begins the story of Sons and Lovers in terms of Paul's perceptions. Part Two, or the story of Paul's life, can only begin once the favoured son William dies and Paul takes his place in his mother's heart. This section of the novel concentrates more on the conflicting inner feelings of its characters than on the straightforward, action- and detail-oriented realism of Part One. It also focuses on the battle between Miriam and Mrs. Morel for Paul's soul.

Sons and Lovers moves chronologically from before Paul's birth through his life as a young man and ends with his mourning the death of his mother. Flashbacks are often used, particularly in Part One, where Lawrence deals with the Morel parents' premarital backgrounds and Paul's early childhood memories.

Part Two involves a series of repeated attempts of male/female unions, exemplified by Paul's relationship first with Miriam, then with Clara. Many readers feel that these relationships take forever to resolve and that when they do, the result is quite unsatisfactory. Other readers believe that the monotonous repetition of the failed Miriam/Paul relationship theme is deliberate. They feel that Sons and Lovers is structured like ocean waves. There's a rhythmic return pattern to various themes, such as the decay of Mr. and Mrs. Morel's love after it has reached its climax. This serves to show that there are no clear-cut resolutions in life. People make the same mistakes again and again. Part Two can be considered a journey from the known, realistic world of Part One into the realm of the unknown, where there are no definitive solutions. Part Two explores the subconscious and mysterious forces that motivate people. Lawrence saw this sort of exploration as far more important than providing his audience with resolutions

Chapter 7

Major Characters

Paul Morel

Paul Morel, the protagonist of Sons and Lovers, is based on the youthful D. H. Lawrence. Paul is a young man in the painful process of growing up. He's also gradually discovering that he's a gifted artist. Most important to the story, Paul is torn between his passion for two young women, the mystical Miriam and the sensual Clara, and his unyielding devotion to a possessive mother.

You may see Paul merely as a fellow under the thumb of a dominating mother. Some readers feel that his feeling for her is more passionate and that his difficulties with Miriam and Clara stem from this unresolved passion. Only her death frees him at the end. Another view of Paul is that he derives great strength from his mother and is inspired rather than crippled by his relationship to her. The failure of his relationship with Miriam, according to this view, is caused more by her horror of physical intimacy, than by Gertrude Morel's superior place in Paul's affections. How you interpret Paul's relationship with his mother will have much to do with your view of her character.

Another of Paul's conflicts centres on his apparent hatred for his father. You can see Paul's abhorrence of Walter Morel's vulgarity and alcoholism, but you can also see his imitation of Walter's carefree spirit and lust for life. Isn't some of Paul's own brutality to Miriam derived from his father's behaviour?

In some people's eyes, masculine virility is only another version of brutality.

Many readers see Paul's inner conflicts as a reflection of his parents' very different personalities and class backgrounds. He combines his father's working-class simplicity, spontaneity, and sensuality with his mother's middle-class steadfastness, intellectualism, and social ambition. Paul can be viewed as the volatile offspring of both the lower and the middle classes.

He can also be seen as a lovable, charismatic character. He's often kind and jovial, especially to his mother and the shop girls at Jordan's. Paul shares a healthy companionship with other men. It helps him appreciate the everyday joys of life and escape his brooding tendencies.

There's also a dark, brutal side to Paul. He can be very cruel, particularly to his girlfriends. He can't bear Miriam Leivers' superspirituality when it interferes with his sexual desires. After she finally gives up her virginity to him, he leaves her. Given the importance of virginity to an unmarried woman in the early twentieth century, Paul's treatment of Miriam seems shockingly inconsiderate. Once the proud Clara falls in love with Paul, he leaves her as well, telling her to go home to her husband. If Paul is such a sensitive, caring young man, why does he do such cruel things?

Paul is a fascinating mixture of extremes: vitality and despondency, spirituality and sensuality, love and hate, sensitivity and cruelty. Do you think any of these contradictions are resolved as the story ends?

Gertrude Morel

Gertrude Morel is one of the most formidable mothers in all of Western literature. To the narrator, and perhaps to Paul Morel, she is both a giving, selfless nurturer of her children and a possessive tyrant.

This small, resolute woman with luxuriant hair and a grim, determined mouth is the axis from which her children, particularly William and Paul, spin out into life. She instills them with self-confidence, social and intellectual ambitions, and a great joy in living. At the same time, she dislikes her sons' girlfriends and makes it difficult for her sons to find happiness with a mate. Gertrude also lets her sons know that she's living just for them, placing enormous pressure on their ability to "cut the apron strings."

Mrs. Morel is a character you must watch carefully. She often seems to be doing wonderful things for her children, but the resulting impact on their lives cripples them. Many readers feel that Mrs. Morel is so important to William and Paul that all other women come up short when compared to her.

These readers believe that William dies, not of pneumonia, but really because he can't resolve the conflict he feels between marrying his girlfriend Gyp and remaining devoted to his mother. Paul, too, will have a hard time feeling satisfied with his lovers. At one point he even says that he'll never find a wife while his mother lives- nor does he. According to modern psychological theory, as formulated by Freud and others, Gertrude Morel has replaced her husband with her sons.

Although Mrs. Morel adores her sons, she is certainly capable of hate. We see this in her relationship with her coarse, uneducated husband and with Paul's first love, Miriam. Gertrude, brought up in the respectable middle class, can't accept her husband's irresponsibility or drinking habits. As a result, she writes him out of her life and puts all her passion into the children.

As you read the novel you'll have to decide for yourself if her hatred of Walter Morel is justified. Gertrude's dislike of Miriam can be viewed as justified or unjustified. Some readers agree with Gertrude that Miriam tries to suck all the energy out of Paul's life and make him into a disembodied spirit. Other readers feel that Gertrude's dislike of Miriam is selfish. She fears the young girl will take her son away from her.

Although Gertrude Morel makes it difficult for Paul to find a suitable mate, she clearly doesn't want him left alone when she dies. She wants him to find satisfaction in work and marriage. Gertrude feels he'll achieve this by marrying a lady and becoming a respectable, successful middle-class husband. But her idea of a suitable lifestyle may not be what Paul actually needs or desires. Mrs. Morel is right, however, to discern that her son needs a wife who equals him in strength, intelligence, and warmth.

While Mrs. Morel comes across as icy and overly pious at times, Paul tells you that at one time she had known true passion with her husband and that it awakened her need for a full, vital life. She hates to give up living, even when she's terminally ill. Mrs. Morel wants to cling to life and realise her social and intellectual aspirations through Paul. When she finally dies, his emptiness seems total. Paul has been both blessed and cursed with such an extraordinary mother.

Walter Morel

Walter Morel is Paul's rough, sensual, hard-drinking father. In many ways, he is his wife's opposite. Walter is from a lower-class mining family. He speaks the local dialect in contrast to his wife's refined English. He loves to drink and dance, practices that Gertrude, a strict Congregationalist, considers sinful.

There are two ways to look at Walter Morel's failure to be a good husband, father, and family breadwinner. You can see him as a man broken by an uncaring, brutal industrial system and an overly demanding wife. You can also see Walter as his own worst enemy, inviting self-destruction through drink and irresponsibility.

You learn a good deal about Walter's good and bad qualities in Sons and Lovers, While Lawrence seems to concentrate on the character's violence and irresponsibility, he also gives you a picture of Walter's warm, lively, loving ways. The key scenes of family happiness revolve around the time when Walter stays out of the pubs and works around the house, hugging his children and telling them tall stories of life down in the mines.

Miriam Leivers

Miriam Leivers, Paul's teenage friend and sweetheart, was modeled after Lawrence's own young love, Jessie Chambers. As Jessie was with Lawrence, Miriam is Paul's devoted helpmate in his artistic and spiritual quests. Although beautiful, she takes no pleasure in her physical attributes. Her whole life is geared toward heaven and a mystical sense of nature.

Paul and Miriam's first bond is their mutual love of nature. Sons and Lovers tells of their many idyllic country walks. However, whereas Miriam wants to absorb nature, Paul just wants to live in harmony with it. Later, Paul will come to feel, as his mother does, that Miriam wants to absorb his life as well.

Miriam is a loner. By her own choice, she has few friends. When Paul thinks that perhaps they should marry for appearance's sake, she's mortally offended. Though Miriam is physically and socially timid, she refuses to live her life in accordance with superficial standards of etiquette.

Most of Paul's family and friends feel put off by Miriam. She's too intellectual and otherworldly even to know how to hold an ordinary conversation. She lacks the normal joys of living. Her life is an extreme of agony or ecstasy. This lack of normalcy and plain fun is one of the things Paul hates about her.

There are two warring sides to Miriam- her love of Paul Morel and her resistance to her sexual feelings toward him. Her mother taught her that sex is one of the burdens of marriage, and though she doesn't want to believe it, she can't help but listen to the woman who's shaped her life. When Miriam finally gives in to Paul, she does it in a spirit of self-sacrifice that disappoints both of them. Miriam's inability to enjoy sex makes her an incomplete person in the Lawrentian world, where sex as well as spirituality is necessary to an individual's fulfillment.

Miriam is a very complex character. At times you feel that Lawrence himself is trying to understand exactly what she's like. The narrator, like Paul, fluctuates between pitying and condemning her. But because there are so many opposing elements to Miriam, you have an opportunity to figure out who she really is and what she wants, through your own investigation and interpretation.

Clara Dawes

Clara Dawes is the sensuous older woman who comes to replace Miriam as the love interest in Paul's life. It is with Clara that Paul learns the importance of sex as humanity's deepest link with nature and the cosmos.

Clara is depicted as a new twentieth-century woman. She's a feminist before it was fashionable. Determined to be independent, she leaves her husband, earns her own living, and has an extramarital affair with Paul. Clara can be viewed as representative of the many post-Victorian women who rebelled against the traditional image of woman as the "weaker sex." Clara is extraordinarily intelligent, with a good critical mind. But you get little demonstration of this aspect of her personality, since the story concentrates on her physical attractiveness to Paul.

Clara, unlike Miriam, is bursting with a lusty, animal passion. She is Paul's match for fearlessness, sensuality, and intelligence. At the same time, she lacks Miriam's spirituality and sensitivity. Without these qualities, can she stimulate Paul's work as an artist?

At first Clara acts condescending to Paul. He's convinced she hates all men. She's certainly bitter about male/female relationships. Her husband Baxter brutalized her and was unfaithful. Does this mean that she hates men, or that she's had an unsatisfying married life?

Later, when Paul delivers a message to Clara at her mother's home, you see quite another side of this proud, independent woman. She's humiliated and exhausted by her sweatshop labour, as she and her mother spend grueling hours making lace. Even though they have the freedom to work at home rather than on an assembly line at one of Nottingham's many factories, these women are still exploited, underpaid victims of the industrial system.

Paul helps Clara get back her old overseer's job at Jordan's, and they become good friends through his generosity. Their subsequent love affair gives them both a new, expansive sense of life. With Clara, Paul finds the sensual fulfillment he can't have with either Miriam or his mother. Paul awakens Clara's sexuality, something she missed with her husband.

Some readers feel that Clara is the least successful of the major characters in Sons and Lovers. They believe she comes across merely as a vehicle for Paul's passion and as a very shallow caricature of the "new woman." How do you think Lawrence succeeds in drawing Clara Dawes? How does he fail?

William Morel

William is Paul's older brother. He's based on Lawrence's own brother Ernest, who was the pride and joy of his family. Like his fictional counterpart, Ernest died in London at an early age.

William is robust and merry like his father. He's also intellectual and responsible like his mother. He's Gertrude's darling because he distinguishes himself early and remains devoted to her. When he goes off to a promising job in London, he meets and falls in love with a shallow-minded beauty, Louisa Lily Denys Western ("Gyp"). She satisfies his passion and fulfills his aspiration to marry someone from a higher social class, but leaves his mind and soul unfulfilled. Some readers think that William chooses such an unsuitable mate because he fears having a woman who might usurp his mother's place in his heart. Lawrence, in an unpublished foreword to Sons and Lovers, ascribes William's death from pneumonia to his internal struggle between his physical passion for a young, frivolous woman and his true love for his mother.

Louisa Lily Denys Western ("GYP")

Gyp is William Morel's fiancée. She's a flighty, foolish, but beautiful young woman whose family has fallen upon hard times. Even though she is forced to work as a secretary, Gyp still treats people like the Morels as inferiors.

The Other Morel Children

Annie Morel is Paul's older sister. She becomes a schoolteacher and marries her childhood friend, Leonard. Arthur Morel is Paul's younger brother. He's much like Walter Morel, un intellectual and fun- loving. He marries Beatrice Wyld, a friend of Annie's.

The Leivers

The Leivers are Miriam's family. They provide a home-away-from-home for Paul. Paul is very close to Mrs. Leivers, a flighty, mystical woman very different from his pragmatic mother. He's also friendly with the strong, rationalistic Edgar, Miriam's oldest brother. The Leivers family give Paul much support.

Chapter 8

Chapter Wise Summary and Analysis

CHAPTER 1: THE EARLY MARRIED LIFE OF THE MORELS

Summary

The first chapter begins with a description of the neighbourhood of "The Bottoms," the miners' dwellings in which the Morels live. We get a small amount of description of Mrs. Morel and learn that her husband is a miner. At this point in the story, the Morel family consists of Mr. Morel and Mrs. Morel (expecting her third child), William (age seven), and Annie (age five). The first action of the novel begins three weeks after the Morels have moved into their new home, on the day of the wakes (a kind of fair).

William goes off to the wakes in the morning and comes back at mid-day for dinner, telling his mother to hurry so that he can return by the time the wakes begin again. He runs off quickly when he hears the music of the merry-go-round, and Mrs. Morel takes Annie later in the afternoon. They run into William and he shows his mother two egg-cups he has won as a present for her. The three of them spend some time together at the fair, and William decides to stay after his mother and sister leave. However, we learn later that he does not enjoy himself after his mother has gone.

After the children go to bed, Mrs. Morel waits for her husband to return from the bar where he is working and reflects on her situation. She cannot afford and does not want her coming child, and she "despises" her husband because of his drinking. Her only solace is in her two children. She wonders if her life will ever change, and reflects that the events in her life seem to take place without her approval. She cleans the house and sits down to sew, and her husband finally comes home. They argue about whether or not he is drunk, he shows her that he has brought gingerbread and a coconut for the children, and she goes to bed.

The next part of the chapter fills in the background to the Morels' marriage. It begins by describing Mrs. Morel, previously Gertrude Coppard, her upbringing in a poor family, and her friendship with a man named John Field, who gave her a Bible when she was nineteen, which she still keeps. The flashback shows her encouraging John Field to stand up for himself and go into the ministry, even though his father wants him to continue the family business. She claims that if she were a man, she would do as she liked. He tells her that being a man isn't everything, and she has finally learned that lesson.

The next part of the flashback describes the meeting between Gertrude Coppard and Walter Morel at a Christmas party when she was twenty-three and he was twenty-seven. It seems the main attraction he holds for her is that he is different from her father. At the party he asks her to dance, she refuses, and he sits down and talks with her instead. The next Christmas they marry, and their early married life seems very happy.

However, after they have been married for seven months, Gertrude finds the unpaid bills for the household furniture in her husband's coat pocket. She confronts him to ask about the bills and he brushes her off, so the next day she goes to see his mother. She tells Gertrude that her husband still owes a good deal of money, and that the house they live in belongs to her. This information changes the way Gertrude feels toward her husband: she becomes colder and more condescending toward him. She begins to feel isolated from her husband, and this causes her to turn toward her child instead.

A key incident happens when Morel cuts William's hair while Mrs. Morel is sleeping. This is one of the major factors in her estrangement from her husband, as the betrayal she feels when she discovers William's haircut remains with her throughout the coming years.

The next important incident, at which the narrative appears to have caught up to the present, occurs on another wakes holiday when Morel goes out with his friend, Jerry Purdy. Jerry is Morel's good friend, but Mrs. Morel does not like him. Jerry and Morel walk to Nottingham, which is ten miles away, and stop at all the pubs along the way. After a nap in a field, Morel does not feel so well. When he finally returns home, he has become irritable and has a fight with his wife, each calling the other a liar. He locks her outside in his anger and then falls asleep at the kitchen table. Mrs. Morel wanders in the yard for a while and eventually, after an hour of knocking at the door, succeeds in waking up her husband.

Commentary

Immediately apparent in the novel, especially to a reader in 1913, is its subject matter of miners. While Lawrence was certainly not the first English writer to depict the lower class, or even miners, he does so out of some personal experience (he maintained that the first part of Sons and Lovers was largely autobiographical) and with a keen ear for the rhythms of their speech Morel's especially and habits.

However, the first chapter is presented mostly from Mrs. Morel's point of view. Lawrence narrates in an omniscient voice that is at times detached‹the opening description of the Bottoms reads almost like the beginning to a fairy tale‹but more frequently zooms in on the interior emotions of each character.

Mrs. Morel's unhappy life is explored thoroughly. She represents intellect that has not been allowed to flourish because she is a woman; her shock that John Field could not do whatever he wanted as a man is a poignant projection of her own repressed ambitions. Her sense of being "buried alive" is a logical complaint for someone whose husband mines underground all day. However, she is just as repressed by their industrial life, a theme Lawrence will explore throughout the novel.

Though the sensual, passionate Morel seems an odd choice for Mrs. Morel, Lawrence demonstrates here, and elsewhere in the novel, how oppositions can attract as often as they repulse. Morel is also in attractive opposition to Mrs. Morel's loathed father. Still, the marriage is clearly a disaster, pitting mind against body, a conflict in which Lawrence was always interested. Morel is also irresponsible in regards to their children; he drinks away his wages, while Mrs. Morel lives only for William and Annie.

Sons and Lovers is informed by, and revises, Sigmund Freud's early psychoanalytic theories of sexuality. Freud's most famous theory, that of the Oedipus complex, in which the son unconsciously desires his mother sexually while murderously hating his father, is given full treatment in the novel (the complex is named after the eponymous character in the Greek play Oedipus Rex). Here, the relationship between Mrs. Morel and William verges on romantic love; William wins her the egg-cups much as a lover proudly wins his girlfriend a prize at a fair, and he cannot enjoy himself once she leaves. Mrs. Morel, too, has projected the disappointment from her marriage into excessive love for her children, especially William. Lawrence uses several psychological symbols to demonstrate the complex relationships. Morel, threatened by his wife's love for their son, cuts off William's curly hair in a symbolic castration. Lawrence describes the act as "the spear through the side of her love for Morel." His metaphor suggests malevolent phallic imagery.

Tellingly, Mrs. Morel's first name, Gertrude, echoes that of the queen in Shakespeare's Hamlet, another work noted for its Oedipal themes.

CHAPTER 2: THE BIRTH OF PAUL, AND ANOTHER BATTLE

Summary

Morel feels ashamed for bullying his wife. He also realises her difficulties and begins to be somewhat more helpful. One morning Mrs. Morel summons her neighbour, Mrs. Kirk, by banging on the back of the fireplace with the poker, and tells her to fetch Mrs. Bower, the midwife. She gives birth to a boy and is very ill. Her husband comes home and is told by Mrs. Bower that he has a son. He asks her for a drink and then, after he has had his dinner, goes up to see his wife and son.

We are then introduced to Mr. Heaton, the Congregational clergyman, who comes to visit Mrs. Morel every day. One day Morel comes home while he is still visiting and begins to make a scene by enumerating the difficulties of working in the mine. Mrs. Morel feels disgusted by her husband's tendency to play for sympathy with those around him.

One evening after a quarrel with her husband, Mrs. Morel takes Annie and the baby and goes for a walk near the cricket fields. She seems at peace and feels strongly for her baby son; she has a sudden instinct to call him Paul.

The next major battle between the Morels begins when Walter comes home late and drunk again and accidentally pulls out a kitchen drawer in his haste to get something to eat. When his wife tells him she will not wait on him, he becomes enraged and flings the drawer at her, cutting her forehead on the corner of the drawer. For the few days after this incident, Morel refuses to get out of bed. When he finally gets up, he immediately goes to the Palmerston, one of his favourite bars, and this is where he spends the next several nights.

One night, however, he finds himself out of money, and therefore takes a sixpence from his wife's purse. She notices that it is missing and confronts him, upon which he becomes very indignant. He then goes upstairs and returns with a bundle and says he is leaving. Mrs. Morel feels sure that he will return that night, but she begins to get worried when he has not returned by dark. However, she finds his bundle hidden behind the door of the coal-shed and begins to laugh. Morel sulkily returns later that evening and his wife tells him to fetch his bundle before going to bed.

Commentary

Just as Mrs. Morel previously transferred her dissatisfaction with her life to her love for William, here we see her redouble those efforts with Paul. For every cruel turn Morel makes toward her, she reacts with overflowing love for her newborn child. This continues the Oedipal theme hinted at in Chapter I, and also bolsters the idea of oppositions playing off each other.

Another feature of oppositions explored here is how contradictory human nature is. Morel is usually heartless and detached, but he sometimes shows flashes of concern and love for his family. A greater contradiction emerges when he leaves, when Mrs. Morel realises that "her heart was bitter, because she had loved him." In her anxiety over her husband's presumed departure, she has understood that she has some fund of love for him (they even share a somewhat romantic moment when he brings her tea in the morning). However, it is possible if she is confusing dependence with love, a mixture she seems to inflict upon her children as well.

Mrs. Morel gains insight into her life while in the meadow. In Chapter I, she was at peace among the flowers in her garden (the flowers will become an important symbol). The Modernist literary movement borrowed the Romantic tradition of transcendence in nature and frequently transplanted it to a number of other settings, including urban ones. James Joyce and Virginia Woolf, especially, were fascinated with how the single moment‹Joyce preferred the term "epiphany"; Woolf, "moments of being"‹could elevate a human beyond his normal mental and spiritual state into a transcendent vision of himself and the world. Lawrence continues to use nature as the setting for these epiphanies, and it seems a logical choice for Mrs. Morel, constrained by her house and the nearby dirty mines.

Lawrence is adept at planting small scenes within larger narrative sweeps to highlight general behaviour. For instance, the scene in which Morel interrupts his wife and Heaton explains, without abstract commentary, Morel's jealousy over Heaton's relationship with his wife and even his child, his bitterness over his job in comparison with the clergyman's, and his growing irritation with his wife.

CHAPTER 3: THE CASTING OFF OF MOREL - THE TAKING ON OF WILLIAM

Summary

Morel begins to fall ill, despite all of his requests for medicine. His illness is attributed to the time he fell asleep on the ground when he went with Jerry to Nottingham. He falls seriously ill and his wife has to nurse him. She gets some help from the neighbours, but not every day. Eventually, Morel grows better, but he has been spoiled during his illness and at first wants more attention from his wife. However, she has begun to cast him off and to turn completely to her children to find a sense of meaning in her life.

During the period of peace following Morel's illness, another baby is conceived, and this child, Arthur, is born when Paul is seventeen months old. Arthur is very fond of his father, and this makes Mrs. Morel happy.

Meanwhile, time is passing, William is growing bigger, and Paul begins to have fits of depression in which he cries for no reason. One day, one of the other women of the neighbourhood, Mrs. Anthony, confronts Mrs. Morel because William has ripped her son Alfred's collar. Mrs. Morel asks William about it, he gives her his side of the story, and she reprimands him. However, Mrs. Anthony also tells Morel about the incident and he comes home very angry with William. This provokes yet another battle between Mr. and Mrs. Morel, as it is only her intervention that prevents him from beating William.

Mrs. Morel joins the Women's Guild, a club of women attached to the Cooperative Wholesale Society, who meet and discuss social questions. When William is thirteen, she gets him a job at the Co-op office. This provokes another argument with her husband, who would have preferred his son to become a miner like himself. However, William does well in his job as he does well in everything. He wins a running race and brings his mother home the prize, an inkstand shaped like an anvil.

However, William clashes with his mother when he begins to dance. Mrs. Morel turns away girls who come to call, much to William's dismay.

At nineteen, William gets a new job in Nottingham and also begins to study very hard. Then he is offered a job in London at a hundred and twenty pounds a year and is ecstatic, failing to see his mother's dismay at his departure. William and his mother have one final shared moment as they burn his love letters, and then he goes to London to start his new life.

Commentary

The third chapter details the effects of the Oedipus complex that has been developing in the first two chapters, but with a twist‹it appears that, with William, there is a reverse Oedipus complex at play. Mrs. Morel seems to be in love with her son, who desires her approval but is not nearly as dependent on her as she is on him. Her jealousy over the girls who visit him and have sent him love-letters is thinly veiled.

The effect William's departure will have on Paul, her more effeminate son, is unclear, but we have seen ample evidence so far that Mrs. Morel has a tendency to transfer dissatisfied feelings from one area of her life (such as her marriage) to another area (her children). We may assume that she will project her longing for William onto Paul, though how that love may mutate is unclear.

Complicating this Oedipal relationship is Morel, who acts in an infantile, dependent manner and becomes, in effect, an ignored middle child. While this temporarily enhances his relationship with his wife, whatever love they had (which she admitted to having in the last chapter) is gone, and he no longer has the power of being an imposing father figure.

Alongside Morel's growing dependence is Mrs. Morel's burgeoning independence (aside from her dependence on her children). She easily defeats and bullies Morel in a fight and, more importantly, joins the Women's Guild and recalls her former intellectual skills that have been out of service for so long.

CHAPTER 4: THE YOUNG LIFE OF PAUL

Summary

This chapter begins by describing the way that Paul, in the absence of William, bonded most closely with his sister Annie. She was a tomboy, who played games with the other neighbourhood children, and Paul would quietly tag along behind her. One day, while Annie's favourite doll is lying covered up on the sofa, Paul jumps off the sofa arm and lands on the doll. Annie is very upset, but her brother is perhaps more upset at her grief. A few days later, Paul suggests that they make a sacrifice of the doll, and they burn and smash its remains.

One evening when Paul comes home, he finds his father and older brother in the midst of an argument, which only fails to come to blows because of Mrs. Morel's intervention.

The family moves out of the Bottoms into a house with an ash-tree, which makes noise when the wind blows through it. Morel likes it, but the children hate it.

Morel still comes home late and drunk most nights, and Paul begins to worry because his mother is worrying about his father. One night he goes out to play, then at night anxiously runs into the kitchen to check on his mother. When he finds that his father has not come, he goes to visit Mrs. Inger, who lives two doors down and has no children of her own. He talks to her for a while, then goes home.

When Morel finally does come home, he is usually rude and irritable. During this time period he becomes more and more shut out from the family affairs, as the children begin to tell their mother everything and their father nothing. This is illustrated by the example of Paul's prize, which his mother convinces him to tell his father about. During their conversation, it becomes apparent that Morel is an outsider in his own family.

The next part of the narration, however, describes the times of happiness between Morel and his children. When he is happily engrossed in his work, he gets along well with his children. He tells stories, like the ones about Taffy the horse. On these nights, when Morel has some job to do, he goes to bed early and the children feel secure when he is in bed.

One day Paul comes home at dinnertime feeling ill and does not go back to school. It turns out that he has bronchitis. His father visits him while he is ill, but he asks for his mother, and sleeping with his mother comforts him.

The next episode is that of Paul going to collect the money for his father's pay on Fridays. When his name is called, he is at the back of the room behind all the men and almost misses his turn. He is saved by Mr. Winterbottom, the clerk, who pauses and asks the men to step aside so that Paul can get through. Paul is embarrassed and flustered by the experience, and he is relieved when it is over, and he is outside. He then goes to the New Inn to meet his father and has to wait a long time before he comes. When he gets home, Paul tells his mother he doesn't want to go collect the money any more. His mother soothes him "in her own way."

On Friday night, Paul stays home and bakes while his mother goes to the market. He likes to draw or read while the baking is being done. His mother gets home, shows her purchases to Paul, and they discuss the bargains she has gotten.

The rest of the family's life in the Scargill Street house is rather happy. The children love playing outside on winter evenings with the other neighbourhood children.

The final part of the chapter concerns the preparations made for William's visit at Christmas. The three other children go to the station to meet him and get very discouraged when the train is more than two hours late. At last, however, the train arrives with William. At home the parents are also anxious and begin to quarrel slightly, but finally the children arrive. William has brought presents for everyone, and everyone feels happy. After he returns to London, William is offered a trip to the Mediterranean over the midsummer holiday. However, he declines in favour of returning home, much to the delight of his mother.

Commentary

Paul's burning of the doll is similar to William's burning his love-letters‹except that William had real girls he was sacrificing as he moved to London, whereas Paul sacrifices the doll out of guilt for jumping on it. However, Paul's action may shed some light on William's; perhaps William felt guilty for dallying with women and making his mother jealous, and burning the letters was his way of assuaging his guilt.

Another similarity between Paul and William develops when Mrs. Morel buys the dish with cornflowers on it. The egg-cup William won for her at the wakes had "moss-roses" on it, and flowers are frequently depicted as calming agents which soothe Mrs. Morel in times of anxiety (she often goes into the garden for respite from her husband). Indeed, the cornflowers delight Paul, and flowers seem to bond other characters throughout the novel.

Previously, Mrs. Morel felt like she was being "buried alive," a logical complaint for someone married to a miner. Here, we learn that the children dislike the vast, open spaces around their new house. While not physically constricting, this space is still a "tight place of anxiety" to the children. No matter where they are, the characters always feel bound by their environment.

The characters are also bound to their love and dependence on William. While Mrs. Morel's dependent love was already well established, we see how his presence can temporarily revive the family, and how his absence can return it to misery.

Lawrence continues to use two forms of temporal shifts here: he laces small scenes into larger narrative sweeps, and uses a flashback for much of this chapter. The purpose is not to construct the temporal movement of the characters' lives, since episodic, achronological narratives are inferior to tight, chronological narratives in that regard. Rather, Lawrence constructs a sense of the characters' emotional movement; an event from years ago may have as much to do with their present feeling as one from last week.

CHAPTER 5: PAUL LAUNCHES INTO LIFE

Summary

Morel is injured at work when a piece of rock falls on his leg. When Mrs. Morel gets the news, she is very flustered while she is preparing to go to the hospital to see him. Paul calms her down and gives her some tea, and she leaves for the hospital. When she returns, she tells the children that their father's leg is injured rather badly. They all feel anxious, but are comforted by the fact that her father is a strong healer. Mrs. Morel feels somewhat guilty because she no longer loves her husband; while she is sorry for his pain and his injury, she still feels an emotional emptiness. She is somewhat comforted by talking to Paul, who is able to share her troubles. True to his nature, Morel does recover, and the family is very happy and peaceful while he is still in the hospital, almost to the point of regretting that he will soon return.

Paul is now fourteen, and it is time for him to find a job. Everyday, his mother sends him to the Co-op reading room to read the job advertisements in the paper. This makes him miserable, but he dutifully writes down a few offers and brings them home. He makes applications for several jobs using a variation on a letter that William had written. He is summoned to call on Thomas Jordan, a manufacturer of surgical appliances, and his mother is overjoyed.

Paul and Mrs. Morel travel to Nottingham one Tuesday morning to respond to the invitation. Paul suffers the whole way there, dreading the interview and the necessity of being scrutinized by strangers. During the actual interview, Mr. Jordan asks Paul to read a letter in French and he has trouble reading the handwriting, becomes flustered, and continually insists that doigts means fingers, although in this case it refers to the toes of a pair of stockings. Nevertheless, he is hired as junior spiral clerk.

After the interview, Paul and his mother have dinner in an eating-house, where it turns out that the food is more expensive than they realised; they order the cheapest dish possible. After dinner they wander around the town, look at some shops, and buy a few things. Paul is happy with his mother.

The next day he applies for a season ticket for the train. When he returns and tells his mother how much it will cost, she says that she wishes William would send them some money to help pay for things like the ticket.

Meanwhile, William is becoming a gentleman in London and is beginning to see a girl, Louisa Lily Denys Western, whom he calls Gipsy. He asks her for a photograph to send to his mother, and when the photo comes it shows her with bare shoulders. Mrs. Morel comments to William that she does not think the photo is appropriate, and the girl sends another one in which she is wearing an evening gown. Mrs. Morel is still not impressed.

The next Monday morning, Paul goes off to work on the train. He arrives at the factory and is introduced to his boss, Pappleworth. Pappleworth shows him how to fetch and copy letters, to write out orders and invoices, and to make up parcels for shipping. He also introduces him to some of the other people who work in the factory, and Paul gets along best with the women, like Polly, the overseer of the sewing crew, and the hunchback Fanny, who works in the finishing-off room. He becomes friends with many of the women and grows to like his job at Jordan's.

Commentary

Lawrence uses the words "prisoner" and "bondage" to describe industrialism's effect on Paul. Immediately contrasting these suffocating words are pastoral images of sunflowers, corn, and woods; flowers once again symbolize a peaceful world apart from the demands and responsibilities of work and family. Ironically, Paul loves work and feels free in the warehouse, showing the first signs of confidence and befriending not only his supervisor but various women.

Though we do not see evidence of Mrs. Morel's jealousy over Paul's relationships with these women yet, again she does not mask her disapproval of William's romantic relationships. Lily's youth, beauty, and wealth threaten her, and it seems doubtful she will ever bless any union of her eldest son.

Moreover, William is drifting further from the family. He is more devoted to his own career, and he uses his money for his personal life. It seems Paul has started working not only to compensate for this loss of income, but to take over William's position as the responsible son. Paul even gleefully announces that he is the "'man in the house'" when his father is in the hospital.

With this new status comes a more confused sexual identity. When Paul and his mother go to Nottingham together, Lawrence describes them as "feeling the excitement of lovers having an adventure together." Paul's Oedipus complex is sketched out in his ambition to share a cottage with his mother after his father dies. Although this does not include the Oedipal desire of murdering the father, the psychological implications are clear.

CHAPTER 6: DEATH IN THE FAMILY

Summary

This chapter begins with a description of Arthur, and tells how, as he grows older, he comes to detest his father. All of the children follow this same trend until they all loathe him. Arthur wins a scholarship to the school in Nottingha, and his mother decides to let him live in town with one of her sisters because of his adversarial relationship with his father. Annie is a teacher in the Board-school, and Mrs. Morel clings to Paul.

William becomes engaged to the girl he has been seeing, and decides to bring her home at Christmas. She comes home with him and puts on airs of high station, treating Annie like a servant. William begins to be annoyed with the way that she acts much grander than his family, and he tells his mother that he only feels fond of the girl when he is around her in the evenings; otherwise, he has no feelings for her.

Paul has Monday afternoons off from work, and one Monday his mother tells him that they have been invited to see Mr. Leivers on his new farm. They decide to go that afternoon. They have a nice walk through the countryside on the way there, and then are welcomed and given a tour of the farm when they arrive. The Leivers boys show Paul how to make the chicken eat out of his hand, and they tease their sister Miriam because she is afraid to try. Paul later finds her shyly reaching her hand toward the chicken and helps her to let it eat out of her hand.

The next time William brings his fiancee home, she once again annoys him and the rest of his family with her attitude toward his sister. He begins to ridicule her in front of others, and discusses with his mother that he no longer really wants to marry her, but feels that he has gone on too long to break it off now. He comes home again, alone, the first weekend in October, and his mother notices that he has not been well. The Tuesday morning after his return, Mrs. Morel gets a telegram saying that he is ill. She takes the train to London, arrives at

William's lodging, and stays with him until he dies late that night. She sends a telegram for Morel to come to London, and when it arrives Paul has to go to the mine to fetch his father. Morel goes to London, and Mr. and Mrs. Morel return on Saturday night. After William's death, Mrs. Morel becomes shut off until one day Paul falls ill with pneumonia. She almost loses him as well, but he somehow pulls through and "Mrs. Morel's life now rooted itself in Paul."

Commentary

William seems to foreshadow his death when he repeatedly mentions that Lily would forsake his love if he died. (Lawrence also says that William proves a "prophet" when Lily does, indeed, forget about William after his death.) Perhaps the one symbolic association we may make with William's death stems from his becoming aware of the erysipelas when he wears a collar. The lifestyle he has adopted in London‹excessively ambitious in the social and working worlds, engaged to a materialistic lady‹has collared and bound him as much as Morel's mining has imprisoned him.

Mrs. Morel, too, dislikes Lily largely because she has somehow escaped this prison. Though Lily, as a secretary, is not at a much higher station in life than Mrs. Morel, nor does she have much intellect, she acts far above Mrs. Morel. Mrs. Morel's jealousy comes out in deceptive, manipulative behaviour. She suggests William break off his engagement, then reprimands him for fighting with Lily in front of her.

We again see flowers acting as a bonding agent for Paul and his mother, when he picks her forget-me-nots in the country. His exuberant appreciation of his mother's outfit‹he claims that if he saw her on the street, he'd say "'Doesn't that little person fancy herself!'"‹exposes some complex psychological masking. He transfers his own "fancying" of his mother‹a guilty, incestuous feeling if he admitted to it‹onto her to assuage his conscience.

Mrs. Morel, however, shows the first glimmers of attraction to a male who is not one of her own sons when she critiques Mrs. Leiver to Paul and proposes that she herself would have made a better wife for Mr. Leiver. She does not fully own up to these desires, calling Mrs. Leiver "'lovable'" at the end, just as she never seems completely aware of how her maternal love borders on romantic love for her sons.

Mrs. Morel now has another emotion to deal with: guilt, for William's death. She compensates for his death, and her feeling that it should have been her, by heaping attention on Paul. That he becomes ill with pneumonia as well allows her to enact the maternal duties of nursing she wishes she could have used for William.

CHAPTER 7: LAD-AND-GIRL LOVE

Summary

This chapter describes the growing intimacy between Paul and Miriam. It begins from Miriam's perspective and describes the way that she aspires to learning, since she cannot have pride in her social status. She is interested in Paul, but scorns him because he only sees the swine-girl side of her and not the princess she believes she is inside. When he falls ill, she feels like he would be weaker than she and that is she could take care of him, she would love him deeply.

Paul enjoys visiting the Leivers' farm because it is so different from his own home. Miriam and her mother both have very strong religious and spiritual convictions, and this strikes Paul as enormously different from his own mother's logical manner.

One evening when he is there for dinner, the boys all become very upset with Miriam because the potatoes are burned. Her mother reprimands her for answering them instead of turning the other cheek, and Paul is puzzled why an insignificant matter like potatoes would cause such conflict.

Miriam and Paul make their connection through nature, as they share the experience of looking at a birds' nest. The narrator tells us, though, that it is a long time before Paul really notices Miriam. He first becomes friends with the boys, most of all Edgar. Then one day Miriam shows him the swing they have in the cowshed, and they slowly grow closer. Paul is troubled by her "intensity, which would leave no emotion on a normal plane". She tells him of her desire to learn, and he agrees to teach her algebra. They are both frustrated by the effort, and Paul finds her simultaneously infuriating and attractive.

One evening when Paul and Miriam are walking home, she brings him into the woods to see a particular bush because she wants to share it with him. This excursion causes him to be late coming home, and his mother is unhappy with him, partly because she is not fond of Miriam. They argue about his relationship with the girl and he insists that they are not courting.

Paul organizes a walk to the Hemlock Stone on Good Friday. During this walk, Miriam notices that Paul is different when she is alone with him. On the way back, she comes upon him alone in the road, trying to fix his umbrella so his mother will not be upset, and she realises that she loves him.

Miriam and Paul get along well during another excursion to Wingfield Manor on Easter Monday. However, after this she begins to feel tormented about whether she should be ashamed of loving him, and she decides she will no longer call at his house on Thursday nights. One evening she does call, and Paul picks some flowers to pin on her dress. Paul still refuses to define his and Miriam's relationship as that of lovers, and he forces his family to accept her as his friend.

When Paul is twenty, he has saved enough money to take his family away for a holiday for two weeks at a cottage called Mablethorpe. The night before they leave, Miriam stays at the house so she doesn't have to walk in the morning. One evening, she and Paul are walking on the beach and see a beautiful view of the moon, and Paul is confused by his instincts: he feels powerful feelings toward Miriam, but does not know how to interpret them. So they return to the cottage, Mrs. Morel admonishes him once more for being late, and the chapter ends with Paul feeling irritated at Miriam because she has made him feel unnatural.

Commentary

Paul dislikes it when Miriam smothers unreturned love on her youngest brother not only because Paul is not the recipient, but because it reminds him of how his mother loved and favoured William. The old feelings of jealousy that must have been present when he observed his mother's closer relationship with William reemerge.

Miriam is also like Mrs. Morel in her desire to learn more and transcend her gender's societal limitations. Mrs. Morel's own jealousy of Miriam, therefore, is not only a product of her ever-present disdain for any girl who shows an interest in one of her sons. Mrs. Morel envies Miriam's independence which she herself has forsaken for a family.

Paul strengthens the connections between the two women when he fuses his mother and Miriam through his painting: his mother provides the artistic inspiration, and Miriam helps him shape the final product. But this blending confuses Paul's sexual desires, evident when the image of his mother, and not Miriam, presides in his head at night. Perhaps Miriam is simply a way for Paul to get to a younger version of his mother, before she was ruined by her husband and William's death.

It is possible to read Miriam's wild-rose bush as a symbol for the female vagina. She and Paul make their way "'Down the middle path'" through the dense undergrowth of the woods to "have a communion together," and they finally reach the bush, which Lawrence twice describes with the sexualized words "splashing" and "splashed." Moreover, the roses, some of which are "expanded in ecstasy," have a "white, virgin scent."

Again, nature and, more specifically, flowers intimately bond characters, as when Paul shows Miriam the celandines, and in their frequent nature walks.

CHAPTER 8: STRIFE IN LOVE

Summary

Arthur enlists in the army on a whim, and then writes a letter to his mother to try to get out of it. She is very upset and goes to the sergeant, but is not able to get him out of it. He does not like the discipline of the army, but he has no choice.

Paul wins two first-prize awards in an exhibition for students' work in the Castle, which makes his mother very proud of him, and she goes to the Castle to see his work on display.

One day Paul meets Miriam in town with Clara Dawes, the daughter of an old friend of Mrs. Leivers. The next time Paul sees Miriam, she asks him what he thinks of Clara. He tells her that he likes her somewhat, and she sulks. He tells her that she is always too intense, and he longs to kiss her but cannot. When he leaves, he invites her and Edgar to tea the next day and she is happy. However, when he gets home and tells his mother, she is not pleased, and they argue.

Paul feels torn between Miriam and his mother, and resents Miriam because she makes his mother suffer. She feels hurt one day when he tells her he will not meet her before a party at his house because "you know it's only friendship."

One Friday night while Paul is doing the baking, Miriam comes to call and, when she hangs up her coat, he feels as though they live in the house together. He shows her a curtain he has made for his mother, and gives her a cushion-cover in the same design that he has made for her. They begin to talk about his work, and this is the time that Paul is happiest with Miriam.

They are then interrupted by Beatrice, a friend of the family, who makes fun of Miriam and flirts with Paul until Miriam reminds him that he is supposed to be watching the bread. He has burned one of the loaves, and then begins to feel somewhat guilty for ignoring Miriam. On some level, though, he feels that she deserves it. They go over her French notebook, they read a little bit, and he walks her home. When he returns, his mother and sister are waiting for him and they have found the burnt loaf of bread. They are angry that he has been with Miriam and his mother is ill. He reconciles with his mother and realises that he loves her more. His father comes home, and they fight, stopping only after Mrs. Morel faints, and Paul takes care of her.

Commentary

The discussion of Morel's body is important, especially coming after various descriptions of the close calls Miriam and Paul have had in physical contact‹Miriam even touches Paul once intimately on his sides. Lawrence shows the importance of the body in romantic relationships, and how that almost makes up for lack of spiritual communion; Mrs. Morel nearly remembers her long-abandoned passion for Morel when she examines his body.

The brief flirtation scene between Paul and Beatrice marks, for the first time, a love triangle of sorts that does not involve Mrs. Morel. Paul has a love/hate relationship with Miriam that affirms Lawrence's theme of oppositions, and he vacillates frequently with her in this chapter. Every time he sees a window open onto their love, he recalls something that instills some hatred in him. His burning the bread also recalls the time Miriam distractedly burnt the potatoes while Paul watched her.

Often, that something is his mother. Mrs. Morel returns to her rightful place in the novel's real love triangle when she openly admits to her reasons for hating Miriam. Her interaction with Paul is sexually charged, full of intimate physical contact. She says "'I've never had a husband‹not really'" almost as a plea for authentic romance in her life, and Paul's desire that she not sleep next to Morel sounds like more than merely a son's concerned view.

Paul's winning the art prizes is similar not only to William's "sporting trophies" for his mother, but to William's winning the egg-cup at the wakes long ago. In all three cases, the sons live for their mother, who lives through them.

CHAPTER 9: DEFEAT OF MIRIAM

Summary

Paul realises that he loves his mother more than Miriam, and Miriam seems also to realise that their relationship will never deepen. One day Paul comes to call and is unusually irritable. When Miriam begs him to tell her what is the matter, he tells her that they had better break off. She does not understand why, and he tries to tell her that, even though they have agreed that they are to be friends, "it neither stops there, nor gets anywhere else." She finally understands that he is telling her that he does not love her and wants to leave her free for another man.

Miriam feels that he is mistaken and that deep in his soul he loves her, and she is angry with him for listening to his mother, who has told him that he cannot go on in the same way unless he means to become engaged. She is angry that he lets his mother and his family tell him what he should do, thinking that she wishes the outside world would let the two of them alone.

Paul misses Willey Farm when he does not go there to call on Miriam, so he continues to go there to be with Edgar and the rest of the family. He no longer spends much time alone with Miriam, but one night he ends up alone with her when Edgar stays for Communion with Mrs. Morel. They are discussing the sermon and he reads to her from the Bible, and they almost attain their previous level of harmony—until Paul begins to feel uncomfortable.

Miriam invites Paul to come to the farm one day to meet Clara Dawes. He accepts and is excited to meet her. He arrives, meets her in the parlor, talks to her and Miriam for a short time, and quickly decides that he does not like her. He goes to meet Edgar on his way back from getting coal. He tells Edgar that Clara should be called 'Nevermore' because she is so disagreeable.

Later, Miriam asks Paul to accompany the two women on a walk. They meet Miss Limb and her horse, and Clara especially is very fond of the horse. After they leave, Paul and Miriam mention that they both feel there is something strange about Miss Limb, and Clara suggests that she wants a man.

Clara walks a little ahead, and Miriam asks Paul if he still finds her disagreeable. He replies that something is the matter with her, and she agrees. They arrive at a field of wildflowers, and enjoy it together. Paul and Miriam pick flowers, and Clara says she doesn't like to pick them because she doesn't want the corpses around her. Paul argues that it is sufficient reason that he likes and wants the flowers and that there are plenty of them, and Miriam says that the spirit in which the flowers are picked is what matters. When Clara bends forward to smell the flowers, Paul scatters cowslips over her hair and neck.

Paul takes his mother to Lincoln to see the cathedral, and he becomes worried about her when she cannot climb the hill because of her heart. He laments the fact that his mother is old and ill and that he was not the eldest son, and his mother tells him that she is only a bit old and not really ill.

At this time Annie is engaged to Leonard, who has a talk with Mrs. Morel because he wants to get married right away. She cautions him that neither he nor Annie has much money, and he tells her that he realises that, but he still wants to marry Annie right away. She trusts him, as she tells Paul, and so the wedding takes place immediately.

Mrs. Morel decides to buy Arthur out of the army, at which he is overjoyed. He comes home and takes up with Beatrice Wyld.

Paul writes Miriam a letter attempting to explain what has happened in their love, and we are told that this is the end of the first phase of Paul's romantic endeavors.

Commentary

Paul makes several differentiations between physical and spiritual love in this chapter. Sensual Clara epitomizes the physical, much as Paul's father does. She is fascinated by the great stallion's physique, roughhouses with Paul, and cuts a striking, full figure.

Miriam, clearly, opposes Clara, much as Mrs. Morel does. She is the far more spiritual figure, as Paul points out. Even Miriam's few instances of physicality are projected through another, purer medium. When she "caress[es] with her mouth and cheeks and brow" the "wild looking daffodil," Lawrence hints at her repressed sexual desires; he explodes this when he writes "Rhythmically, Miriam was swaying and stroking the flower with her mouth, inhaling the scent which ever after made her shudder as it came to her nostrils." The numerous double entendres are easy to pick out, and Paul is the phallic "wild looking daffodil" she so strongly desires.

Flowers otherwise continue to play an important role in the novel. When Clara refuses to pick them because she thinks they become like "'corpses'" when they are picked; this is indicative of her liveliness and sensuality. Paul picks them because "'I like them, and want them.'" He, too, indirectly expresses his true desire for Clara through the flowers.

Paul says he likes Clara because she is "'defiant'" and "'angry,'" but perhaps what really appeals to him is her own reference to her "'free and independent'" life. This alludes to her separation from her husband, and we see that Clara is the one woman in the novel who is unfettered by the men in her life. She is exactly what Mrs. Morel could never be, an independent woman who does not need her unloving husband.

Mrs. Morel is downplayed here as she seems to age well beyond her years, except when Paul takes her out to dinner and says "I'm a fellow taking his girl for an outing.'" He is still obsessed with his mother, wanting to live with her yet wanting something else out of life, and romantic confusion over her and Clara‹seven years his senior‹seems inevitable.

CHAPTER 10 - CLARA

Summary

Paul sends a painting to an exhibition at Nottingham Castle, and one morning Mrs. Morel gets very excited upon reading a letter. It turns out that he has won first prize and that the painting has been sold for twenty guineas to Major Moreton. Paul and his mother rejoice at his success, and he tells her that she can use the money to buy Arthur out of the army. Paul is invited to some dinner parties and tells his mother he needs an evening suit. She gives him a suit that was William's.

Paul's newfound success prompts discussions with his mother about class and happiness. She wants her son to ascend into the middle class, but he says that he feels closest to the common people. Mrs. Morel wants her son to be happy, which seems mostly to mean finding a good woman and beginning to settle down. Paul argues that he worries a normal life might bore him.

Paul maintains his connection with Miriam, able neither to break it off entirely nor to go the full way to engagement. He feels that he owes himself to her, but he begins to drift slightly away from her.

Arthur is married to Beatrice, and she has a child. At first he is irritable and unhappy, but eventually he begins to accept his responsibilities and care for his wife and child.

One day a mutual friend asks Paul to take a message to Clara Dawes. He goes to her house, meets her mother, and observes them working on making lace. He delivers his message, has a pleasant conversation with Clara and her mother, and leaves, having gotten a humbling view of Clara, whom he had previously believed to be so high and mighty. Paul finds out that Susan, one of the girls at Jordan's, is leaving to get married, and so he gets Clara her job. The other girls do not like Clara because she acts like she is above them; they call her the Queen of Sheba.

One day Paul is rude to Clara; later, he regrets his rudeness and brings her chocolates as an apology. On his birthday Fanny surprises him with a gift of paints that all the girls except Clara, who they do not include in their planning, have chipped in to buy him. Paul goes out walking at dinnertime with Clara, and she complains that the girls have some secret from her. Paul tells her that the secret was the planning for his birthday present, and, that evening, she sends him a book of verse and a note. This incident brings Paul and Clara closer together.

They discuss what happened between Clara and her husband, and somehow the subject of Miriam comes up. Paul says that Miriam wants his soul, which he cannot give her. Clara, however, informs him that Miriam does not want his soul, only Paul himself.

Commentary

This chapter details various class tensions. Paul believes he doesn't want to belong to the middle-class although, as his mother points out, the people he prefers to associate with‹especially Miriam‹are middle-class.

Clara's superiority at work, and her reluctance to converse with the working-class women, on the other hand, suggests that Paul is much closer to the working-class than he might otherwise be. He is good friends with all the girls, and their gift to him of paints‹a decidedly middle-class, artistic gift‹indicates their hope that he will rise beyond the factory and someday paint for a living.

Paul's attraction to Clara's body continues. When he watches Clara at work, there are some similarities to when Miriam bent over the daffodils in Chapter IX: "She bent over her machine, grinding rhythmically, then stooping to see to see the stocking that hung beneath He watched the handsome crouching of her back." Miriam's actions with the daffodils were nearly sexually explicit but, in the end, virginal and pure, whereas even Clara's manual labour is tinged with sexuality.

Paul calls Clara "Penelope," a direct reference to Penelope in Homer's Odyssey. While Paul makes the connection with Clara's habit of waiting and weaving, the name also recalls the theme of fidelity in the Odyssey. Penelope held off her suitors for twenty years as she waited for her husband's return, while Clara is separated from her husband but not legally divorced. Exposition about the marriage complicates this allusion; Clara's husband was unfaithful to her, not the other way around. Though Paul vows to remain only friends with her, we sense that soon she and Paul will develop a sexual relationship.

CHAPTER 11: THE TEST ON MIRIAM

Summary

Inspired by Clara's advice, Paul realises that he must go back to Miriam. He reflects that the problems between the two of them may have been caused by the lack of sexuality in their relationship. He feels no aversion to her; rather, he feels that his desire for her has been overwhelmed by his stronger shyness and virginity.

He begins to spend more time with Miriam again, much to the dismay of his mother. One day he begins a serious discussion with her about marriage, and asks her if she thinks they have been "too fierce" in their purity toward each other. He tells her that he loves her, that he has been obstinate, and he kisses her. On their way home, he asks her (not in so many words) if she will sleep with him, and she tells him that she will, but not now.

Miriam feels that her submission to Paul will be a sacrifice, and it is a sacrifice she is willing to make for him. He begins to treat his relationship with her as a romantic relationship. One evening they go into the woods and "she relinquished herself to him," but with some horror and with her soul somewhat apart.

Miriam goes to stay at her grandmother's cottage, and Paul visits her often. One holiday he goes to spend the whole day with her. She prepares dinner, for that day they feel as though they live together in that cottage. They take a walk outside after dinner, and then come back inside and make love. Paul feels that he is sacrificing Miriam and that she is allowing herself to be sacrificed because she loves him so much.

During the next week, he asks her why she is so hesitant toward him, and she replies that she feels it is not quite right because they are not married. He tells her that he would like to marry her, but she feels they are too young. He begins to feel a sense of failure and to draw somewhat away from Miriam again. He begins to spend more time with his men friends and also once again with Clara.

Paul tells his mother that he will break off with Miriam, because he does not love her and does not want to marry her. She is somewhat surprised, and encourages him to do whatever he thinks is best. He goes to Miriam and tells her they should break off because he does not want to marry. She is upset, tells him he is a child of four, and tells him that she knew all along that it would not work out between them. This upsets Paul and he begins to feel that she has deceived him, she had only pretended to love him. They part, each full of bitterness.

Commentary

This chapter is the most explicit thus far in terms of sexuality, but Lawrence's descriptions are still a far cry from his later work. The preponderance of sexual euphemisms‹"'You will have me,'" "'belong to each other,'" "'his satisfaction,'" "relinquish," "sacrifice"‹reflect both what the prudish Paul and Miriam would say and what was permissible in literature in Lawrence's repressive time. He was instrumental in breaking literary sexual boundaries, but Sons and Lovers seems to suffers in accuracy from its puritanical language; while Miriam "relinquished[s]" herself to Paul in the woods, they have intercourse for the first time in the cottage, so it is unclear exactly what "relinquish" means.

Lawrence also uses a number of other techniques to comment indirectly on the budding sexuality of his characters. The cherry is a symbol of virginity‹specifically of the hymen‹and Paul's throwing the cherries at Miriam is an aggressive act that releases his frustrations over their virginity. To break the hymen metaphor open even more, Lawrence has

Paul accidentally rip his shirt-sleeve. Miriam, ever the pure virgin, promises to mend it, but not before exploring his warm skin underneath, an action indicative of her sexual curiosity.

The colours of the sunset while Paul picks the cherries also mirror the climax of orgasm: "Gold flamed to scarlet, like pain in its intense brightness. Then the scarlet sank to rose, and rose to crimson, and quickly the passion went out of the sky." The use of weather to reflect a character's disposition‹known as pathetic fallacy‹is frequently used in literature, but Lawrence's erotically charged images allow him to explore the nature of sexuality without appearing indecent.

When Paul breaks up with her, Miriam frequently returns to the word "bondage." She feels enslaved to Paul, and is upset that he has so much power over her. This bondage, which we have seen in Mrs. Morel, is one of Lawrence's main concerns: how does a woman remain liberated yet still enjoy the romantic and sexual company of a man?

CHAPTER 12: PASSION

Summary

Paul begins to spend much of his time with his mother again. They go to the Isle of Wight for a holiday, and Mrs. Morel has a bad fainting fit caused by too much walking. She recovers, but Paul still feels anxious about her condition.

Paul also returns to spending a great deal of time with Clara. He tells her that he has broken off with Miriam. One Saturday evening Paul and Clara go for a walk and he kisses her, then, upon leaving, he is suddenly consumed by passion for her and cannot wait for Monday to come so that he can see her again. On Monday they go walking in the afternoon and take a tram out to the country.

They walk near a river and decide to go down to the bank, but because of the rain, the path is gone. They encounter two fishermen while walking along the riverbank and keep walking until they find a secluded clearing slightly above the river level. After they leave, they climb up to the top again and they stop while Paul cleans off Clara's boots. She distracts him with kisses, but he finally finishes. They stop for tea at the house of an old woman, who gives Clara some flowers.

Paul returns home and tells his mother that he has been with Clara. She cautions him because Clara is a married woman, and he tells her not to worry. He asks if she would like to meet Clara, and decides to invite her to tea at their house one Sunday afternoon.

He still sees Miriam occasionally, and they talk about Clara and why she left her husband. Miriam tries to compare them to Mr. and Mrs. Morel, but Paul disagrees; he says that his mother felt passionately toward his father and that's why she stayed with him. He feels that Clara never had this type of passion for Baxter. Miriam understands that he is trying to initiate himself into passion. He tells her that Clara is coming to tea at his house on Sunday to meet his mother, and she understands that this is an indication of his seriousness.

When Clara comes to tea, she gets along well with his mother. Morel also meets her and impresses her with his politeness. Clara and Paul are in the garden looking at the flowers when Miriam arrives to say hello to Clara. She sees them together, and feels as though they are married. Mrs. Morel is not pleased to see Miriam, whom she still dislikes. All three go to chapel and, afterward, when Paul and Clara are walking home, she asks him if he will give Miriam up. He tells her that he thinks he will always be friends with Miriam, and she draws away from him slightly and mocks him, telling him to run after Miriam. He gets angry with her and kisses her in rage. They go off into the fields, where they look at the lights of the town until Clara realises she must go to make her train. They run and she just makes the train.

The next week Paul takes Clara to the theatre. She tells him to wear his evening suit, and she arrives dressed in a green evening dress. After the play, Paul realises that he has missed his train, and Clara tells him to come home with her instead of walking. They arrive, and Clara's mother, Mrs. Radford, makes fun of their fancy clothes. Paul and Clara sit up playing cribbage, and Mrs. Radford waits up for them. Finally Paul goes to bed, but he cannot sleep for want of Clara. After he hears Mrs. Radford go to sleep and realises that Clara is waiting downstairs, he goes down to her and asks her to come to his bed instead of going to sleep with her mother. She refuses, and he goes back to bed.

Mrs. Radford wakes him up in the morning, and he realises that she is fond of him. He asks if she and Clara would like to go to the seaside with him and is amazed when she accepts.

Commentary

Lawrence again omits explicit sexual information when Clara and Paul go to the river. Their descent down the wet riverbank mimics the act they are about to perform, and to indicate intercourse, Lawrence merely starts a new paragraph with "When she arose" The coquettish conversation afterward also impiies sex, with Paul's denial that Clara is a "'criminal'" or "'sinner.'"

Lawrence again focuses on Paul's obsession with Clara's body. It seems that Paul spends as much thought on Clara's body as he did on Miriam's personality. We can see the reasoning behind this preoccupation; not only does her body arouse in him a new, sensual being, he is transformed into her. He loses himself in her body, identifying with her specific parts: "He was Clara's white heavy arms, her throat, her moving bosom." Paul gains access to a femininity previously unknown to him.

Oddly, Mrs. Morel is not jealous of her son's relationship with Clara, at least at first. Perhaps this is because Clara does not want to compete with her, and though the girls at work think Clara is snobby, Clara does not threaten her in the same way Miriam did. Mrs. Morel sees that Paul desires Clara most for her body, and not his spiritual connection with her, as he did with Miriam. However, as Mrs. Morel's own body decays in old age, she returns to her jealous ways when she says Paul's attraction to Clara will not last. Clara represents a displacement of her as a maternal figure for Paul, but a far younger, healthier, and more beautiful maternal figure.

Another mother figure is presented in greater depth here, Mrs. Radford. Her hostility towards Paul seems to stem from her sadness over her husband's death, alluded to just once.

CHAPTER 13: BAXTER DAWES

Summary

Paul is in a bar with some friends when Baxter Dawes enters, Clara's husband from whom she has been separated for years. Paul offers him a drink, since he is the superior at Jordan's, but Dawes refuses. Dawes begins to talk about Paul being at the theatre with a 'tart,' and Paul is about to leave when Dawes says something that causes Paul to throw a glass of beer in his face. Dawes rushes at Paul but is held back, and he is thrown out of the bar. Paul's friends at the bar tell him that he should learn to box, so that he can take care of Dawes. When he leaves, one of the men walks with him.

He tells Clara what has happened, and she does not seem surprised, saying that Baxter is a low sort of person. She wants Paul to carry a gun or a knife for protection and is angry when he refuses.

One day at the factory, Paul runs into Dawes. Dawes threatens him while he carries on with his work. Finally Dawes grabs Paul's arm, and Thomas Jordan comes out of his office to see what is happening. He tells Dawes to leave and, when he does not, grabs his arm. Dawes jerks his elbow and sends Jordan flying backward through a spring-door and down half a flight of steps. Jordan is not hurt, but he dismisses Dawes.

Paul discusses love with his mother and says that perhaps something is the matter with him and that he can't love. She says that he has not met the right woman, and he replies that he will never meet the right woman while she is alive. Clara asks him about the future, and he tells her he will go abroad and then come back to be with his mother. He tells her not to ask about the future but just to be with him now, and they surrender to their passion. She does not want a divorce from Baxter and therefore cannot belong to him completely. They both realise that they will go separate ways.

One evening they pass Dawes as they are walking, and Paul does not realise who it is until after they have passed him, and Clara says it was Baxter. Another night some time later, Paul is walking alone and encounters Dawes waiting for him. They fight and Paul is hurt. He struggles to get himself home and goes to sleep, and his mother is there to take care of him when he awakes. While he is ill, Clara and then Miriam come to visit him, and he tells his mother that he doesn't care about them.

After he is better, he goes on a holiday with his friend Newton and arranges to meet his mother at Annie's house in Sheffield. When he arrives there, Annie opens the door and he realises that his mother is ill. They discover that she has a tumor, and Paul goes to see her doctor in Nottingham. He agrees to come to Sheffield, looks at the tumor, and says that he may be able to cure it. Mrs. Morel stays in Sheffield for two months, and then the family hires a motor-car to drive her home, at which she is very glad.

Commentary

Another bearer of jealousy emerges in this chapter, Baxter Dawes. His brand of jealousy is a more conventional kind in literature, that of the jilted (in his eyes, at least) lover. Other conventional actions emerge from this: threats, insults, the humiliating encounter (when Dawes makes himself unnoticeable), the comparisons by the woman between the two men, and the fight.

Paul's pacifism, and his lack of knowledge of even how to fight, disappoints Clara, who seems to relish the idea of two men fighting for her. However, generally she is far more subdued now, no longer an elusive, mysterious figure to Paul. Now Paul is the more magnetic character. There is a great deal of description of Paul's body in this chapter as seen through her eyes, a contrast to previous chapters in which Paul's point of view focused on Clara's body.

Interestingly, the description of Paul's body coming alive in the fight is similar to the description of his body during love-making. Perhaps the fight releases his pent-up hatred for both Clara and Miriam as well as for Dawes. Meanwhile, Mrs. Morel's body continues to decay, and death is now imminent.

There is also much discussion in this chapter of possessiveness and bondage. Clara is bound to Paul, who does not feel the same degree of bondage toward her, or any woman, except his mother. Clara also feels Dawes belongs to her, which is why she cannot divorce him.

Lawrence refers to Paul as "Morel" during his fight with Dawes. This change emphasizes that the battle is between two men, rather than a man (Dawes) and a boy (Paul).

CHAPTER 14: THE RELEASE

Summary

Dr. Ansell tells Paul that Baxter Dawes is in the fever hospital in Sheffield, and Paul decides to visit him. Paul tells Dawes that he can recommend him a convalescent home in Seathorpe. He tells Clara that he has been to visit Dawes in the hospital, and she becomes upset and realises that she has treated her husband badly. She goes to see him to try to make amends, but at first they do not get on well. Paul also visits Dawes a few times, and the two men begin to develop a sort of friendship.

Paul does not spend much time with Clara now, because he is occupied with his mother's illness. Mrs. Morel gets gradually worse, and Paul spends much time caring for her. When Clara reminds him that it is her birthday, he takes her to the seashore, but spends most of the time talking about his mother and how he wishes that she would die.

The next time he sees Dawes, Paul mentions that he has been with Clara, and this is the first mention the two men make of Clara. He tells Dawes that he will go abroad after his mother dies.

Time passes, and Mrs. Morel stays the same. Miriam writes to Paul and he visits her. She kisses him, believing he will be comforted, but he does not want that kind of comfort from her and finally manages to get away. Paul and Annie share the nursing of their mother. They begin to feel as if they can no longer go on, and Paul decides to give her an overdose of morphia to put an end to all their suffering. He crushes all the pills they have into his mother' milk, and she drinks it obediently, believing it to be a new sleeping draught. She lasts through the night and finally dies the next morning.

Dawes is now in a convalescent home, and Paul goes to see him again and suggests that he has plenty of life left in him and that he should try to get Clara back so that he can regain something of his former life. The next day, he and Clara bring Dawes to his lodging and Paul leaves them together.

Commentary:

The two illnesses in this chapter demonstrate how the sick body can either cripple or restore relationships that were, on some level, dependent on the body.

Mrs. Morel's illness and death has an adverse effect on both Morel and Paul. Morel is unable to deal with his wife's death, refusing to look at her in sickness and death. He wants only to remember her as his "young wife" with whom he shared a passionate, physical relationship, and not as the cancerous woman who loathed him.

Paul's physical relationship with his mother, on the other hand, has lasted longer than Morel's and is more deeply rooted. The effect of his mother's dying, therefore, has a more complicated effect. He is unable to stand seeing her waste away, and his overdosing her is as much for his and Annie's sake as their mother's. Moreover, his action reverses that of Oedipus; rather than kill his father, Paul kills his mother. Though he is still beholden to his mother, he is beginning to understand he must live without her.

Paul's reaction to his mother's death is intense‹he repeats "My love‹my love‹oh, my love!"‹but Lawrence spends little time discussing the death at first. When Paul visits Mrs. Morel's body again at night, however, his near-necrophiliac kissing and stroking reveals his pent-up desires. He wants her to be "young again" not only so she can be a youthful mother but, one suspects, so she can be the perfect romantic object Paul has not found in Miriam or Clara. His relinquishing Clara to Dawes can be seen as Paul's understanding that Clara is not a substitute for his mother, and that he must move on in life. He tells Dawes that none of his women has ever wanted to "'belong'" to him, and though it seems that Miriam gladly would have wanted this, it is clear that no one ever wanted it as much as his mother.

Conversely, Dawes's illness restores his relationship with Paul and, eventually, Clara. The friendship the two rivals form is curious but plausible; perhaps Paul feels he can befriend Dawes since he is no longer threatened by the older man's formerly strong body (the other reason, as Paul explains, is that the passion has died out in his romance with Clara).

CHAPTER 15: DERELICT

Summary

Clara goes back to Sheffield with her husband, and Paul is left alone with his father. There is no point in keeping their house any longer, so they each take lodgings nearby. Paul is lost without his mother. He can no longer paint, and he puts all of his energy into his work at the factory. He has debates within himself, telling himself that he must stay alive for his mother's sake. However, he wants to give up.

One Sunday evening, however, he sees Miriam at the Unitarian Church. He asks her to have supper with him quickly and she agrees. She tells him that she has been going to a farming college and will probably be kept on as a teacher there. She says that she thinks they should be married, and he says he's not sure that would be much good. He says he does not want it very much, and so she gives up. That is the end between them. She leaves him, realizing that "his soul could not leave her, wherever she was."

Paul, alone, yearns for his mother and considers following her into death. However, he decides to leave off thinking about suicide, and instead walks toward the town.

Commentary:

The brief concluding chapter is despairing until the very end, when Paul finally releases himself from the hold of his mother and chooses to return to life.

A hold, indeed, for much of Sons and Lovers is about bondage to someone else. Here, Paul refuses to be bound, to belong, to Miriam, but not because he fears bondage. Miriam is too sacrificial and passive; he wants a woman who will claim him as strongly for herself as his mother did. For him, this is the only kind of relationship that can duplicate the intense love he had with his mother. Paul does not seem to understand until the final moments of the novel, however, that his mother's love was smothering, jealous, and ultimately destructive. His release from her feels like a victory; he may now be able to love someone else.

Flowers reappear here, but now they symbolize Paul's parting from Miriam, and not a bond. The other imagery that is important is the city's "gold phosphorescence" in the final paragraph. Frequently in the novel, Lawrence paints scenes of happiness and love with light colours of the sky. The return of these light colours here signifies Paul's choice of life over the "darkness" of death.

Chapter 9

Study Questions

Q1. What are the major themes discussed in " Sons and Lovers"

Or

Q. What are the issues Lawrence deals with in " Sons and Lovers"

Or

Q. To what extent does Lawrence succeeds in introspecting into love and society in " Sons and Lovers"

THEMES

Sons, Mothers, and the Oedipus Complex

You can look at Sons and Lovers as a story of the unnatural devotion of Paul Morel to his possessive mother. Many readers see the novel as a fictional study of the "Oedipus complex," described by Lawrence's contemporary, the founder of psychoanalysis, Sigmund Freud. Freud took the old Greek myth of Oedipus, in which the hero unknowingly kills his father and marries his own mother, as a reflection of man's subconscious sexual desires. Freud rebelled against the Victorian idea that children are asexual. He believed that a child's earliest sexual attraction (at about three to five years of age) is to the parent of the opposite sex. Freud concluded his theory with the warning that if a boy did not eventually suppress this attraction and begin to identify with his father, he would never be able to transfer his early love for his mother to a suitable partner.

Paul Morel seems very much like a man suffering from an Oedipus complex. At times Paul's relationship with Gertrude is disturbingly passionate. He hates his father and dreams of living exclusively with his mother. Paul has grave problems finding a satisfying relationship with any woman other than his mother. The novel traces his unsuccessful attempts to reconcile spiritual love, sexual passion, and filial devotion. Mrs. Morel encourages her son's dependence and is envious of Miriam, her rival for his affection.

Along with the Oedipus complex, you'll want to consider the positive aspects of Paul's relationship with his mother. She encourages his art, education, and social advancement. In many ways, Mrs. Morel embodies the Victorian concept of the ideal mother. She lives for her sons and will do anything to see them make their way in the world. Paul's life on his own is just beginning at the novel's end. Do you think Mrs. Morel's influence on her son will prove to be for better or for worse?

Man/Woman Love

Sons and Lovers is an investigation of love between men and women. Paul has a spiritual love with Miriam and a sexual one with Clara. Both relationships leave him unfulfilled because Paul needs a love that combines both spiritual and sexual elements in one woman. Lawrence clarified and developed his ideas on the importance of man/woman love in his later novels. Still, in this novel you get a strong feeling that survival in modern, industrial society depends on strong heterosexual relationships. Such a relationship is only possible when both man and woman are spiritually and physically vital. Paul Morel's unfulfilled quest for this sort of relationship is a major theme of Sons and Lovers.

Sex is a bone of contention between Paul and his two loves, Miriam and Clara. Both women want a personal, emotional relationship, whereas Paul views sex as rather impersonal. The woman isn't exactly an object, but a catalyst for man's mystical communion with nature. Clara and Miriam both feel that Paul doesn't make love to them as individuals, but as symbols of womanhood. They feel used, while Paul fears they're trying to possess and smother him. Lawrence felt that modern, industrial life caused such sexual warfare between men and women. Sex, which the author viewed as a healthy expression of man's link to God and nature, had been perverted by Victorian morality and the dehumanization of mechanized, industrial life.

Lawrence's sense of sex as good was alien to the Victorian belief that it was evil and beastly. Sex was not supposed to be a topic of conversation between a man and a good woman. The character of Miriam is a depiction of repressed sexuality common in the Victorian woman. Many other writers were encouraged by Lawrence's bold descriptions of the sexual act and continued his revolutionary work in their own novels.

The Maturation of an Artist

Sons and Lovers tells the story of an individual growing up to become a talented painter and a deeply sensitive, troubled young man. The novel traces Paul's discovery of his need and ability to paint. Art for Paul is inspired by nature and women. The beauty of the countryside stimulates his creativity, as do the gentle, devoted encouragement of Miriam, the sensuality of Clara, and the protective, sensible nurturing of Mrs. Morel.

As the novel progresses, Paul becomes more and more confident in his paintings. He starts to believe he'll make a great artist someday. What's most interesting about Paul as an artist is the way he sees things. He imbues raindrops, birds, and wildflowers with a supernatural vitality. They appear to him like miraculous affirmations of brilliant, individualistic lives struggling against eternal darkness and chaos.

The artist's mission in life, according to Lawrence, is to help others see beyond the commonplace and into life's mystery and wonder. At Jordan's factory, Paul draws the local shop girls in such a way as to make each of them appear unique. He makes the girls see their own inner beauty and special ness.

Class Conflict

You can see Sons and Lovers as a novel that epitomizes the conflict between the unskilled, ill- educated working class and the rigidly moral, emotionally and sexually inhibited middle class. Walter Morel, a symbol of the working class, has the positive qualities of instinct, warmth, and spontaneity. His wife, Gertrude, a symbol of the middle class, embodies their work ethic and their intellectual and social aspirations. Gertrude and Walter ought to complement one another with their very different positive points, but in fact they, like the lower and middle classes, can't get along. In Sons and Lovers, the lower class's hatred of snobbery and phony propriety and the middle class's concern with money and social advancement cause Gertrude and Walter to come to blows. Lawrence in his own life and later novels sought a way of bringing these two social realms into harmony.

Sons and Lovers can also be viewed as a working-class novel, a novel that focuses on the everyday lives, trials, and tribulations of unskilled, poor labourers. Through Lawrence's words, you get a vivid picture of what it was like to be a miner or a factory worker around the turn of the century.

Industrial Life Vs. Nature

We have a sense in Sons and Lovers that modern industrial life perverts people. They're cut off from nature and their own instinctive sexuality. Industrialism and its rigid moral code enslaves nature and discounts the sensual and aesthetic needs of humans. As you read the novel, pay close attention to the narrator's description of Jordan's factory and the way that Clara and Paul, on a brief escape from work, view the cityscape as a scar on the countryside. Factory life with its enforced confinement and long working hours isolates man from the natural world that is his true connection to the life force. Flowers, water, and other natural images are identified with sensuality and beauty, while the mines bury the fields in dust and darkness.

OPPOSING FORCES: LIGHT AND DARK

Sons and Lovers deals constantly in oppositions, such as light and dark. Lawrence believed that oppositions in the grand scheme of things form a completeness, rather than a vicious, irreconcilable struggle. Light stands for rational life and day-to-day reality. It is most strikingly associated with Mrs. Morel. Darkness symbolizes the wonder and mystery of existence, as well as the human subconscious and brute instinct. This quality is exemplified in Walter Morel, who every day descends deep into the earth.

To Lawrence, light and dark, like life and death, opened naturally into each other. When you come to William's death in Chapter 6, you'll notice that the coffin is brought from the dark into the family's lighted parlor. Lawrence, always ill and close to dying himself, felt that death was a natural extension of life and should be treated as such. To deny death, he believed, was truly to deny life.

Bondage

Lawrence discusses bondage, or servitude, in two major ways: social and romantic. Socially, Mrs. Morel feels bound by her status as a woman and by industrialism. She complains of feeling "'buried alive,'" a logical lament for someone married to a miner, and even the children feel they are in a "tight place of anxiety." Though she joins a women's group, she must remain a housewife for life, and thus is jealous of Miriam, who is able to utilize her intellect in more opportunities. Ironically, Paul feels free in his job at the factory, enjoying the work and the company of the working-class women, though one gets the sense that he would still rather be painting.

Romantic bondage is given far more emphasis in the novel. Paul (and William, to a somewhat lesser extent) feels bound to his mother, and cannot imagine ever abandoning her or even marrying anyone else. He is preoccupied with the notion of lovers "belonging" to each other, and his true desire, revealed at the end, is for a woman to claim him forcefully as her own. He feels the sacrificial Miriam fails in this regard and that Clara always belonged to Baxter Dawes. It is clear that no woman could ever match the intensity and steadfastness of his mother's claim.

Complementing the theme of bondage is the novel's treatment of jealousy. Mrs. Morel is constantly jealous of her sons' lovers, and she masks this jealousy very thinly. Morel, too, is jealous over his wife's closer relationships with his sons and over their successes. Paul frequently rouses jealousy in Miriam with his flirtations with Agatha Leiver and Beatrice, and Dawes is violently jealous of Paul's romance with Clara.

Contradictions and Oppositions

Lawrence demonstrates how contradictions emerge so easily in human nature, especially with love and hate. Paul vacillates between hatred and love for all the women in his life, including his mother at times. Often he loves and hates at the same time, especially with Miriam. Mrs. Morel, too, has some reserve of love for her husband even when she hates him, although this love dissipates over time.

Lawrence also uses the opposition of the body and mind to expose the contradictory nature of desire; frequently, characters pair up with someone who is quite unlike them. Mrs. Morel initially likes the hearty, vigourous Morel because he is so far removed from her dainty, refined, intellectual nature. Paul's attraction to Miriam, his spiritual soul mate, is less intense than his desire for the sensual, physical Clara.

The decay of the body also influences the spiritual relationships. When Mrs. Morel dies, Morel grows more sensitive, though he still refuses to look at her body. Dawes's illness, too, removes his threat to Paul, who befriends his ailing rival.

Nature and flowers:

Sons and Lovers has a great deal of description of the natural environment. Often, the weather and environment reflect the characters' emotions through the literary technique of pathetic fallacy. The description is frequently eroticized, both to indicate sexual energy and to slip pass the censors in Lawrence's repressive time.

Lawrence's characters also experience moments of transcendence while alone in nature, much as the Romantics did. More frequently, characters bond deeply while in nature. Lawrence uses flowers throughout the novel to symbolize these deep connections. However, flowers are sometimes agents of division, as when Paul is repulsed by Miriam's fawning behaviour towards the daffodil.

Q2. D.H. Lawrence was aware of Freud's theory, and Sons and Lovers famously uses the Oedipus complex as its base for exploring Paul's relationship with his mother. Do you agree?

Or

Q. In what ways " Sons and Lovers" uses,twists and exemplify Oedipus complex.

Oedipus Complex

Perhaps Sigmund Freud's most celebrated theory of sexuality, the Oedipus complex takes its name from the title character of the Greek play Oedipus Rex. In the story, Oedipus is prophesied to murder his father and have sex with his mother (and he does, though unwittingly). Freud argued that these repressed desires are present in most young boys. (The female version is called the Electra complex.)

D.H. Lawrence was aware of Freud's theory, and Sons and Lovers famously uses the Oedipus complex as its base for exploring Paul's relationship with his mother. Paul is hopelessly devoted to his mother, and that love often borders on romantic desire. Lawrence writes many scenes between the two that go beyond the bounds of conventional mother-son love. Completing the Oedipal equation, Paul murderously hates his father and often fantasizes about his death.

Paul assuages his guilty, incestuous feelings by transferring them elsewhere, and the greatest receivers are

Miriam and Clara (note that transference is another Freudian term). However, Paul cannot love either woman nearly as much as he does his mother, though he does not always realise that this is an impediment to his romantic life.

The older, independent Clara, especially, is a failed maternal substitute for Paul. In this setup, Baxter Dawes can be seen as an imposing father figure; his savage beating of Paul, then, can be viewed as Paul's unconsciously desired punishment for his guilt. Paul's eagerness to befriend Dawes once he is ill (which makes him something like the murdered father) further reveals his guilt over the situation.

But Lawrence adds a twist to the Oedipus complex: Mrs. Morel is saddled with it as well. She desires both William and Paul in near-romantic ways, and she despises all their girlfriends. She, too, engages in transference, projecting her dissatisfaction with her marriage onto her smothering love for her sons. At the end of the novel, Paul takes a major step in releasing himself from his Oedipus complex. He intentionally overdoses his dying mother with morphia, an act that reduces her suffering but also subverts his Oedipal fate, since he does not kill his father, but his mother.

Q3. Individualism and Paradox remain the major issue of discussion in the Works of D. H. Lawrence. Do you agree?

Or

Q. Lawrence criticizes not the humanity as a whole but rather a specific group—perhaps the vacationing, upper-middle class. Comment.

Or

Q. Lawrence's works reflect his existence in a complex world full of difficult questions like ours. Discuss in relation to "Sons and Lovers".

When you read something by D. H. Lawrence, you often end up wondering the same thing: does he hate people? Lawrence has a profound interest in us human beings, but it's the fascination of a child picking at a scab that drives him, rather than a kind of scientific or spiritual quest for some mythical "social truth." Some of Lawrence's works—"Insouciance," for example—question mankind's tendencies outright: what good is served by a world of "white-haired ladies" wasting time "caring" and sounding intelligent and cultured and talking about pretentious, bourgeois issues?

But this work is blatant in its negative descriptions of people and their behaviour in society. At one point in "Insouciance," the narrator—Lawrence—comes right out and pontificates for several paragraphs on the defects of "modern" society. But for me, it is the more subtle pieces that hold greatest power. When Lawrence hints, insinuates, or implies his views, he is, in a way, letting us discover the kernel of truth, however upsetting or controversial.

This process, utilized in "Mercury," is of far greater interest than the almost direct missive from Lawrence used in "Insouciance," that flatly states his view of what "living" really is. For not only must we discover the meaning; we must also decide whether our interpretation is really Lawrence's intent—perhaps we have confused some inadvertent seepage of Lawrence's personnel venom with his intended meaning. It is a risk we will have to take as we analyse works such as "Mercury".

Instead of condemning society in "Mercury," Lawrence actually tries to leave it, ascending to "the top of the Merkur," where he has a new vantage point on the world. He develops some of the same ideas as in "Insouciance," but at the end of the work, Lawrence redeems society, or at least apologizes for it, adding new fire to our question. By the end we cannot, with certainty, tell whether Lawrence hates people or not—and this reflects a sort of internal struggle for Lawrence.

One could lessen the scope and dilute the importance of this topic by suggesting that the "Sunday people" Lawrence criticizes are not humanity as a whole but rather a specific group—perhaps the vacationing, upper-middle class Schlegels, perhaps the aspiring, pseudo-intellectual Leonard Basts of the lower middle class, who think culture lies in a misunderstood walk through the woods. So an important related question to our topic is this: if he does hate people, who are they?

For me, Lawrence's "hate" extends to some extent to everyone, even me. In fact, I'm probably a perfect example of the kind of person that Lawrence hates: conforming, petty, ambitious and a little greedy, as most people are. Worst of all, from Lawrence's perspective, I idealize: I care as much about "the news" as I do the squirrels who are constantly fighting outside my dorm; I ignore personal relationships so I can write essays on one defunct writer or another—all because it is expected. In almost all of Lawrence's work I see a little of myself, and it is not a pretty reflection. I'd like to imagine that Lawrence turns the magnifying glass on himself too, but "Mercury" does not really suggest this.

But despite what I think, this secondary question of who is difficult to answer definitively. Though it is of great importance to my subject, I cannot claim to know the answer—I can only pose the question. We each must come to a personal conclusion as we study Lawrence—try to keep this question in mind as I describe the story and its relation to our original question: does Lawrence hate people?

"It was Sunday, and very hot." From the very first line of "Mercury", Lawrence makes a buried commentary on society, religion in this case. There is something ironic in the hot, almost hellish Sunday that Lawrence describes—he continues to make extensive use of heat imagery throughout the first half of the story: "The hot sun burned overhead, and all was in steam." I suppose that from a certain angle the idea of a special, pious day is somewhat ridiculous, as if that could possibly excuse our nastiness on the other six days. And then there's the matter of the old tablet-stone and altar, which the Sunday-people set aside and ignore.

Here we see what happens to religions once a new, improved "brand" comes about—a pitiful fate for once important religious iconography. Whether or not Lawrence is actually anti-religion seems difficult to determine from the information presented in "Mercury"; however, it seems clear that the religious status quo does not entirely satisfy him.

And when we reach the top of the hill of Mercury, "there is nothing for us to do."

What matter? We have come a stride beyond the world. Let it steam and cook its half-baked reality below there. On the hill of Mercury we take no notice. Even we do not trouble to wander and pick the fat, blue, sourish bilberries. Just lie and see the rain-pure tree-trunks like chords of music between the two worlds.

As Lawrence has put it, "we have come a stride beyond the world." We look down on the valley—that steaming, "half-baked reality below"—and seem to realise that we are somewhere between the heavens and the earth. Below we see the valley, with its bustling humanity—above, the unchanging heavens, whose permanent, ethereal qualities appear through the description of the circular movement of the sky and the upper tree trunks. And, in between these worlds, with a "stride" either way, we find that there is "nothing to do." Without the trivial action and the self-important motion of humanity, what is there to do?

If we were to abandon humanity altogether, as we might in the occasional daydream, would we be better off? Or would things be unbearably boring? Is God, in the lonely company of those eternal circles of Aristotle and Hipparchus, bored? The fact that there is nothing to do at the Merkur's peak prompts so many questions that we really must consider the almost existential conundrum: "what is there to do?" Certainly humanity, for all it's defects, serves the important purpose of giving us all something to do. And Lawrence takes this question seriously. So here we must "chalk one up" for humanity—we have yet to find a clear answer.

Before making any conclusions, though, we must consider the most dramatic part of the story: the sudden lightning and hail-storm which sweeps in. The "Sunday crowd" instantly becomes "curiously unified" (in fear perhaps) as they, like cattle, come under the control of the most basic social instincts and rush for safety as one, practically stampeding for the veranda's shelter, pressing "closer, in the darkness and the suspense." And then, in one of those chance moments of unexplained complexity, perhaps a moment which scientists would call "Heisenberg uncertainty," the kind of moment in which God, luck, evil and magic still live, we see the figure of Mercury, the winged messenger. With lightning-made wings at his ankles, "he is going somewhere, swiftly." Later we realise that the apparition of Hermes was one of the funicular-operators, struck down by Zeus's bolt. The crowd in "Mercury" comes together in horrified amazement.

These people no longer have "nothing to do." It is times like this, when we are most helpless, that we need to band together, wide-eyed, if only to murmur "Absolute winter!" to each other in the face of such a defining moment. Yes people are silly and petty and largely insignificant, but it is at these moments of "absolute winter" when we both need society and community and realise its shortcomings. The "absolute" and the "ideal" are concepts which Lawrence hates-there is no question about that—but during this brief but anticlimactic ending, we hardly seem to notice his subtle commentary. We are as much in shock as the "Sunday crowd."

So it seems we cannot really discern (from this work at least) the answer to our question: does Lawrence hate people? Our uncertainty stems from Lawrence's uncertainty, reflecting his existence in a complex world full of difficult questions like ours. His answer, if he had a definite one, would probably depend on his mood at the moment. One thing is clear though: he has a particular disgust for those who find their answers in tested, socially honoured sources like religion, society, and "properness" itself. In this Lawrence is much like Emerson, though from the opposite angle. Where Emerson gives us direct guidance, Lawrence gives us his view of what is "wrong." Surprisingly, they get similar results: Nature, instinct and self are the highest, truest powers. Both tell us to be "self-reliant." Of course, this is a bit paradoxical—someone telling you to listen only to yourself.

Q4. Paul Morel's Quest is for Manhood." Do you agree?

Or

Q. Critically analyse the character of Paul Morel.

Or

Q. Whether influenced by psychoanalytical conventions or not, Lawrence creatively portrays the true nature of psychical impotence throughout this work. Discuss.

The profound relationships that the characters share in D. H. Lawrence's Sons and Lovers serve as the powerful core of the novel. Whether influenced by psychoanalytical conventions or not, Lawrence creatively portrays the true nature of psychical impotence throughout this work. Though this is the central issue of the novel, the rather short relationship that Paul shares with Baxter Dawes is worthy of speculation. This relationship could be Paul's attempt to resolve his unconscious oedipal problems that he has suffered throughout his life.

Baxter Dawes is much like Paul's father Walter Morel. Baxter and Clara, much like Walter and Gertrude, married prematurely. Clara, much like Gertrude, did not take the time to really get to know the true nature of her husband. Baxter mirrors Walter as a man who cannot reveal his true feelings to his spouse. Both men feel neglected by their wives, acting out their frustrations in negative ways. Rather than revealing their true feelings, they try to bully their wives into loving them. Consequently, Baxter and Walter only succeed in pushing their wives further away.

Paul seems fascinated by Baxter Dawes. At first, their relationship is hateful and violent. Gradually, Paul begins to feel guilty for being with Clara. Paul eventually feels sorry for Baxter who is lost in life without Clara as much as Paul is lost with Clara. The emptiness of life is the essence the two men share in their relationship. Eventually, Paul takes it upon himself to get to know and console Baxter Dawes. Conceivably, Paul is sub-consciously making a connection between Baxter and Clara's failed relationship and that of his own parents. Whether Paul realises it or not, he wants to make things right between Clara and Baxter just as he would have had his parents truly love each other.

If Paul can help Baxter become strong again towards Clara, he will fill in the void where he could not help his father's relationship with his mother. Hypothetically, by successfully uniting Baxter and Clara in reality, Paul takes one step towards sub-consciously resolving the division that he nurtured between his parents. Thus, subconsciously he is making peace with his father who he has hated all his life. Psychoanalytically speaking, this success could sub-consciously replace/erase the failed relationship that caused him to hate his father and intimately love his mother.

Q5. Discuss relationships as shown and perceived in " Sons and Lovers"

Or

Q. Does Sons and Lovers painfully and revelatory portrays the complexity of human relationships ?

What I find to be truly interesting about Sons and Lovers is the intensely painful and revelatory portrayal of the complexity of human relationships, a concept that I expect to see repeated and reevaluated in much of Lawrence's work that I have yet to read.

I especially value the ideas in this book because there are no absolutes, no certainties-nothing that I feel compelled to accept as definite truth. It's amazingly freeing to read such literature when one is used to "siding" with a particular character or force in a book simply for the sake of argument. It is nearly impossible to do that with Lawrence. His words are as ambiguous and frustrating as reality; they repeatedly kick you in the head. One of the subjects I am most drawn to in Sons and Lovers is the matter of marriage, whether it is literal (Mr. and Mrs. Morel) or merely hypothetical, as I think of it in the unions between Miriam and Paul and Clara and Paul. I understand marriage to be quite destructive in terms of one's autonomy.

It is a personality constrictor, which prevents the realization of one's full potential. Independence is necessary in order to preserve control, and yet, human beings instinctively need to feel a sense of rooted ness or belonging. This notion appears numerous times in the book: Paul belongs to Miriam, Clara recognizes that she "never fully had [Paul]," and he no more belongs to Clara than she belongs to him, Clara feels that Dawes belongs to her, and Walter is described as looking as though "nobody owned him."

This desire to own and be owned, to "have and to hold," is rather mechanical-an irrationalized acceptance of society's expectations. Miriam, however hard she tries to snub such conventions, cannot fully liberate herself from them. Clara, on the other hand, has already managed to extricate herself from "the institution's" dominant pattern; she exists on the fringe of society in her rather lowly divorced, suffragette state. In this state Clara is not a threat to Paul's independence, so they are free to "receive the baptism of life, each through the other".

Within the confines of her societal sanctioned marriage to Dawes however, Clara reverts to the "self-sacrificial" notion of marriage as a voluntary surrender of one's own will; the same concept that Miriam follows in her relationship with Paul. Miriam seems proud to sacrifice herself to Paul, yielding to it as if it were an inherent duty.

Paul, however, cannot comply because she wants his soul so desperately that it ceases to be his decision to give it. All Oedipal theory aside for a moment, I wonder if Mrs. Morel isn't just a convenient reason for Paul to remain detached from other women. The differences between men and women are illuminated in the male and female characters' perception of marriage and belonging. As Simone de Beauvior said, "marriage diminishes man but it almost always annihilates woman." Could it be that women are more interested in and have a greater need for close human relationships than man? I would argue that possibility wholeheartedly in accordance to the ideas presented in Sons and Lovers if it weren't for one sentence on page 413: "None of [Paul] himself remained-no

Clara, no Miriam, no mother that fretted him." Paul defines himself in terms of these women, as if he were incomplete without them.

He too is a mundane figure of reality with the need to submit his identity in order to gain wholeness. Society is a complex and horribly controlling thing. It forever persists in the crevices of the subconscious as something to measure oneself up against. One thing I have learned for certain in Sons and Lovers is this: it may be simple to question and criticize social obligations, but it is always difficult to discount them.

Q6. Discuss Society and Ideology in Sons and Lovers.

Or

Q. For Lawrence, writing Sons and Lovers between 1910 and 1913, before experiencing the mass insanity of the War, before really understanding his characters' problems as problems of contemporary society, was this individualist perspective was convincing?

Or

Q. Lawrence's exaggerated sense of individual autonomy led him to distort his representation of reality.Is this so in Sons and Lovers?

The difference in speech between Walter and Gertrude Morel, marking as it does their differences in class background and education, corresponds to an underlying conflict in outlook and aspiration. Mrs Morel comes from solid bourgeois stock, stout Congregationalists all. In the memory of her grandfather, a failed lace manufacturer, she possesses an image of lost social eminence that might be regained. From her father, an engineer whose chief concern seems to have been the size of his salary, and who was well-educated and stern-minded, she formed her ideal of manhood. As a young woman she had all but married one John Field, 'the son of a well- to-do tradesman', also an educated man who aspired to the ministry and settled upon merchandising. She is well-educated herself, having taught school for some time.

This side of her character emerges in chats with the vicar over starched table-cloths, in her activities with the Women's Guild, and in her promotion of the Morel children's education. Through her sons, for whom she wants middle-class jobs, comfortable homes and 'ladies' to wive, she attempts to regain some of the status which she has lost through marriage to Morel.

Morel on the other hand, who left school at age ten to work in the mine, is barely literate, spelling painfully through the headlines and seeing no value whatsoever in the reading of books. He has no use for Mrs Morel's religion, preferring the pub to chapel, and falls to understand either her highfalutin ideas or Paul's art. Unlike his wife, he does not feel specially pinched by poverty, never dreams of clawing his way into the middle class, nor does he envision a very different future for his children. Little beyond Bestwood attracts him, and little within Bestwood repels him.

Morel clearly does not live up to Mrs Morel's ideal of manhood, and she communicates her judgment to the children... [who] learn from her to mock their father's manners, to belittle his work at the mine, to sneer at his lack of formal education and in general to degrade his manhood. Even though specific grievances often emerge during money squabbles, it is evident that something more basic than customary domestic wrangles over shillings and pence - vital as shillings and pence are - has motivated this total assault upon Morel as father and husband.

Of course he scants her budget, but so do the other miners when times are bad. It is far more significant that he does not share her education, religion, social aspirations, aesthetic training, economic motivations, manners, language, moral views or political interests. Their marriage is wrecked by differences that are primarily social rather than personal.

In the scene in Chapter 3 where William's career is at issue, Mrs Morel calls attention to these differences by contrasting herself with Morel's mother: she is not going to put *her* sons down the pit, whatever the old lady had decided to do with the likes of Walter. In the opening chapter these women meet, and from that encounter we learn that while living in a rented house, sitting on mortgaged chairs and eating off mortgaged tables might suit old Mrs Morel, it is far from suiting Gertrude Coppard Morel.

Such a cramped financial state pinches her bourgeois soul. She had persuaded herself, we are told, that she was marrying a financially independent man, owner of two houses and a houseful of furniture, possessor of a bank account, a miner with the drive to 'get on'. As it happened she married a man indebted, Marx's classic labourer, owner of nothing but his body.

Her disenchantment with the marriage dates from this experience: 'She said very little to her husband, but her manner had changed towards him. Something in her proud, honourable soul had crystallized out hard as rock.' Because she remains aloof from the other miners' wives, who beard her for having put a stop to Morel's career as dancing master, and by implication for having fettered his free spirit with her puritan scruples, she feels increasingly isolated, 'miles away from her own people'. Her own people, of course, are the ministers, engineers, teachers and the like whom she knew as a girl. We are told that this marks the beginning of their marital battle, a beginning which Lawrence depicts with perfect clarity in social terms. But then what conclusion does he draw?

> She fought to make him undertake his own responsibilities, to make him fulfill his obligations. But he was too different from her. His nature was purely sensuous, and she strove to make him moral, religious. She tried to force him to face things. He could not endure it - it drove him out of his mind.

The narrator has translated social differences into moral and psychological terms: the wife is responsible, aware of obligations, bearing the reformer's burden: the husband is irresponsible, blind to obligations, the crude soil which she is to cultivate; he is sensuous, the body; she is religious, the spirit. Two pages later we read:

Nevertheless, she still continued to strive with him. She still had her high moral sense, inherited from generations of Puritans. It was now a religious instinct, and she was almost a fanatic with him, because she loved him, or had loved him. If he sinned, she tortured him. If he drank, and lied, was often a poltroon, sometimes a knave, she wielded the lash unmercifully. The pity was, she was too much his opposite. She could not be content with the little he might be; she would have him the much that he ought to be. So, in seeking to make him nobler than he could be, she destroyed him. She injured and hurt and scarred herself, but lost none of her worth. She also had the children.

Their differences in expectation are translated into valued 'opposites': she has a high moral instinct, he by implication has a low; he sins and she redeems; he is content with mediocrity while she aspires to noble heights; she strives to shape him, he remains the passive clay; although he is destroyed, she, miraculously 'loses, none of her worth'. The passage, like the novel as a whole, assumes Mrs Morel's purpose and standards. Thus concrete differences between particular human beings, differences which are comprehensible in social terms, serve as the basis for constructing a metaphysic which opposes the body to the mind.

Time after time in those early pages Lawrence proffers moral or psychological explanations of incidents which he has already given us evidence for interpreting sociologically. Consider the hair-clipping scene in the opening chapter. Borrowing clothes from her sisters, Mrs Morel arrays baby William in white coat and hat, complete with ostrich feather, and she lets his hair burgeon in curls to complete this transformation of the miner's son into Little Lord Fauntleroy.

One morning Morel takes the boy aside and clips his hair. No son of his should be considered a sissy in the village - but this is precisely what Mrs Morel wanted, because the child's appearance was a prop for her performance as lady in the mining community. In his description of the aftermath, however, Lawrence ignores this social dimension, referring to the incident as an 'act of masculine clumsiness'. Morel appears totally cowed, his wife appears the martyr.

Having taken the pledge at the time of his marriage, Morel resumes his drinking after these early battles, but not more heavily than many miners, so we are told, nor anything stronger than beer. In various scenes we learn that the pub offered him a form of community, free from authority, that could be found neither in mine nor home. His pub-sitting was a regular part of the miner's life, a compensation for numbing and back-breaking work, often the only social activity other than chapel (where Nonconformist ministers reconciled an embittered flock to their barren pasture) which was available to an uneducated and exhausted man in an industrial village. Despised by his wife, shut out from his family, Morel has added reason for drinking.

But in scene after scene, when he appears drunk and brutal, we hear nothing of his reasons for drinking, but only of his ruin and of his wife's bitter suffering. After these early scenes, which pretend to justify the father's damnation by the mother, and, following her, by the children, Lawrence treats Morel from the outside as a broken man who is responsible for his own ruin, one who is redeemed only in fleeting moments by his singing or tinkering. The narrator's judgment is consistent with that of the mother: 'his manhood broke', 'he broke himself', he became 'more or less a husk', he 'fell into a slow ruin', he 'lapsed slowly', he 'denied the God in him'.

There seems to be a division between the narrator who is compassionately recording the miner's life, and the narrator who is judging that life. After all, the triumph of realism is also Lawrence's triumph as a writer: he conveys a sense of the pressures, deformations and joys of life in that mining community with a loving attention and a vigour of language which is unrivalled in English literature. In a scene midway through the novel Morel observes his own body while bathing, a body prematurely aged, twisted and broken from years of hacking at the coal-face and from scores of accidents, a body scarred blue with coal-dust, and instead of damning the mines which have crippled him, 'he felt the ruin he had made during these years. He wanted to bustle about, to run away from it'. Lawrence simultaneously records a fact and implies a judgment. That Morel *felt* responsible for his own ruin seems convincing and disturbing. But the narrator by his silence at this point appears to accept this judgment, implying that Morel's social fate, a fate shared with millions of labourers, was a sign of personal guilt.

The narrator consistently views the father through the mother's eyes:

> As he bent over, lacing his boots, there was a certain vulgar gusto in his movement that divided him from the reserved, watchful rest of the family. He always ran away from the battle with himself.

Lawrence was later to use the contrast between reserve and gusto as a means of distinguishing the neurotically repressed middle classes from the instinctive and sensuous common people. But here the miner appears 'vulgar', elsewhere we have found him described as a 'knave', 'poltroon', 'nasty' and 'brutal'. When he returns home sweaty and exhausted from the mines, to find the Congregational minister sipping tea over a table-cloth in the kitchen, and when he is treated as a crude beast by his wife, Morel understandably grows furious.

The minister is one of Mrs Morel's 'own people', he is an educated man, a spiritual man, possessed of proper manners. He is a reincarnation of John Field, a middle-class substitute for her husband. Enough has passed before to persuade us that Morel appreciates the significance of the minister's presence and of his wife's behaviour; certainly the reader does. Yet the narrator endorses Mrs Morel's opinion that, by fussing and complaining, the miner is just showing off; even young William is made to hate him, 'with a boy's hatred for false sentiment, for the stupid treatment of his mother'. We are told that as Morel ages he acts in increasingly 'dirty and disgusting ways', but all we learn of this behaviour is that 'His manners in the house were the same as he used among the colliers down pit'. Yet what was the determining reality for this miner, cut off from the rest of his family, if it was not that gathering of colliers down pit? His ways were disgusting from Mrs Morel's point of view, according to her middle-class upbringing, and it is this point of view which Lawrence employs throughout the novel, in matters great and small.

Even Morel's lack of education is turned against him. In one important scene Paul reluctantly tells his father of winning a prize in a writing competition for a child's paper:

> Morel turned round to him.
>
> 'Have you, my boy? What sort of a competition?'
>
> 'Oh, nothing - about famous women.'
>
> 'And how much is the prize, then, as you've got?'
>
> 'It's a book.'
>
> 'Oh, indeed!'
>
> 'About birds.'
>
> 'Hm - hm!'
>
> And that was all. Conversation was impossible between the father and any other member of the family. He was an outsider. He had denied the God in him.

The breach between father and son appears as an educationally conditioned difference in language. What after all is Morel to say about famous women, resurrected from histories and dressed up in an essay? What conversation is he to make about the prize book which he cannot read? Still a child, Paul has already outstripped his father in formal if not in practical knowledge. Nor is that surprising in view of the miner's upbringing.

Yet this demonstration of Morel's educational backwardness (previous scenes have demonstrated his drunkenness, his brutality, his ignorance of bourgeois manners and his indifference to bourgeois culture, his refusal to stand up for his own rights and his inability 'to get on' at work) is made occasion for the judgment that he is *personally* guilty of failing to become a whole human being: 'He had denied the God in him.'

Although it is difficult to see how any but an exceptional man could have overcome his disadvantages - poverty, inadequate education and limited class expectations, work that is physically exhausting while mentally undemanding, cramped housing and political impotence - nevertheless Mrs Morel condemns him for failing to achieve precisely this miraculous escape. Paul accepts her class-bound judgment. Lawrence, having himself freshly escaped at the time he wrote the novel, accepted it as well.

In making that judgment Mrs Morel applied what can best be called a 'bourgeois' perspective, wholly consistent with her Protestant ethics, a perspective which treats the individual as the unit of success or failure, without regard to the conditions which shape him, without regard to the collective social reality within which he dwells. Like St Paul, whom her father admired more than any other man, and like the great Reformation theologians who looked to St Paul for their authority, Mrs Morel held the individual responsible for his salvation or damnation.

Her individualist perspective dominates the book, as her feelings dominate Paul, as her values dominate the Morel household. Suffering from the capitalist ethic on the job and from the Protestant ethic in his own home, Morel neatly illustrates Max Weber's proposition of a link between the two spheres of ideology. Both the religious and the economic ideology treat mankind as a collection of atomic individuals, each person seeking his own salvation or profit, motivated solely by rational self-interest - according to Adam Smith's formulation - each isolated Robinson Crusoe remaining solely responsible for his worldly condition.

Thus both William and Paul make their escape, such as it is, alone, leaving their community unchanged; their alienation would seem to be the natural state of man according to Mrs Morel's individualist perspective.

For Lawrence, writing *Sons and Lovers* between 1910 and 1913, before experiencing the mass insanity of the War, before really understanding his characters' problems as problems of contemporary society, this individualist perspective was convincing. After all, had he not scrambled out of the working class, had he not escaped the industrial system, had he not wooed a lady? Individual autonomy, at least for those who were willing to give a tug at their own bootstraps, seemed to him a proven fact.

Enjoying an exile's comparative social independence, he exaggerated man's freedom, since anyone estranged from the conditions and institutions of his society, whether physically exiled like Rousseau, or emotionally like Blake, is prone to stress man's freedom rather than his bondage. Of course the exile is at once the most and the least free of men; his very isolation from all social groups prevents him from effectively acting upon his ideas.' Such isolation commonly leads - as has been shown by Emile Durkheim, who named this condition *anomie* - to frustration and disgust, equally with oneself and one's society. Like Swift and Orwell, two other emotional exiles, Lawrence was by spells the aloof yet penetrating observer, and the misanthrope, manifesting by turns the profoundest concern for his countrymen and the most consummate disgust, each alike the fruit of social isolation.

Lawrence's exaggerated sense of individual autonomy led him to distort his representation of reality - especially in *Sons and Lovers,* but to a varying degree in all his novels - by isolating personal existence partly or wholly from social existence. Although *Sons and Lovers* abounds in references to social conditions and historical movements, these are not used to account for the quality, the changes and crises, of individual lives.

That is to say, Lawrence explains the problems of his characters psychologically rather than historically, in terms of a personal rather than a collective past. When in a later essay he wrote that 'I feel it is the change inside the individual which is my real concern. The great social change interests me and troubles me, but it is not my field', he posited a dichotomy between individual psychology and social existence which would have seemed alien to George Eliot, Dickens or Austen, and to all of the great Continental realists such as Stendhal, Balzac or Tolstoy. Of course he was entitled to occupy himself primarily with subjectivity, and did so, but when he set himself the task of *explaining* subjectivity, or of passing judgments on individuals, he often failed, as in the case of Morel, to take the social dimension into account.

Morel's failure should be grounds for criticizing the industrial and economic system which has maimed him, rather than for criticizing the man. Mrs Morel's bitter repudiation of her married state expresses more than class prejudice. Her outrage and Morel's ruin were to be translated by Lawrence into a basic critique of the social order which had produced this humanly degraded way of life.

This woman is determined not only to help her children escape the financial straits in which she finds herself, but also to liberate them from the brutal working conditions and from the domestic squalor which the industrial order has imposed upon generations of Morels. To her son she transmits both outrage and frustration, and she teaches him to defend precisely those values which the industrial system - with its associated politics, economics, housing and schools - denies.

The son of Mrs Lawrence was to protest - in plays and essays and novels - the evil which had been committed against the human spirit in Eastwood's mines and streets. When Lawrence returned to the same emotional terrain at the end of his life, in *Lady Chatterley's Lover* and 'Nottingham and the Mining Country', he judged his father differently. He had become aware by that time of the larger social forces which had intersected in the lives of the Morels, Leivers and Dawes, and in particular those forces which had mutilated his father.

I have dwelt upon the conflict between Mr and Mrs Morel because it is the clearest example in the novel of a socially and historically comprehensive problem which is nevertheless interpreted by Lawrence in personal, psychological terms, and because it demonstrates the triumph of Mrs Morel's individualist perspective, which rules the novel as a whole. The class differences between Mr and Mrs Morel are evident. The novel 'follows this idea', Lawrence wrote to his agent in 1912, 'a woman of character and refinement goes into the lower class, and has no satisfaction in her own life'.' Lawrence was very much aware of the corresponding class differences between his own parents, and he frequently referred to this social conflict, built into his family, as a means of explaining certain aspects of his own character and thought.

My mother was a clever, ironical delicately molded woman of good, old burgher descent. She married below her. My father was dark, ruddy, with a fine laugh. He is a coal miner. He was one of the sanguine temperament, warm and hearty, but unstable: he lacked principle, as my mother would have said. He deceived her and lied to her. She despised him - he drank.

He wrote those words late in 1910, while his mother was dying. In a later poem, much of the sympathy which he had once felt toward his mother's class having vanished, he wrote more bitterly of the social fissure which had divided his childhood:

My father was a working man
and a collier was he,
at six in the morning they turned him down
and they turned him up for tea.

My mother was a superior soul
a superior soul was she,
cut out to play a superior role
in the god-damn bourgeoisie.

We children were the in-betweens
little non-descript were we,
indoors we called each other you,
outside, it was tha and thee.

Aware though he was of this parental class conflict, I do not believe Lawrence fully realised how very near the heart of his work that conflict lay, how fundamentally the contrast between his father's life and his mother's ideas had influenced his own representation of reality....

We have observed that the conflict between Walter and Gertrude Morel is often described in the novel as an opposition between flesh and spirit, an opposition which is reflected by differences in speech: Morel's language is highly sensory and formulaic, presenting a direct account of his emotional responses to immediate experience; Mrs Morel on the other hand demonstrates that, while sharing her husband's capacity for concreteness, she possesses the additional capacity for abstraction, for transcending the present situation towards past and future, for articulating something more than immediate sensations.

By the time of writing *Studies in Classic American Literature,* Lawrence had come to view the analogous contrast between his own parents as the paradigm of conflict between body and mind:

> My father hated books, hated the sight of anyone reading or writing. My mother hated the thought that any of her sons should be condemned to manual labour. Her sons must have something higher than that. She won. But she died first. He laughs longest who laughs last. There is a basic hostility in all of us between the physical and the mental, the blood and the spirit. The mind is 'ashamed' of the blood. And the blood is destroyed by the mind, actually.

Here manual labour is explicitly opposed to labour of the mind. Morel's work is almost purely physical; the role of planning, purpose, control - of *consciousness* - is minimal. Only at night or on holiday, when he is mending boots or blacksmithing, does Morel become the conscious, self-directing craftsman idealized by Ruskin and Morris; but these are only spare time activities, fitfully pursued. He is not a craftsman but an industrial worker. Mental functions in the mines have been transferred to the owners and managers.

Like Mrs Morel, they are the educated ones, and they are the ones whose projects and orders are carried out by men such as Morel. There is in the mines a *functional* division between body and mind, which corresponds - as Marx and other nineteenth-century critics of industrial civilization observed - to the division of labour between workers and managers.

This division was for Lawrence the dominant feature of industrial society: it crops up again and again in his writing. Aside from the account of opposition between workers and owners in *The White Peacock* and *Sons and Lovers*, the manager reappears as a creature of dominating will and mind in such characters as Tom Brangwen, Jr, Gerald Crich, Clifford Chatterley, Fraser (in *The Daughter-in-Law*), and the mine owners of *Aaron's Rod*....

Although Lawrence's critique of industrial society has not yet become explicit in *Sons and Lovers*, the raw materials, the conditions which he would later condemn, are all there. During the nineteenth century, as the scale of economic organization increased, as automation fragmented the work process, as control over the process itself receded ever further from the worker and as the relations between workers became increasingly mechanized, the individual human being was reduced to the role of an instrument of production. We can observe the effects of these economic changes upon the life of Bestwood.

The men become interchangeable tools in the production process. There is no opportunity for creativity in their work, nor does their labour seem to produce any durable results, since the indistinguishable tons of coal are quickly consumed. Slack times in the pit mean hard times in the home, and there is no redress. The penniless and the powerless in the novel are intimidated by train stations and restaurants, by waitresses and paymasters; they queue for Saturday morning charity treatment at the doctor's surgery; like Mrs Morel they develop 'that peculiar shut-off look of the poor who have to depend on the favour of others'.

Paul's feeling of terror and humiliation when fetching his father's pay expresses a child's dread of the 'system', when first seeking work as a lad fresh out of school, he balks at entry into the 'business world, with its regulated system of values, and its impersonality', because this means becoming a 'prisoner of industrialism'. In order to work, a man must submit to an alien system, which operates according to its own impersonal laws.

The working people of Bestwood have little sway over those forces which fundamentally shape their lives - supply and demand of the market, weather, pay offers, strikes, government decisions, educational policy, development of industrial uses for coal, accidents in the mine, or the distribution of resources in the earth's bowels.

They are not masters of their condition, either individually or collectively. As a group they function within an encompassing political and economic system over which they have practically no control. For them the larger society has become, to use Marx's term, *reified:* it seems to be a substantially independent world, inhabited by irrational, unpredictable and uncontrollable forces which determine people's lives while remaining oblivious to their desires.

There are striking similarities between this experience of society and Lawrence's representation of nature as an autonomous process over which the individual has no control, but in which he is deeply enmeshed by virtue of his animality, his existence as a physical creature. This is the view of nature which is implicit, for example, in the scene in which Paul and Miriam confront a rose tree at evening:

> It was very still. The tree was tall and straggling. It had thrown its briers over a hawthorn-bush, and its long streamers trailed thick right down to the grass, splashing the darkness everywhere with great spilt stars, pure white. In bosses of ivory and in large splashed stars the roses gleamed on the darkness of foliage and stems and grass. Paul and Miriam stood close together, silent, and watched. Point after point the steady roses shone out of them, seeming to kindle something in their souls. The dusk came like smoke around, and still did not put out the roses.

The rose tree is an active subject, the master of transitive verbs, and is not simply alive but *independently* alive, acting on the young lovers who are bound together, as they themselves acknowledge, by something common in nature, something which they recognize to be continuous with their own passions, instincts and desires, something that calls forth a response from their 'souls'. Consistently, Lawrence's human agents for the most part respond passively to impersonal forces which transcend them and which, in sexual relations particularly, are overwhelming.

This subjection of the human to impersonal nature recurs in passages throughout *Sons and Lovers:* the account of Paul and Miriam's first sexual encounter, in which a cherry tree, a sunset and a fir register the harmony between the course of external nature and the course of their young blood; the scene by the flooded Trent, where the surging river functions as objective correlation for the emotions that master Clara and Paul; the scene in which Paul emerges from lovemaking to hear pewits scream:

It was all so much bigger than themselves that he was hushed. They had met, and included in their meeting the thrust of the manifold grass-stems, the cry of the peewit, the wheel of the stars; and finally another lovemaking scene in which he merges in consciousness with the encircling natural world:

Just as he was, so it seemed the vigourous, wintry stars were strong also with life. He and they struck with the same pulse of fire, and the same joy of strength which held the bracken-frond stiff near his eyes held his own body firm. It was as if he, and the stars, and the dark herbage, and Clara were licked up in an immense tongue of flame, which tore upwards and upwards.

After one such encounter Paul reflects that 'It was as if they had been blind agents of a great force': the natural process, like the social, becomes reified, appearing as an autonomous realm of irrational and impersonal forces. just as unpredictable and uncontrollable social forces rule the lives of common people, so natural forces govern the course of personal relationships. The one realm of impersonal forces is no more hospitable than the other. And just as economic forces reduce human beings to instruments of production, so instinctual forces reduce human beings to instruments of gratification.

Thus Paul justifies his calculated use of Clara by arguing that their intercourse is mutually rewarding - yet she is nonetheless his instrument, serving his needs. To his mother he confesses that, 'Sometimes, when I see her just as *the woman, I* love her, mother; but then, when she talks and criticizes, I often don't listen to her.' When Clara charges him with treating her as an object, rather than as a person with her own needs and desires, he excuses himself by appealing to the relentless urge of passion. His relationship with Miriam, though fuller, is corrupted by the same instrumental attitude:

> He had always, almost willfully, to put her out of count, and act from the brute strength of his own feelings. And he could not do it often, and there remained afterwards always the same sense of failure and of death.

When in a fit of pique he accuses her of trying to 'absorb' him, he is merely echoing his mother's jealous sentiments. Although Lawrence was later to swear by the 'truth' of judgments uttered spontaneously and passionately (basing his faith on the instincts), the judgments which actually appear in his novels, as in the present instance, often merely express unexamined prejudices. When Paul declares an end to his love affair with Miriam - which for his part has been based on intellectual and sexual domination - he is shocked by the girl's bitterness, since he has justified his actions all along by reference to the holy and undeniable passions.

In its crudest forms this appeal to the sanctity of instinct becomes in the later Lawrence a variety of sexual determinism, differing little in its ethical implications from the biological determinism of the Social Darwinists. The instrumentalisation of human beings and the mechanization of personal relationships is equally vicious, whether enforced by an industrial-economic order, or by a natural order....

The sentimental education of a working-class boy, the lives of a mining family, a farming family and a suffragette: these appear to be the chief subjects of *Sons and Lovers.* We are presented with the drama of 'an organic disturbance in the relationships of men and women', to use Dorothy Van Ghent's phrase,[1] and with the Oedipal dilemma of a miner's son. But these materials have an historical content which Lawrence, on account of his psychological focus, did not fully acknowledge.

That is to say, the true underlying subject of the novel is a larger historical reality, the movements and qualities of which are concretely focused in the lives of individual characters, who are 'typical' in the sense defined by Lukacs.

The psychology of these characters can be interpreted as a response to social conditions; their motives and behaviour are comprehensible in terms of their social existence. Whether we examine Mrs Morel's frustrated bourgeois aspirations, Morel's brutalization, Mrs Leivers' bitterness, Miriam's compensating religiosity, Clara's feminism, Dawes's demoralization, or the middle-class values and emotional lameness of Paul, we find evidence of crucial trends in contemporary society: the deprivations of working-class life; the increasing mechanization of society which was to result in the horrors of the 1914-1918 War; the conflict between bourgeois and proletarian ideologies which would lead to revolutions after the war; the proliferating sense of *anomie;* and the movement of women for emancipation.

To claim this is not to deny the richness of the novel's world, but on the contrary to indicate the ground of its coherence, to reveal the matrix of social trends which gives it unity. Indeed the novel derives its significance as much from this larger historical reality as from the individual lives through which history is concretely grasped. Although Lawrence focuses on personal relations and subjectivity, it is a subjectivity permeated by social forces, which registers the stress of growing up within a working community that was being transformed by industry, the schools, and the awakening of social consciousness.

Furthermore, Lawrence's own psychology, like that of his characters, is rooted in the social and moral conditions which govern the world of *Sons and Lovers.* Like them, his values and thought developed within the bounds of a specific social existence. His ideas and his art, whatever enduring interest they may possess, represent first and foremost a coherent response to a concrete historical situation.

I have suggested certain correspondences between the plane of consciousness and the plane of social existence: the origins of Lawrence's individualistic perspective in bourgeois ideology, with his consequent substitution of psychological for historical explanation; the relation of his mind/body dualism to the dualism of mental and physical functions enforced by the division of labour; the additional parallel between the mind/body dualism and the conflict (practical and ideological) between middle and working classes; the similarity between the representation of nature and of society, each realm being impersonal, autonomous and irrational, and each one reducing the individual to the status of an object in a process which he cannot control. There is at least this much similarity between the structure of his social experience and the structure of ideas which he uses to account for that experience.

Q7. Write a not on language style in D.H. Lawrence Sons and Lovers

Or

Q. Discuss the language pattern in Sons and Lovers.

Introduction

At the turn of the century, many writers both in Britain and America tried to make experimentations upon the traditional literary techniques, such as James Joyce, Virginia Woolf, Oscar Wilde, etc.. Though D.H. Lawrence did not go so far as to pay much attention to literary forms, he is still one of them. The unique language style in *Sons and Lovers* is a telling proof. Firstly, Lawrence's language style is the natural result of his intentions in the novel.

His style is one of explanations using direct statement and the expression of his own views about Paul Morel's life in relation to his family. Secondly, he is also trying to express his sense of the importance of life and even sacredness of nature of the human body and of the human relationships. It presents us a style that is at times poetic, rich and resonant. Thirdly, Lawrence implies dialect according to different cultural background of the people in order to make the novel highly realistic and revealing.

Frankness

In *Sons and Lovers,* Lawrence's tendency to be frank is obvious. He uses short, blunt sentences to express as directly as possible the movement of Paul's mind. For example, he tells us of Morel, the father, who "denied the God in him". This statement, however, does not emerge from the novel as a possibility to be discussed. It is simply handled as a truth. For the most part, Lawrence's frankness in *Sons and Lovers* is rather persuasive. The following quotation from Chapter XI is a good example, in which we are told that Paul's love with Miriam is an inevitable failure:

> He continued faithful to Miriam. For one day he had loved her utterly. But it never came again. The sense of failure grew stronger. At first it was only sadness. Then he began to feel he could not go on. He wanted to run, to go abroad, anything. Gradually he ceased to ask her to have him.

Lawrence uses these short, simple sentences to express how Paul feels about his relationship with Miriam. His tone is somehow solid and monotonous and it conveys a sense of his failure with Miriam and his feelings of frustration and desperation. A good deal part of *Sons and Lovers* is taken up with conversations, and here again Lawrence has a direct approach that cuts out all unnecessary words and gives us the important part of any given dialogue. One of the reasons for this may be that in the Midland working-class environment of the novel people are not given too many words anyway and there is a kind of "nonsense" approach to life, which shortens the speech even of mother and son, as this example shows:

One day he (Paul) came home at dinner time feeling ill. But it was not a family to make any fuss. .

"What's the matter with you?" his mother asked sharply.

"Nothing", he replied.

But he ate no dinner.

"If you eat no dinner, you're not going to school", she said.

"Why?" she asked.

"That's why?" (ibid)

And with "That's why" as the answer, here it means that Mrs. Morel refuses to offer any explanation, Paul goes to sleep on the sofa. The dialogue is brief and clear. No doubt mother and son exchanged more words on this occasion but Lawrence only gives us the words important for his purposes.

The conversation at the Morels, and among the miners, is brief and vivid. The conversation between Paul and Miriam or Paul and Clara is slightly more elaborate but, again, it is economically handled. Lawrence picks up a piece of dialogue just long enough for us to follow the argument that is going on and then drops it and goes back to his usual description or analysis. This is another way in which he moves from the general descriptions or analysis to the specific part of one particular conversation as described above. Here is an example showing that Clara is "mad with desire" for Paul and is turned down when she tries to kiss him at work:

"But what do you always want to be kissing and embracing for?" he said, "Surely there's a time for everything".

She looked up at him and the hate came into her eyes.

"Do I always want to be kissing you?" she said.

"Always, even if I come to ask you about the work. I don't want anything to do with love when I'm at work. Work's work...."

"And what is love?" she asked. "Has it to have special hours?" "Yes, out of work hours."

"And you'll regulate it according to Mr. Jordan's closing time?" "Yes.... It is only to exist in spare time?"

The conversation that is quoted here is clear and brief. On one side, the author intends to explain how Clara becomes irritated to Paul with her insistence on constant passion; on the other side, the author explains the reaction of Paul to Clara's anger and irritation.

What he aims at in presenting this brief dialogue is not to develop the plot or even to put much emphasis on this particular conversation; his purpose is to give us another insight into the whole quality of their relationship. Thus Lawrence throws everything in, moving backward and forwards in time, to reveal as much as possible about their relationship.

Poeticness

Lawrence believes industrialism can warp and pervert naturally healthy organisms. He thinks Man is in harmony with nature; on the land a man lives by natural rhythms of birth, growth, death and renewal. In certain aspects, Lawrence himself has a religious, sacred quality, which Lawrence tries to catch by adopting a style that is more elevated, more poetic and richer than his direct style.

This is particularly apparent when Lawrence is concerned with nature and with sex. In Chapter VII, Paul and Miriam are walking together in the woods at night, Lawrence then describes the dew, the mist, a "cloud" of white flowers, Miriam's eagerness as she looks for her rose bush, and the "communion" she will be able to have with Paul once she finds it. They walk on into the wood until they find the bush.

It was very still. The tree was tall and straggling. It had thrown its briers over a haw thorn-bush, and its log streamers trailed thick, right down to the grass, splashing the darkness everywhere with great spilt stars, pure white. In bosses of ivory and in large splashed stars the roses gleamed on the darkness of foliage and stems and grass. Paul and Miriam stood close together, silent, and watched. Point after point the steady roses shone out to them, seeming to kindle something in their souls. The dusk came like smoke around, and still did not put out the roses.

Paul and Miriam look into each other's eyes and have the "communion" that she wants. The cool scent of the white roses, however, is "a white, virgin scent" which makes Paul feel "anxious and imprisoned". The rich words used here tend to bring together the magic of nature and the magic of sexual attraction between them. It is necessary for Paul to be present if Miriam is to experience her roses fully.

There is a strong religious current in the episode and altogether Lawrence manages to make the spiritual "communion" a certain relationship between Paul and Miriam: their "Kindled" souls. The author employs many nature words to describe the nature vividly and poetically. The whole episode occupies about a page and a half, "dark" or "darkness" appear six times, "white" five times, "roses" five times, "silent" or "silence" four times, "dusk", "ivory", "holy", "honeysuckle", "communion", "stars", "pines" and "grass" twice each.

The magic atmosphere of the dusky wood with scent-laden air is emphasized by these repetitions that take us a long way into the realities of Morel's inner word. Poetic style comes not only from nature words but also from imagery used in the episode that strengthens this impression. White flowers appear "in a cloud", the sky is "like mother-of-pearl", the roses "splash" the darkness, gleaming and shining, the dusk is "like smoke", and the roses seem like "butterflies". Everything seems to echo everything else: the mist is white as are the champion-flowers, and the sky, the roses, and the ivory all remind us of certain sorts of butterflies.

Miriam's soul and virginity, and the dresses of children at "communion" are all poetically presented. Lawrence adopts this "poetic" style at several points in the novel and usually these are the significant moments, especially from a sexual point of view in Paul's relationship. Thus there is an extensive description of the natural surroundings on the occasion of Paul and Clara's first lovemaking in Chapter XII in which Lawrence concludes the episode again in poetic imagery:

> When she arose, he, looking on the ground all the time, saw suddenly sprinkled on the black wet beech roots many scarlet carnation petals, like splashed drops of blood; and red, small splashes fell from her bosom streaming down her dress to her feet.

Lawrence's poetic style reaches its most elevated level in Chapter XIII in which Paul is beginning to experience the impersonality of passion. He is simply man and Clara is simply woman and they become one with the natural world in which they make love. There is a section in the middle of this chapter, which is devoted to a poetic treatment of this passionate communion with nature. At its climax, Lawrence writes:

> And after such an evening they both (Clara and Paul) were very still, having known the immensity of passion. They felt small, halt afraid, childish' and wondering, like Adam and Eve when they lost their innocence and realised the magnificence the power which drove then out of paradise and across the great night and the great day of humanity. It was for each of them an initiation and a satisfaction.... If so great a magnificent power could overwhelm them, identify them altogether itself, so that they knew they were only grains in the tremendous heave that lifted every grass-blade its little height, and every tree, and living thing, then why fret about them selves.

For Lawrence, the harmony of nature and the human being, the whole universe, has become a living body and life communion between parts of this body is like the pulse and flow of blood. This sexually tinged metaphor in this "blood intimacy" gives sex a sacramental colour, because sexual act is not considered as a human concept, but as the most vital means for life communion with the universe.

This poetic presentation, together with its dynamic prose, takes us back to the first point made about Lawrence's style it is like a piece of preaching, it is like a lecture delivered in passionate tones and with the poetry of rhetoric.

Dialect

Besides the direct language and poetic styles, *Sons and Lovers* also abounds in Nottingham shire dialect. To some extent, Lawrence's use of this Midland dialect is highly realistic and revealing. For Nottingham shire miners, they do not speak Standard English or the English of London; in 1913 the differences were even greater than they are today. However, there is more than just presenting the dialect. The dialect represents and symbolizes certain changes and developments of characters in relation to their class and mood and cultural backgrounds. Mrs. Morel, for example, speaks better English than Morel who always speaks in dialect, being "thee'd and thou'd" by Morel; part of the reason for this is the way in which they used to speak attracts her.

They fall in love with each other almost at first sight when they meet at a dance party. Gertrude, a girl from a middle-class family, lovely and well-educated, is full of dreams and aspirations, whereas Walter Morel, a miner, is handsome, passionate and energetic. Gertrude is attracted by his warm physical nature and he is impressed by her refined speech and manner. These two people have lived in the same society, geographically close to each other, but each of them inhabits a world, which is unknown to the other.

In the former chapters, the children (William and Annie) speak in dialect but William soon drops his accent. As he moves up in the world, he only speaks normal English. His snobbish Miss Western speaks like a lady and the readers can fell the contract between her speech and Morel's when they are introduced. The young Paul speaks in dialect but rapidly loses it so that there is a strong contrast, later in the novel, between him and Naxter Dawes, who always speaks dialect. Interestingly, he reverts to dialect after he has made love to Clara for the first time.

His first words are "Your flowers are smashed" (normal English), then he says "why dost look so heavy?" (Why do you look so sad?); "Nay! Never thee bother! "(No! You should not mind!); "Dunna thee worrit" (Don't you worry.). But when he and Clara have climbed back up to the top of the Grove, he says "Now we're back at the ordinary level" (normal English). It seems that the "ordinary level" means not only the path at the top of the steep riverbank but also the level of daily life, which is "ordinary", compared with the level of lovemaking. The dialect, then, seems suitable for the earthly but wonderful level of passion (even Morel has the virtue of being passionate and he is earthly too) but the "ordinary level" requires normal English. Miriam, significantly, always speaks normal English.

It seems that Lawrence uses both normal English and dialect in the novel to reveal a contrast between flesh and spirit. Every character has his or her own identity of languages, which reflects another kind of conflict of this novel: the conflict between people and environment. It might also suggest the contrast between reason and passions, or between artificiality and simplicity. These contrasts add power to *Sons and Lovers.*

Conclusion

In a word, Lawrence reveals the truth by using direct comments. While talking about nature and sex, he tries to adopt a style that is more poetic and richer than his direct style. Also, the dialect used among the different characters and cultural background is a reflection of this novel's multi-contrast. Thus the transfer use of language has made the novel become one of the famous literary works of modern times.

Q8. Ho far is Lawrence successful in searching individualism through Sons and Lovers.

Or

Q. All the relationships in Sons and Lovers are involved with power struggles. Do you agree?

Q. Critically analyse character of Paul as Lawrence perceives it.

D. H. Lawrence's perpetual search for the archetypal human relationship affects all his fiction and particularly Sons and Lovers, his coming of age novel. It is here that his preoccupation with the love ethic and the profound split caused by the imbalance or "power cast," of most relationships are so nakedly revealed.

The incomplete and imperfect relationships of Sons and Lovers are among the most discussed and analysed in English Literature. Paul Morel's imprisoning relationship with his mother cripples all his other relationships. Early on it is evident that Mrs. Morel substitutes attachment fir her sons for the broken connection with her husband, and what results is her certain domination over Paul in particular. What begins as a warm, wholesome attachment between mother and child later becomes shaded with incestuous overtones and ends as the controlling force in Paul's life.

When Paul is born his has already turned away from physical responsiveness to her husband, and indeed to everything, except for her love of flowers and the flowers of her womb, her children. The movement of the mother away from normal relationships lies heavily on Paul, and caught, as it is in the life cycle of blooming and dying vegetation, seems doomed toward death. The result for Paul seems to be the inability to respond to the women in his life both sexually and unself-consciously.

With Miriam, his first love, Paul's primary contact is spiritual and cerebral, and the once mutual attraction crumbles into bitterness, hurt and rejection, because neither can respond to their "physical life force" or integrate it into their attempted communion of souls. Part of the difficulty in this relationship, Lawrence seems to be implying, is that Miriam's attraction to Paul is attracted, that she rejects the spontaneous physical response available to them and prefers "the higher level of affection and spiritual communion and intellectual interchange." This obstruction seems a consequence of her sex, class and environment resulting in a kind of liberalization of womankind through education, a theme which Lawrence continues to treat in later novels.

When Paul, physically aroused, finds no natural response in the girl who seems to love him, he is confused, helpless, and becomes even cruel. Unable to assert himself, or even to accept as natural his unquenched longings he is unable to continue in the mental/spiritual relationship with the girl—because his mother alone already owns his soul. The relationship is ruptured, Paul's personality suffers a kind of tearing or splitting, another favourite image in Lawrence, and in his next relationship Paul realises at some unconscious level he must leave his soul somewhat free for his mother and participate on a kind of detached physical level.

Thus, in his relationship with Clara, it is the primarily bodily maleness of Paul bonding with the primarily bodily femaleness. Obviously the danger is to oversimplify the Paul/Miriam and Paul/Clara relationships. It is true that the contact with Clara puts Paul at least temporarily into richer contact with his own body, his phallic consciousness, as Lawrence would say, whereas in his sterile relationships with his mother and Miriam Paul has had to forego this fuller consciousness. Now he experiences what he believes is a kind of paradisiacal kind of love and fulfillment. After lovemaking he refers to coming "out of some dark current of unconsciousness" to be "carried by life" in love.

Yet, a novice, Paul fears the powers Clara has over him and finally lets their relationship wither as the demands of a sick and dying mother call him home. At this time in his life, when Paul seems most aware of his mother's hold on him, when he himself is apparently sucked into the drift toward death at her side, he is drawn into another relationship perhaps as fruitless and death-signifying, the one with Baxter Dawes.

Is this relationship with Dawes Paul's initiation in homosexual love? It seems so only in the most general sense. True, Paul fights bodily with Dawes, often a metaphor for homosexual bonding: an accepted kind of surrogate sexual experience between men.

The bloody and almost unconscious participation in the fight does seem to initiate him into a more vital awareness of his own physical presence. After Paul recuperates from this violent loss of a virginity of sorts, a kind of courtship with Dawes begins, with Paul visiting the ailing man, bringing gifts, even showing affection and setting him up in new lodgings and a job.

Frank O'Connor sees the Paul/Dawes relationship as possibly one in which Paul Morel reencounters the father of his life, and thus his own masculinity through the presence of a virile, less spiritual person in whom the "dark consciousness" reigns. This analogy seems plausible considering Paul's efforts at reconciling Dawes and his wife, a kind of substitution for reconciling his own mother and father.

But this aspect of the relationship, Paul as reconciler, becoming almost passive and non-participant in the ensuing relationship seems one more way Lawrence symbolizes a true coming together of persons, as if only through Paul can the broken relationship come again to be melded together.

In any case, all the relationships in Sons and Lovers seem to involve power struggles:Mrs. Morel wrenches power from her husband by turning from his sexual presence and then dominating, even emasculating her sons; she controls Paul's devotion through the imposition of her values and aspirations and thus weights down that relationship.

Miriam, apparently passive and devoted to Paul, is in effect constantly trying to assert her will over his. To possess him, he fears, and that love disintegrates. Clara accuses Paul of controlling how much of himself he will give to her or takes back of her in return, complaining that he can't or won't "come out" to her. And Paul controls their relationship time wise, dissolving it when it seems superfluous to him.

He also initiates the relationship with Dawes, except for the older man's early attempts to engage him in combat, thus drawing him out of passivity and finally only allowing him to reassert his rights with Clara under his (Paul's) domination.

The balance of power in relationships sees to be an essential concern of D. h. Lawrence, since it is appears over and over again to be responsible for the death of love. Lawrence's men and women will not be controlled, possessed or lost in another individual's reality. Relationship to them must not be a mere matter of perfect blending with the resultant loss of selfhood, they are telling us. Nor can strong relationships be wrought of outright possession of one by the other, but rather, through a delicate balance, achieved somehow in terms of recognition of otherness and of the primal selfness. Which itself can only be recognized, even shaped, in encountering the other, unencumbered, and free.

Lawrence's life itself would illustrate the struggle to achieve balance in relationships, and definition of the self as wrought against the outlines of another being. But that is material for another essay, surely with its own echoes of Sons and Lovers.

Q9. Critically analyse D.H Lawrence Sons and Lovers.

Or

Q. To what extent Sons and Lovers is an autobiographical novel.

Sons and Lovers was the first modern portrayal of a phenomenon that later, thanks to Freud, became easily recognizable as the Oedipus complex. Never was a son more indentured to his mother's love and full of hatred for his father than Paul Morel, D.H. Lawrence's young protagonist. Never, that is, except perhaps Lawrence himself. In his 1913 novel he grappled with the discordant loves that haunted him all his life—for his spiritual childhood sweetheart, here called Miriam, and for his mother, whom he transformed into Mrs.

Morel. It is, by Lawrence's own account, a book aimed at depicting this woman's grasp: "as her sons grow up she selects them as lovers—first the eldest, then the second. These sons are urged into life by their reciprocal love of their mother—urged on and on. But when they come to manhood, they can't love, because their mother is the strongest power in their lives."

Of course, Mrs. Morel takes neither of her two elder sons (the first of whom dies early, which further intensifies her grip on Paul) as a literal lover, but nonetheless her psychological snare is immense. She loathes Paul's Miriam from the start, understanding that the girl's deep love of her son will oust her: "She's not like an ordinary woman, who can leave me my share in him. She wants to absorb him."

Meanwhile, Paul plays his part with equal fervor, incapable of committing himself in either direction: "Why did his mother sit at home and suffer?... And why did he hate Miriam, and feel so cruel towards her, at the thought of his mother. If Miriam caused his mother suffering, then he hated her—and he easily hated her." Soon thereafter he even confesses to his mother: "I really don't love her. I talk to her, but I want to come home to you."

The result of all this is that Paul throws Miriam over for a married suffragette, Clara Dawes, who fulfills the sexual component of his ascent to manhood but leaves him, as ever, without a complete relationship to challenge his love for his mother. As Paul voyages from the working-class mining world to the spheres of commerce and art (he has fair success as a painter), he accepts that his own achievements must be equally his mother's. "There was so much to come out of him. Life for her was rich with promise. She was to see herself fulfilled... All his work was hers."

The cycles of Paul's relationships with these three women are terrifying at times, and Lawrence does nothing to dim their intensity. Nor does he shirk in his vivid, sensuous descriptions of the landscape that offers up its blossoms and beasts and "shimmer ness" to Paul's sensitive spirit. Sons and Lovers lays fully bare the souls of men and earth. Few books tell such whole, complicated truths about the permutations of love as resolutely without resolution. It's nothing short of searing to be brushed by humanity in this manner.

D. H. Lawrence is considered one of the Twentieth Century's greatest and most visionary English novelists. He was born in 1885 in Eastwood, a mining community in Nottinghamshire, England (DeMott iii). His father was an uneducated miner and his mother had been a schoolteacher before she married. According to England's rigid class system, his mother's marriage to his father was considered a step down, since she came from a well-educated middle-class family. Thus the vast differences between his parents was cause for "the fabric of his parents' marriage [to be] ripped by bitterness, violence and hate" (DeMott vii).

Lawrence's first great novel, Sons and Lovers, is clearly autobiographical: "there's no denying the closeness of the resemblance between Paul Morel's life and that of his creator" (DeMott vii). The novel tells the story of Gertrude Morel, a mother whose possessive love for her sons hinders their ability to establish fulfilling relationships with other women.

Lawrence himself had an unusually close attachment to his mother. The novel also depicts the working class of England at the turn of the century, when industrialism was rearing its ugly head and was creeping upon the English countryside. Set in a town similar to the one where he was born, Sons and Lovers gives a detailed and realistic portrayal of the hardships and conflicts of the Morels, a mining family.

Gertrude Morel, the character based on Lawrence's mother, has married below her station; she is a religious woman who is serious and believes in hard work and adherence to a strict code of morals. She is unhappy and disillusioned with the lower-class mining-family lifestyle and is "sick of it, the struggle with poverty and ugliness and meanness". But she is resolved to stay in her unhappy marriage "and all the time... thinking how to make the most of what she had, for the children's sake".

She met Walter Morel at the age of twenty-three: "his cheeks were ruddy, and his red, moist mouth was noticeable because he laughed so often and so heartily." Upon meeting him, she watches him with fascination, for he is "so full of colour and animation... Soft, non-intellectual, [and] warm". He is a simple miner with simple needs and no real ambition to better himself. Physical attraction leads her to marry him, but when the attraction fades, the marriage becomes bitter and stormy. Her frustration with him stems from the fact that he is completely unable to live up to her bourgeois expectations.

Consequently, Mrs. Morel turns away from her husband and invests all her love and energy in her two eldest sons, William and Paul. William, the eldest, is ambitious and finds a lucrative job in London, but dies soon after marrying a frivolous woman. Mrs. Morel then turns all her attentions upon Paul, the character based on Lawrence himself, in an abnormally close relationship.

As Walter Morel turns to drinking and spends his evenings at the pub, spending his family's much-needed money, "his pride and moral strength" disappear. As a result, Mrs. Morel directs all of her attentions to her children, especially Paul, and treats her husband as a failure. Paul is a pale and quiet child, old for his years.

Even as a newborn child, Paul has "dark, brooding pupils, as if a burden were on his heart...quite sorrowful". Paul, always withdrawn, follows his mother around like a shadow, establishing himself a special place in her favour. Mrs. Morel is the centre of Paul's life, and "his heart contracted with pain of love of her". Paul sides with his mother against his father and views life from her point of view.

He is completely dependent upon her, even as he ventures out to find his first job. Paul feels distraught, for he feels that "the business world, with its regulated system of values, and its impersonality... is monstrous". Paul feels "a prisoner of industrialism," and only wants a simple life. His only wish is to earn a small salary and when his father dies, to have a cottage with his mother, paint, and live happily ever after.

But Paul appeases his mother and goes along with her plans for him. Paul's going to work in industry is the fulfillment of his mother's dreams. As her son goes into the world, Mrs. Morel sees him as a reflection of herself. And so the two travel together on the way to the interview, "feeling the excitement of lovers having an adventure together". Mrs. Morel lives each moment through Paul, as though his life were her own.

Part Two of the novel begins with a new life for Paul, in his friendship and eventual relationship with Miriam. Paul, coming into manhood, is fascinated by the revelations he finds in Miriam. The awakening in Miriam of her sensuality draws her to Paul, and she hopes to be with him in a spiritual union. But Miriam shrinks from any thoughts of physical passion between them.

Meanwhile, Paul is waking up to his feelings of sexuality and feels uneasy: "Paul hated [Miriam] because, somehow, she spoilt his ease and naturalness. And he writhed himself with a feeling of humiliation". Miriam is in many ways like Paul's mother—she is religious, pure and possessive. However, their relationship cannot work, for Paul's closeness to his mother inhibits him from forming any successful and lasting relationships with other women. Mrs. Morel is resentful of the closeness that Paul and Miriam share, and she treats Miriam with disdain. Mrs. Morel, with her strength and domination, feels as though she possesses Paul's soul and will now allow room for Miriam in Paul's life.

Next, there is the older, sensual woman that arrives in Paul's life: Clara Dawes. She enters his life when Paul is becoming aware of his need for a physical relationship with a woman. Her sense of mystery intrigues Paul, and they begin a love affair. Clara fulfills a need for Paul, stemming from his unsatisfying relationship with Miriam. Clara possesses a sensuous and intuitive quality that Miriam lacks and makes Paul feel like a man.

However, Paul's attachment to his mother ends this relationship as well. No other woman can compare to his mother, and though Paul resents her, he cannot separate himself from her. Mrs. Morel's intense possessiveness of Paul has made it impossible for him to feel a normal desire, sexually or emotionally, for any other woman.

Even when near death, Mrs. Morel does not want to die, for she feels that she must finally leave Paul. Upon her death, Paul feels nothing but a longing for his own death. He must then learn to live a life of his own, independent of the influence (and support and encouragement) of his mother. However, the spirit in Paul persuades him to turn away from death and walk towards the town and a new beginning.

Paul Morel, like Lawrence himself, is a man alone. As an artist, searching for identity and meaning in his world, Paul must find his own answers from his background in the mining community, from industrial England, and from the strong influence of his mother. Paul has lived a life of struggle and despair in the mining community, but he has also wondered at the beauty and miracle of the earth and all the growing things that surround him in the pastoral countryside.

It is obvious that Lawrence preferred the agrarian England as opposed to the dehumanizing and mechanized modern world. Lawrence addresses "the human costs" of an industrialized society in Sons and Lovers and many of his other works, including his infamous Lady Chatterley's Lover (DeMott viii). Industrial British society has turned away from its agrarian roots and is destroying England, and the old way of life is seen as much more vibrant and complete. Lawrence, a genius in his own time, prophesied "that the West is on a disaster course and that all of us must change our lives" before we destroy the beauty of our world, and in the process destroy our own souls.

Q10. Critically analyse character of Miriam.

Or

Q. How does Lawrence portray Miriam in Sons and Lovers?

The girl was romantic in her soul.

And she was cut off from ordinary life by her religious intensity which made the world for her either a nunnery garden or a paradise, where sin and knowledge were not, or else an ugly, cruel thing.

And in sacrifice she was proud, in renunciation she was strong, for she did not trust herself to support everyday life.

"You don't want to love—your eternal and abnormal craving is to be loved. You aren't positive, you're negative. You absorb, absorb, as if you must fill yourself up with love, because you've got a shortage somewhere."

With very few exceptions, the commentators on Lawrence's *Sons and Lovers* have tended to accept the view of Miriam's character as thus described by the narrator and by Paul Morel. Mark Spilka, for example, in his stimulating book, bases his interpretation of the novel on the assumption that Miriam has "an unhealthy spirituality," is truly "negative," that she really "wheedles the soul out of things," as Paul Morel says, and that "because of the stifling nature of Miriam's love, Paul refuses to marry her"—justifiably, since "Miriam's frigidity is rooted in her own nature." But I believe that the portrait of Miriam is far more complex than either Paul or the narrator will allow, and that a study of her part in the book will cast some light upon the puzzling and peculiar technique of narration that Lawrence adopts when he comes to the central section of his novel, the five tormented chapters (7-11) running from "Lad-and-Girl Love" through "The Test on Miriam."

As everyone has noticed, part 1 of the novel (the first third of the book, concluding with the death of William) is written in the manner of Victorian realism: the omniscient narrator, working with firm control, sets forth the facts objectively. The countryside, the mining village, the family conflicts, the daily life of the household— all is given in clear, precise, convincing detail. The use of local dialect, the echoes of biblical style, the short, concise sentences combine to create in us a confidence in the narrator's command of his materials.

His fairness to everyone is evident. If the father is predominantly shown as brutal and drunken, in those savage quarrels with the mother, he is also shown in his younger glory as a man who might have flourished with a different wife: "Gertrude Coppard watched the young miner as he danced, a certain subtle exultation like glamour in his movement, and his face the flower of his body, ruddy, with tumbled black hair, and laughing alike whatever partner he bowed above." Even when the wife has turned away from him she can enjoy his music:

Quite early, before six o'clock, she heard him whistling away to himself downstairs. He had a pleasant way of whistling, lively and musical. He nearly always whistled hymns. He had been a choir-boy with a beautiful voice, and had taken solos in South well cathedral. His morning whistling alone betrayed it.

His wife lay listening to him tinkering away in the garden, his whistling ringing out as he sawed and hammered away. It always gave her a sense of warmth and peace to hear him thus as she lay in bed, the children not yet awake, in the bright early morning, happy in his man's fashion.

We watch Morel's relish in getting his breakfast and his joy in walking across the fields to his work in the early morning; we learn of those happy times when Morel is cobbling the family's boots, or mending kettles, or making fuses; we recognize his faithful labour at his grueling job; and particularly we notice the love for him felt by the youngest child Arthur: "Mrs. Morel was glad this child loved the father." All these things give a sense of balance and proportion to part 1, making it clear that Paul's view is partial, unfair to the father, ignoring his basic humanity.

Paul's blindness towards his father's very existence as a human being is cruelly shown in the scene where Morel emerges from the pit to hear of William's death:

"And William is dead, and my mother's in London, and what will she be doing?" the boy asked himself, as if it were a conundrum.

He watched chair after chair come up, and still no father. At last, standing beside a wagon, a man's form! The chair sank on its rests, Morel stepped off. He was slightly lame from an accident.

"Is it thee, Paul? Is 'e worse?"

"You've got to go to London."

The two walked off the pit-bank, where men were watching curiously. As they came out and went along the railway, with the sunny autumn field on one side and a wall of trucks on the other, Morel said in a frightened voice:

"'E's niver gone, child?"

"Yes."

"When wor't?"

The miner's voice was terrified.

"Last night. We had a telegram from my mother."

Morel walked on a few strides, then leaned up against a truck side, his hand over his eyes. He was not crying. Paul stood looking round, waiting. On the weighing-machine a truck trundled slowly. Paul saw everything, except his father leaning against the truck as if he were tired.

"Paul saw everything, except his father." Only the omniscient narrator reveals the man Morel, battered from his work, frightened for his son's life, sunk in dumb agony at the news, while his intimate dialect plays off pitifully against the formal language of Paul, to stress the total division between the two.

Part 1, then, is a triumph of narration in the old Victorian style. It is a long prologue, in which the issues are clearly defined, and in which, above all, the mother's overpowering influence is shown in the death of one son, while she turns toward Paul as her only remaining hope: "'I should have watched the living, not the dead,' she told herself."

Meanwhile, as William is engaged in his fatal courtship, the figure of Miriam has been quietly introduced, in the natural, harmonious setting of the farm: "Mother and son went into the small railed garden, where was a scent of red glovers. By the open door were some floury loaves, put out to cool. A hen was just coming to peck them. Then, in the doorway suddenly appeared a girl in a dirty apron. She was about fourteen years old, had a rosy dark face, a bunch of short black curls, very fine and free, and dark eyes; shy, questioning, a little resentful of the strangers, she disappeared." Shortly after this follows the vivid incident in which the brothers jeer at Miriam for being afraid to let the hen peck the corn out of her hand:

"Now, Miriam," said Maurice, "you come an' 'ave a go."

"No," she cried, shrinking back.

"Ha! baby. The mardy-kid!" said her brothers.

"It doesn't hurt a bit," said Paul. "It only just nips rather nicely."

"No," she still cried, shaking her black curls and shrinking.

"She dursn't," said Geoffrey. "She niver durst do anything except recite poitry."

"Dursn't jump off a gate, dursn't tweedle, dursn't go on a slide, dursn't stop a girl hittin' her. She can do nowt but go about thinkin' herself somebody. 'The Lady of the Lake.' Yah!" cried Maurice.

We are bound to align this with the later incident of the swing, both of which might be taken "as revelations of Miriam's diminished vitality, her tendency to shrink back from life, whether she is making love, feeding chickens, trying to cope with Mrs. Morel's dislike of her, or merely looking at flowers." But we should note that immediately after the passage just quoted Paul witnesses another aspect of Miriam:

As he went round the back, he saw Miriam kneeling in front of the hen-coop, some maize in her hand, biting her lip, and crouching in an intense attitude. The hen was eyeing her wickedly. Very gingerly she put forward her hand. The hen bobbed for her. She drew back quickly with a cry, half of fear, half of chagrin.

"It won't hurt you," said Paul.

She flushed crimson and started up.

"I only wanted to try," she said in a low voice.

"See, it doesn't hurt," he said, and, putting only two corns in his palm, he let the hen peck, peck, peck at his bare hand. "It only makes you laugh," he said.

She put her hand forward, and dragged it away, tried again, and started back with a cry. He frowned.

"Why, I'd let her take corn from my face," said Paul, "only she bumps a bit. She's ever so neat. If she wasn't, look how much ground she'd peck up every day."

He waited grimly, and watched. At last Miriam let the bird peck from her hand. She gave a little cry—fear, and pain because of fear—rather pathetic. But she had done it, and she did it again.

"There, you see," said the boy. "It doesn't hurt, does it?"

She looked at him with dilated dark eyes.

"No," she laughed, trembling.

The scene shows more than timidity; it shows, also, her extreme sensitivity, along with her shy desire for new experience: she wants to try, she wants to learn; if rightly encouraged she will and can learn, and then she can respond with laughter and trembling excitement. This first view of Miriam, seen through the eyes of the objective narrator, is astir with life: for all her shyness and shrinking she is nevertheless capable of a strong response. The whole initial sketch is suffused with her "beautiful warm colouring" and accompanied by her "musical, quiet voice." She is a girl of rich potential.

As part 2 opens we become at once aware of a drastic shift in method. The first two pages are given over to an elaborate interpretation of Miriam's character before she again appears, "nearly sixteen, very beautiful, with her warm colouring, her gravity, her eyes dilating suddenly like an ecstasy." No such extended analysis of anyone has appeared in part 1; there the characters have been allowed to act out their parts before us, with only brief guiding touches by the objective narrator.

But here we sense a peculiar intensity in the analysis: the narrator seems to be preparing the way for some new and difficult problem, and in so doing he seems to be dropping his manner of impartiality. He is determined to set our minds in a certain direction, and this aim is reflected in the drifting length and involution of the sentences. The style of writing here seems designed to reflect the "mistiness" of the character he is describing, her remoteness from life:

> Her great companion was her mother. They were both brown-eyed, and inclined to be mystical, such women as treasure religion inside them, breathe it in their nostrils, and see the whole of life in a mist thereof. So to Miriam, Christ and God made one great figure, which she loved tremblingly and passionately when a tremendous sunset burned out the western sky, and Ediths, and Lucys, and Rowenas, Brian de Bois Guilberts, Rob Roys, and Guy Mannerings, rustled the sunny leaves in the morning, or sat in her bedroom aloft, alone, when it snowed.
>
> That was life to her. For the rest, she drudged in the house, which work she would not have minded had not her clean red floor been mucked up immediately by the trampling farmboots of her brothers. She madly wanted her little brother of four to let her swathe him and stifle him in her love; she went to church reverently, with bowed head, and quivered in anguish from the vulgarity of the other choir-girls and from the common-sounding voice of the curate; she fought with her brothers, whom she considered brutal louts; and she held not her father in too high esteem because he did not carry any mystical ideals cherished in his heart, but only wanted to have as easy a time as he could, and his meals when he was ready for them.

She is also a girl who is "mad to have learning whereon to pride herself"; and for all these causes she neglects and ignores her physical being: "Her beauty—that of a shy, wild, quiveringly sensitive thing—seemed nothing to her. Even her soul, so strong for rhapsody, was not enough. She must have something to reinforce her pride, because she felt different from other people."

At the same time, her misty emotions lead her towards a desire to dominate Paul: "Then he was so ill, and she felt he would be weak. Then she would be stronger than he. Then she could love him. If she could be mistress of him in his weakness, take care of him, if he could depend on her, if she could, as it were, have him in her arms, how she would love him!"

In all this the narrator is anticipating the views of Miriam frequently expressed by Paul himself: that she is too spiritual, too abstract, that she shrinks away from physical reality, and that she has a stifling desire to absorb and possess his soul. The incident of the swing that follows shortly after would seem to bear out some of this: she is afraid to let Paul swing her high, and Lawrence phrases her fear in language that has unmistakable sexual overtones: "She felt the accuracy with which he caught her, exactly at the right moment, and the exactly proportionate strength of his thrust, and she was afraid. Down to her bowels went the hot wave of fear. She was in his hands.

Again, firm and inevitable came the thrust at the right moment. She gripped the rope, almost swooning." Yet she has led Paul to the swing, and she is fascinated by his free swinging: "It roused a warmth in her. It were almost as if he were a flame that had lit a warmth in her whilst he swung in the middle air." Who can say that Miriam is unable to learn this too, as she has learned with the hen, and as she is later shown to overcome her fear of crossing fences?

Occasionally she ran with Paul down the fields. Then her eyes blazed naked in a kind of esctasy that frightened him. But she was physically afraid. If she were getting over a stile, she gripped his hands in a little hard anguish, and began to lose her presence of mind. And he could not persuade her to jump from even a small height. Her eyes dilated, became exposed and palpitating.

"No!" she cried, half laughing in terror—"no!"

"You shall!" he cried once, and, jerking her forward, he brought her falling from the fence. But her wild "Ah!" of pain, as if she were losing consciousness, cut him. She landed on her feet safely, and afterwards had courage in this respect.

Certainly she wants to learn; only a few lines after the swing episode we find this all-important passage:

> But the girl gradually sought him out. If he brought up his sketchbook, it was she who pondered longest over the last picture. Then she would look up at him. Suddenly, her dark eyes alight like water that shakes with a stream of gold in the dark, she would ask:
>
> "Why do I like this so?"
>
> Always something in his breast shrank from these close, intimate, dazzled looks of hers.
>
> "Why do you?" he asked.
>
> "I don't know. It seems so true."
>
> "It's because—it's because there is scarcely any shadow in it; it's more shimmer, as if I'd painted the shimmering protoplasm in the leaves and everywhere, and not the stiffness of the shape. That seems dead to me. Only this shimmer ness is the real living. The shape is a dead crust. The shimmer is inside really."
>
> And she, with her little finger in her mouth, would ponder these sayings. They gave her a feeling of life again, and vivified things which had meant nothing to her. She managed to find some meaning in his struggling, abstract speeches. And they were the medium through which she came distinctly at her beloved objects.

It seems as though she is learning to reach out towards the "shimmer ness" that is the "real living"; with his help she is coming out of her "mist" towards a distinct sight of "her beloved objects." She is learning, while he shrinks away from her intimate, shimmering eyes ("like water that shakes with a stream of gold in the dark"). She senses the meaning of his "abstract speeches," she gets "so near him," she creates in him "a strange, roused sensation"—and as a result she enrages him for reasons that he cannot grasp. Is it because he is refusing to face the shimmer that is really inside Miriam?

So, when he sees her embracing her youngest brother "almost as if she were in a trance, and swaying also as if she were swooned in an ecstasy of love," he bursts out with his irritation:

"What do you make such a *fuss* for?" cried Paul, all in suffering because of her extreme emotion. "Why can't you be ordinary with him?"

She let the child go, and rose, and said nothing. Her intensity, which would leave no emotion on a normal plane, irritated the youth into a frenzy. And this fearful, naked contact of her on small occasions shocked him. He was used to his mother's reserve. And on such occasions he was thankful in his heart and soul that he had his mother, so sane and wholesome.

One senses, as Miriam does at a later point, an alien influence here, twisting the mind of Paul and the narrator away from Miriam. Two pages later we see a dramatic juxtaposition of two warring actualities:

He used to tell his mother all these things.

"I'm going to teach Miriam algebra," he said.

"Well," replied Mrs. Morel, "I hope she'll get fat on it."

When he went up to the farm on the Monday evening, it was drawing twilight. Miriam was just sweeping up the kitchen, and was kneeling at the hearth when he entered. Everyone was out but her. She looked round at him, flushed, her dark eyes shining, her fine hair falling about her face.

"Hello!" she said, soft and musical. "I knew it was you."

"How?"

"I knew your step. Nobody treads so quick and firm."

He sat down, sighing.

"Ready to do some algebra?" he asked, drawing a little book from his pocket.

Who is sane and wholesome, we may well ask? And whose thoughts are abstracted from life? We are beginning to learn that we cannot wholly trust the narrator's remarks in this central portion of the book, for his commentary represents mainly an extension of Paul's consciousness; everywhere, in this portion of the book, the voice of the narrator tends to echo and magnify the confusions that are arising within Paul himself.

These are the contradictions in which some readers have seen a failure or a faltering in the novel, because "the point of view is never adequately objectified and sustained to tell us which is true." But I feel rather that Lawrence has invented a successful technique by which he can manage the deep autobiographical problems that underlie the book. We are watching the strong graft of a stream of consciousness growing out of the live trunk of that Victorian prologue, and intertwining with the objectively presented action.

The point of view adopted is that of Paul; but since confusion, self-deception, and desperate self-justification are essential to that point of view, we can never tell, from that stream of consciousness alone, where the real truth lies. But we can tell it from the action; we can tell it by seeking out the portrait of Miriam that lies beneath the over-painted commentary of the Paul-narrator.

This technique of painting and over painting produces a strange and unique tension in this part of the novel. The image of Miriam appears and then is clouded over; it is as though we were looking at her through a clouded window that is constantly being cleared, and fogged, and cleared again. It is an unprecedented and inimitable technique, discovered for this one necessary occasion. But it works.

How it works, we may see by looking once again at the frequently quoted passage where Miriam leads Paul, despite his reluctance ("They grumble so if I'm late") into the woods at dusk to find the "wild-rose bush she had discovered."

The tree was tall and straggling. It had thrown its briers over a hawthorn-bush, and its long streamers trailed thick, right down to the grass, splashing the darkness everywhere with great split stars, pure white. In bosses of ivory and in large splashed stars the roses gleamed on the darkness of foliage and stems and grass. Paul and Miriam stood close together, silent, and watched. Point after point the steady roses shone out to them, seeming to kindle something in their souls. The dusk came like smoke around, and still did not put out the roses.

Paul looked into Miriam's eyes. She was pale and expectant with wonder, her lips were parted, and her dark eyes lay open to him. His look seemed to travel down into her. Her soul quivered. It was the communion she wanted. He turned aside, as if pained. He turned to the bush.

"They seem as if they walk like butterflies, and shake themselves," he said.

She looked at her roses. They were white, some incurved and holy, others expanded in an ecstasy. The tree was dark as a shadow. She lifted her hand impulsively to the flowers; she went forward and touched them in worship.

"Let us go," he said.

There was a cool scent of ivory roses—a white, virgin scent. Something made him feel anxious and imprisoned. The two walked in silence.

What is this "something" that makes him "feel anxious and imprisoned"? Is he like the hawthorn-bush, caught in the trailing streamers of the rose-bush? Is it because she has insisted on a moment of soul communion which represents her tendency towards "a blasphemous possessor ship"? The narrator seems to be urging us in this direction. Yet in itself the scene may be taken to represent, amid this wild profusion of natural growth, a moment of natural communion in the human relationship, a potential marriage of senses and the soul. This is, for Miriam, an "ecstasy" in which nature is not abstracted, but realised in all its wild perfection. Paul breaks the mood and runs away towards home. And when he reaches home we may grasp the true manner of his imprisonment:

Always when he went with Miriam, and it grew rather late, he knew his mother was fretting and getting angry about him—why, he could not understand. As he went into the house, flinging down his cap, his mother looked up at the clock. She had been sitting thinking because a chill to her eyes prevented her reading. She could feel Paul being drawn away by this girl. And she did not care for Miriam. "She is one of those who will want to suck a man's soul out till he has none of his own left," she said to herself; "and he is just such a gabby as to let himself be absorbed. She will never let him become a man; she never will." So, while he was away with Miriam, Mrs. Morel grew more and more worked up.

She glanced at the clock and said, coldly and rather tired:

"You have been far enough to-night."

His soul, warm and exposed from contact with the girl, shrank.

Miriam offers him the freedom of natural growth within a mature relation, though Paul soon adopts the mother's view of Miriam's "possessive" nature. He cannot help himself, but there is no reason why readers of the book should accept the mother's view of Miriam, which is everywhere shown to be motivated by the mother's own possessiveness. The mother has described only herself in the above quotation; she has not described Miriam, who is quite a different being and has quite a different effect on Paul.

The fact is that Paul needs both his mother and Miriam for his true development, as he seems to realise quite early in the conflict: "A sketch finished, he always wanted to take it to Miriam. Then he was stimulated into knowledge of the work he had produced unconsciously. In contact with Miriam he gained insight; his vision went deeper. From his mother he drew the life-warmth, the strength to produce; Miriam urged this warmth into intensity like a white light." Or earlier we hear that Miriam's family "kindled him and made him glow to his work, whereas his mother's influence was to make him quietly determined, patient, dogged, unwearied."

But the mother cannot bear to release him. Miriam must be met by her with cold, unfriendly curtness, while the married woman, Clara, may receive a friendly welcome from the mother. Clara offers no threat: "Mrs. Morel measured herself against the younger woman, and found herself easily stronger." "Yes, I liked her", she says in answer to Paul's inquiry. "But you'll tire of her, my son; you know you will." And so she encourages the affair with Clara: the adulterous relation will serve the son's physical needs, while the mother can retain the son's deeper love and loyalty. Mrs. Morel senses what she is doing, but evades the facts:

Mrs. Morel considered. She would have been glad now for her son to fall in love with some woman who would—she did not know what. But he fretted so, got so furious suddenly, and again was melancholic. She wished he knew some nice woman—She did not know what she wished, but left it vague. At any rate she was not hostile to the idea of Clara.

The mother's devices are pitiful, and at the same time contemptible, as we have already seen from the painful episode in which she overwhelms her son with raw and naked emotion:

He had taken off his collar and tie, and rose, bare-throated, to go to bed. As he stooped to kiss his mother, she threw her arms around his neck, hid her face on his shoulder, and cried, in a whimpering voice, so unlike her own that he writhed in agony:

"I can't bear it. I could let another woman—but not her. She'd leave me no room, not a bit of room—"

And immediately he hated Miriam bitterly. "And I've never—you know, Paul—I've never had a husband—not really—"

He stroked his mother's hair, and his mouth was on her throat.

"And she exults so in taking you from me—she's not like ordinary girls."

"Well, I don't love her, mother," he murmured, bowing his head and hiding his eyes on her shoulder in misery. His mother kissed him a long, fervent kiss.

"My boy!" she said, in a voice trembling with passionate love.

"At your mischief again?" says the father, "venomously," as he interrupts this scene of illicitly possessive passion. Mischief it is, corrosive and destructive to the marriage that Paul needs, the full relationship that Miriam offers, with her intimate love for nature.

It will be evident that I do not agree with the view that Spilka and others have taken of that flower-picking episode with Miriam and Clara, the view that takes the scene as a revelation of a basic flaw in Miriam: "She kills life and has no right to it."

"Ah!" cried Miriam, and she looked at Paul, her dark eyes dilating. He smiled. Together they enjoyed the field of flowers. Clara, a little way off, was looking at the cowslips disconsolately. Paul and Miriam stayed close together, talking in subdued tones. He kneeled on one knee, quickly gathering the best blossoms, moving from tuft to tuft restlessly, talking softly all the time. Miriam plucked the flowers lovingly, lingering over them. He always seemed to her too quick and almost scientific. Yet his bunches had a natural beauty more than hers. He loved them, but as if they were his and he had a right to them. She had more reverence for them: they held something she had not.

The last clause has a wonderful ambiguity. If we take Paul's point of view, we will say that she is "negative," that she lacks true life. If we ponder the whole action of the book, we will say that what she lacks is the full organic life of the flower, sexually complete within itself. She cannot grow into her full life without the principle that Paul, with his masculine creativity, here displays. The passage shows a man and a woman who are true counterparts, in mind and body. When, a little later, Paul sprinkles the flowers over Clara, he is performing an exclusively sensuous ritual that threatens more than a pagan love-death:

Her breasts swung slightly in her blouse. The arching curve of her back was beautiful and strong; she wore no stays. Suddenly, without knowing, he was scattering a handful of cowslips over her hair and neck, saying:

"Ashes to ashes, and dust to dust,

If the Lord won't have you the devil must."

The chill flowers fell on her neck. She looked up at him,

with almost pitiful, scared grey eyes, wondering what he

was doing. Flowers fell on her face, and she shut her eyes.

Suddenly, standing there above her, he felt awkward.

"I thought you wanted a funeral," he said, ill at ease.

It is Paul, under his mother's domination, who kills life, by refusing to move in organic relation with Miriam:

He would not have it that they were lovers. The intimacy between them had been kept so abstract, such a matter of the soul, all thought and weary struggle into consciousness, that he saw it only as a platonic friendship. He stoutly denied there was anything else between them. Miriam was silent, or else she very quietly agreed. He was a fool who did not know what was happening to himself. By tacit agreement they ignored the remarks and insinuations of their acquaintances.

"We aren't lovers, we are friends," he said to her. "*We* know it. Let them talk. What does it matter what they say. "

Sometimes, as they were walking together, she slipped her arm timidly into his. But he always resented it, and she knew it. It caused a violent conflict in him. With Miriam he was always on the high plane of abstraction, when his natural fire of love was transmitted into the fine steam of thought. She would have it so.

The last sentence is a fine example of the way in which the commentary of the Paul-narrator can contradict the tenor of the action: "She slipped her arm timidly into his." Clara knows better and tells Paul the truth in that revealing conversation just before "the test on Miriam." Paul has been describing how Miriam "wants the soul out of my body": "I know she wants a sort of soul union."

"But how do you know what she wants?"

"I've been with her for seven years."

"And you haven't found out the very first thing about her."

"What's that?"

"That she doesn't want any of your soul communion.

That's your own imagination. She wants you."

He pondered over this. Perhaps he was wrong.

"But she seems—" he began.

"You've never tried," she answered.

This is not to deny that Miriam is shy, intense, spiritual, and, as a result of her upbringing, fearful and evasive of sexual facts. All these qualities belong to her character, for she is young, sensitive, and modest. My point is that her portrait does not consist simply of a static presentation of these aspects: her portrait is being enriched dynamically and progressively before our eyes, over a long period of years, from her early adolescence, through an awakening and potential fulfillment, to the utter extinction of her inner life and hope.

The truth of Clara's view has been borne out long before, as far back as that scene where Paul accuses Miriam of never laughing real laughter:

"But"—and she looked up at him with eyes frightened and struggling—"I do laugh at you—I *do*."

"Never! There's always a kind of intensity. When you laugh I could always cry; it seems as if it shows up your suffering. Oh, you make me knit the brows of my very soul and cogitate."

Slowly she shook her head despairingly.

"I'm sure I don't want to," she said.

"I'm so damned spiritual with *you* always!" he cried.

She remained silent, thinking, "Then why don't you be otherwise." But he saw her crouching, brooding figure, and it seemed to tear him in two.

And then, on the next page, as Paul repairs the bicycle tire, we have an unmistakable glimpse of the vital image of Miriam, her strong physical feeling for him, and her true laughter:

"Fetch me a drop of water in a bowl," he said to her. "I shall be late, and then I s'll catch it."

He lighted the hurricane lamp, took off his coat, turned up the bicycle, and set speedily to work. Miriam came with the bowl of water and stood close to him, watching. She loved to see his hands doing things. He was slim and vigourous, with a kind of easiness even in his most hasty movements. And busy at his work, he seemed to forget her. She loved him absorbedly. She wanted to run her hands down his sides. She always wanted to embrace him, so long as he did not want her.

"There!" he said, rising suddenly. "Now, could you have done it quicker?"

"No!" she laughed.

He straightened himself. His back was towards her. She put her two hands on his sides, and ran them quickly down.

"You are so *fine!*" she said.

He laughed, hating her voice, but his blood roused to a wave of flame by her hands. She did not seem to realise *him* in all this. He might have been an object. She never realised the male he was.

Those last three sentences, the outgrowth of his torment, and the earlier remark, "so long as he did not want her," provide clear examples of the way in which the over painted commentary tends to obscure the basic portrait of Miriam. It is the same in the episode at Nether mere: "He could not bear to look at Miriam. She seemed to want him, and he resisted. He resisted all the time. He wanted now to give her passion and tenderness, and he could not. He felt that she wanted the soul out of his body, and not him."

He went on, in his dead fashion:

"If only you could want *me*, and not want what I can reel off for you!"

"I!" she cried bitterly—"I! Why, when would you let me take you?"

His bursts of anger and "hate," his feeling that Miriam is pulling the soul out of his body, are only his own tormented reactions to the agony he feels in being pulled so strongly away from his mother, as Daniel Weiss has said: "It is that for the first time in his life he is facing a mature relationship between himself and another woman, not his mother, and that a different mode of love is being demanded from him. It is Miriam's refusal to allow him to regress to the Nirvana, the paradise state of the infant, her insistence that he recognize her, that fills him with anguish."

As though to warn us against accepting Paul's responses and interpretations, Lawrence inserts in the middle of the crucial chapter, "Strife in Love," a long, vigourous, attractive, and surprising scene where the father is shown totally in command of the household, on a Friday evening, when the miners make their reckoning in Morel's house. Complaining with warm, vigourous dialect about the cold room, as he emerges from his bath, Morel draws even his wife into laughter and reminiscent admiration:

Morel looked down ruefully at his sides.

"Me!" he exclaimed. "I'm nowt b'r a skinned rabbit. My bones fair juts out on me."

"I should like to know where," retorted his wife.

"Iv'ry-wheer! I'm nobbut a sack o' faggots."

Mrs. Morel laughed. He had still a wonderfully young body, muscular, without any fat. His skin was smooth and clear. It might have been the body of a man of twenty eight, except that there were, perhaps, too many blue scars, like tattoo-marks, where the coal-dust remained under the skin, and that his chest was too hairy. But he put his hand on his sides ruefully. It was his fixed belief that, because he did not get fat, he was as thin as a starved rat.

Paul looked at his father's thick, brownish hands all scarred, with broken nails, rubbing the fine smoothness of his sides, and the incongruity struck him. It seemed strange they were the same flesh.

"I suppose," he said to his father, "you had a good figure once.

"Eh!" exclaimed the miner, glancing round, startled and timid, like a child.

"He had," exclaimed Mrs. Morel, "if he didn't hurtle himself up as if he was trying to get in the smallest space he could."

"Me!" exclaimed Morel—"me a good figure! I wor niver much more n'r a skeleton."

"Man!" cried his wife, "don't be such a pulamiter!"

"'Strewth!" he said. "Tha's niver knowed me but what I looked as if I wor goin' off in a rapid decline."

She sat and laughed.

"You've had a constitution like iron," she said; "and never a man had a better start, if it was body that counted. You should have seen him as a young man," she cried suddenly to Paul, drawing herself up to imitate her husband's once handsome bearing.

Morel watched her shyly. He saw again the passion she had had for him. It blazed upon her for a moment. He was shy, rather scared, and humble. Yet again he felt his old glow. And then immediately he felt the ruin he had made during these years. He wanted to bustle about, to run away from it.

Paul is the "outsider" here, the one who does not enter into the family warmth, as we have seen a few lines earlier from his cold comment on his father's vigourous exclamations ("Why is a door-knob deader than anything else?"), and as we see a little later from the way in which he turns "impatiently" from his books and pencil, after his father has asked him "humbly" to count up the money. And at the close of the episode he dismisses his father viciously: "It won't be long," he says to his mother. "You can have my money. Let him go to hell." Morel does not deserve this, we feel, after all the warmth and vigour of his action here. Paul is cruel to anyone who threatens his mother's dominion, however briefly.

This Miriam feels instinctively, a few minutes later, when she looks at the stenciled design that Paul has made for his mother:

"Ah, how beautiful!" she cried.

The spread cloth, with its wonderful reddish roses and dark green stems, all so simple, and somehow so wicked looking, lay at her feet. She went on her knees before it, her dark curls dropping. He saw her crouched voluptuously before his work, and his heart beat quickly. Suddenly she looked up at him.

Why does it seem cruel?" she asked.

"What?"

"There seems a feeling of cruelty about it," she said.

"It's jolly good, whether or not," he replied, folding up his work with a lover's hands.

He has also made a "smaller piece" for Miriam; but when he sees her fingering the work "with trembling hands" he can only turn with embarrassment to tend the bread in the oven, and when she looks up at him "with her dark eyes one flame of love" he can only laugh "uncomfortably" and begin to talk "about the design." "All his passion, all his wild blood, went into this intercourse with her, when he talked and conceived his work. She brought forth to him his imaginations. She did not understand, any more than a woman understands when she conceives a child in her womb. But this was life for her and for him." But, as the imagery of conception ironically implies, such talk is not all of life for either of them.

Immediately after this, the physical scuffle and flirtation with Beatrice shows another need, which Miriam recognizes and would like to satisfy: "His thick hair was tumbled over his forehead. Why might she not push it back for him, and remove the marks of Beatrice's comb? Why might she not press his body with her two hands? It looked so firm, and every whit living. And he would let other girls, why not her?" A moment later, as usual, Paul tries to "abstract" their relationship into a French lesson, only to find that her French diary is "mostly a love-letter" to him:

"Look," he said quietly, "the past participle conjugated with *avoir* agrees with the direct object when it precedes."

She bent forward, trying to see and to understand. Her free, fine curls tickled his face. He started as if they had been red hot, shuddering. He saw her peering forward at the page, her red lips parted piteously, the black hair springing in fine strands across her tawny, ruddy cheek. She was coloured like a pomegranate for richness. His breath came short as he watched her. Suddenly she looked up at him. Her dark eyes were naked with their love, afraid, and yearning. His eyes, too, were dark, and they hurt her. They seemed to master her. She lost all her self control, was exposed in fear. And he knew, before he could kiss her, he must drive something out of himself.

And a touch of hate for her crept back again into his heart. He returned to her exercise.

Miriam does not bear the slightest blame for the failure of this relationship: she is "like a pomegranate for richness," like the bride in the Song of Solomon; she combines a pure beauty of sensuous appeal with all the soul that Paul the artist needs for his further development. And like that bride she is not passive, she tries to draw Paul out of his imprisonment, tries to draw his attention towards the wild beauty of "the yellow, bursten flowers." His response is to level at her the most cruel of all his desperate charges:

"Aren't they magnificent?" she murmured.

"Magnificent! it's a bit thick—they're pretty!"

She bowed again to her flowers at his censure of her praise. He watched her crouching, sipping the flowers with fervid kisses.

"Why must you always be fondling things!" he said irritably.

"But I love to touch them," she replied, hurt.

"Can you never like things without clutching them as if you wanted to pull the heart out of them? Why don't you have a bit more restraint, or reserve, or something?"

She looked up at him full of pain, then continued slowly to stroke her lips against a ruffled flower. Their scent, as she smelled it, was so much kinder than he; it almost made her cry.

"You wheedle the soul out of things," he said. "I would never wheedle—at any rate, I'd go straight."

He scarcely knew what he was saying. These things came from him mechanically. She looked at him. His body seemed one weapon, firm and hard against her.

"You're always begging things to love you," he said, "as if you were a beggar for love. Even the flowers, you have to fawn on them—"

Rhythmically, Miriam was swaying and stroking the flower with her mouth, inhaling the scent which ever after made her shudder as it came to her nostrils.

"You don't want to love—your eternal and abnormal craving is to be loved. You aren't positive, you're negative. You absorb, absorb, as if you must fill yourself up with love, because you've got a shortage somewhere."

She was stunned by his cruelty, and did not hear. He had not the faintest notion of what he was saying. It was as if his fretted, tortured soul, run hot by thwarted passion, jetted off these sayings like sparks from electricity.

The shortage is in Paul; and she fondles the flowers so warmly because they offer solace from his ruthless rejection of her natural being. Her closeness to flowers throughout the book shows her as an innocent Persephone who needs only to be carried away by the power that Paul might possess if he were a whole man. But he is not. He is a child, with a child's limited outlook. His mother's influence has reduced all other human beings to unreality. This the narrator makes plain in one of his rare moments of illumination:

> He had come back to his mother. Hers was the strongest tie in his life. When he thought round, Miriam shrank away. There was a vague, unreal feel about her. And nobody else mattered. There was one place in the world that stood solid and did not melt into unreality: the place where his mother was. Everybody else could grow shadowy, almost non-existent to him, but she could not. It was as if the pivot and pole of his life, from which he could not escape, was his mother.

So then for Paul the warm reality of Miriam must fade away into spirituality and soulfulness, and she must suffer the cruel accusation summed up in the falsely composed letter that he writes at the end of the chapter, "Defeat of Miriam"—a letter of stilted, inflated rhetoric, false in every way:

> May I speak of our old, worn love, this last time. It, too, is changing, is it not? Say, has not the body of that love died, and left you its invulnerable soul? You see, I can give you a spirit love, I have given it you this long, long time; but not embodied passion. See, you are a nun. I have given you what I would give a holy nun—as a mystic monk to a mystic nun. Surely you esteem it best. Yet you regret— no, have regretted—the other. In all our relations no body enters. I do not talk to you through the senses—rather through the spirit. That is why we cannot love in the common sense. Ours is not

an everyday affection. As yet we are mortal, and to live side by side with one another would be dreadful, for somehow with you I cannot long be trivial, and, you know, to be always beyond this mortal state would be to lose it. If people marry, they must live together as affectionate humans, who may be common-place with each other without feeling awkward—not as two souls. So I feel it.

So she feels it too, and the hopeless rejection of her true character gives a death-blow to her inner vitality. "'You are a nun—you are a nun.' The words went into her heart again and again. Nothing he ever had said had gone into her so deeply, fixedly, like a mortal wound."

After such a wound, his later effort to carry on sexual relations with her is bound to be a failure. She tries, as she always has tried, but her inner life is ebbing. This is not the marriage that she yearns for, not the union that he needs. Paul hardly knows that she is there, as a person; indeed he does not want to know her as a human being. "He had always, almost willfully, to put her out of count, and act from the brute strength of his own feelings."

The title of the chapter, "The Test on Miriam," is bitterly ironic, for what the chapter presents is the test on Paul's ability to free himself from the imprisonment which he feels, but does not understand. This is clear from Paul's stream of consciousness at the very outset of the chapter: "There was some obstacle; and what was the obstacle? It lay in the physical bondage. He shrank from the physical contact. But why? With her he felt bound up inside himself. He could not go out to her." His only refuge is to turn towards a sort of mindless evasion of his torments, a rejection of his own humanity.

He courted her now like a lover. Often, when he grew hot, she put his face from her, held it between her hands, and looked in his eyes. He could not meet her gaze. Her dark eyes, full of love, earnest and searching, made him turn away. Not for an instant would she let him forget. Back again he had to torture himself into a sense of his responsibility and hers.

Never any relaxing, never any leaving himself to the great hunger and impersonality of passion; he must be brought back to a deliberate, reflective creature. As if from a swoon of passion she called him back to the littleness, the personal relationship.

So Paul, near the end of this chapter, is reduced to pitiful, even contemptible, littleness. Miriam, in her violent despair, at last cries out the essential truth: "It has been one long battle between us—you fighting away from me." His response is shock and utter amazement: in his self-absorption he has never even begun to see it from her point of view. And he turns at once towards a painful series of self justifications, throwing the blame on her: "He was full of a feeling that she had deceived him. She had despised him when he thought she worshipped him. She had let him say wrong things, and had not contradicted him. She had let him fight alone.... She had not played fair." Yet at the very end of the chapter, the bitter truth of what he has done to her emerges poignantly out of self-deception:

"She never thought she'd have me, mother, not from the first, and so she's not disappointed."

"I'm afraid," said his mother, "she doesn't give up hopes of you yet."

"No," he said, "perhaps not."

"You'll find it's better to have done," she said.

"*I* don't know," he said desperately.

"Well, leave her alone," replied his mother.

So he left her, and she was alone. Very few people cared for her, and she for very few people. She remained alone with herself, waiting.

Chapter 10

Further Study Questions

Revision Questions on Chaps. 1-2

1. Explain Mrs Morel's reactions when she is actually in the garden. What do you find unusual in the author's description?
2. Give an account of the day of Paul's birth from the standpoint of (a) Mr Morel and (b) Mrs Morel.
3. What is Mrs Morel's reaction to the birth of Paul?
4. For whom do you feel the most pity, Morl or Mrs Morel, after the scene when Mrs Morel's eye is cut by the drawer? Give reasons for your answer.
5. Do you find anything humourous in Chapter 2?
6. Explain, as fully as possible, Mrs Morel's attitude towards (a) husband and (b) her family.
7. What do you think Walter Morel enjoys most in life? You may, of course, refer to the day of the 'wakes', but need not confine yourself to this.
8. Indicate the main difference in the characters of Mr and Mrs Morel.

Revision Questions on Chaps. 3-4

1. How does Mrs Morel 'relax'? Is this in any way connected with her ambitions for William?
2. Trace William's career from his schooldays to his finally getting the job in London. Does Mrs Morel

demonstrate any possessive love for him during this time?

3. What is the significance of (a) Annie's doll Arabella and (b) the ash-tree in the life of Paul?
4. Give an account of the children's reactions to the disagreements between their father and mother.
5. Is Morel a good father in any ways? Give reasons for your answer.
6. Give three examples of Paul's sensitivity from Chap. 4.
7. Although husband and wife are not close, show how Mrs Morel is a good wife to her husband.
8. How does Mrs Morel demonstrate that she has much more character than her husband.

Revision Questions on Chaps. 9-10

1. Explain why Paul thinks it is necessary to break with Miriam.
2. Are your sympathies generally with Paul or with Miriam at this stage? Give reasons for your answer.
3. Give an account of Pual's visit to Lincoln with his mother. What does it reveal of his character?
4. Why do you think Paul is drawn towards Clara?
5. What does Paul learn of Clara from his visit to her home? Does this knowledge reinforce his own views of her or contradict them?
6. Define Clara's attitude to the girls and Paul when she goes back to Jordan's.
7. What effect does the 'birthday incident' have on the relationship of Paul and Clara?
8. Give a short character sketch of Clara's mother, Mrs Radford.

Topics for Your Research Paper

1. Sons and Lovers as an Autobiography
2. Oedipus Complex in Sons and Lovers

3. Feminist Approach to Sons and Lovers
4. Industrialism as Treated in Sons and Lovers

Topics for Discussion and Presentation

1. Consider the character of Mr. Morel and the reasons why hell develops into such a broken, failed man.
2. What is Lawrence's appraisal of industrialization?
3. Compare and contrast Baxter Dawes and Walter Morel.
4. Discuss how and to what effect Lawrence uses realism in the novel.
5. What is the relation between *Sons and Lovers* and Lawrence's own life?
6. What use does *Sons and Lovers* make of the Oedipus complex?
7. Discuss Paul's self-discovery as an artist and show how this applies to Lawrence's view of the artist's role in society.
8. What are the many different symbolisms evoked by flowers? How do flowers figure differently in the fates of the various characters?
9. Discuss the significance of the ending of *Sons and Lovers*.
10. Compare Mrs. Morel's feelings for both Miriam and Clara.
11. Do you consider the love of Paul for his mother and hers for him as being abnormal? (You should consider, with regard to this, Paul's relation with Miriam and with Clara.)
12. Estimate the part played by Walter Morel in the novel, indicating clearly whether or not you sympathize with him, and defining the author's attitude towards him.
13. In what way is William (a) like his father, and (b) like his mother? Refer closely to the text in your answer.

14. Do you consider that Miriam is unsympathetically portrayed? Give reasons for your answer.

Study Questions:

- The novel is arranged in a series of episodes, not necessarily in chronological order. This type of narrative is called *episodic*. What are the advantages and disadvantages of this type of narration? One effect this technique has is the blending of different time periods. Another element that contributes to the blending of time periods is the use of the iterative mode, which causes confusion about whether events happened one or many times. Think about the effects these techniques have on the text.
- Think about the role the chapter titles play in the novel. Do they reveal too much information about the story? Contrast them with chapter headings in eighteenth-century episodic novels like Henry Fielding's *Tom Jones* or Laurence Sterne's *Tristram Shandy*, both of which have elaborate chapter headings describing everything that happens in the chapter. Also think about if the novel would have been different if the chapters had no titles.
- What role do the shifting narrative perspectives play in the novel? Trace the shifting perspective throughout the novel to determine from which character's point of view the story seems to be narrated at each point.
- What function does the division of the novel into two parts serve? One possible interpretation: the first part of the novel focuses on Mrs. Morel and the second part focuses on Paul. Does this seem like a valid distinction? What other factors seem to distinguish the two sections of the novel from each other?
- Much of the novel is concerned with Paul's relationship with women, most importantly his mother, Miriam, and Clara. Examine Paul's

interactions with the other male characters in the novel. Consider his father, his brothers, Mr. Pappleworth, Edgar Leivers, Baxter Dawes.

- Paul's close relationship with his mother has provoked many Freudian and Oedipal readings of this novel. Is this type of reading valid? If not, what do you make of the relationship between Paul and his mother, which seems to be the one constant force throughout the novel?
- Is Mrs. Morel the most important woman to Paul throughout the novel, or are there moments at which his relationships with Miriam or Clara take precedence? If so, what is the significance of these moments? Why does he always come back to his mother in the end? You may also want to trace the theme of a higher level of understanding between Paul and his mother throughout the novel, possibly beginning with his illness immediately after William's death.
- What goes wrong between Paul and Miriam? Is it just that she cannot compete with his love for his mother, or is there some other problem?
- Why does Paul change his mind so often? Trace his on- again, off-again feelings for Miriam and Clara throughout the novel.
- Think about the religious aspects of this novel. Consider in particular Miriam's notions of sacrifice and of "baptism of fire in passion."
- Morel speaks in a dialect throughout the novel. Why might Lawrence have chosen to make Morel use a dialect? Does it set him apart from the other characters? Are there any other characters who speak in this dialect, and, if so, what purpose does this serve? What is the function of language as communication in the novel?

Chapter 11

Critical Essays

Anger in the Work of D. H. Lawrence

D. H. Lawrence was probably a very angry man. His writings are full of extremely intense feelings of anger and hate which do not seem to belong. This anger is usually connected to love, but can be classified by what other emotions it is also linked to. For example, in "Second Best," there is no real reason for Anne to feel great fury, yet she does towards the mole. Anne somehow equates the mole with a barrier to her success in love, so she hates it. In "The Shadow in the Rose Garden," the intense anger is connected to jealousy. The husband is extremely jealous of his wife's prior involvement with Archie. In "The White Stocking," the anger is also associated with jealousy. Ted does not like the fact that Elsie has been accepting gifts from Sam Adams. The sisters in "The Christening" have intense resentment towards their youngest sister Emma, who ruined the family reputation. This translates into anger directed at her and the world in general. Lastly, the title character and the Orderly in "The Prussian Officer" have a love-hate relationship, except one hates, the other loves. The Orderly, as recipient of unwanted love, feels great resentment and anger towards the Officer, so much so that he kills him.

Lawrence uses anger as an all-purpose front for and manifestation of deeper negative feelings. For this reason, the anger often seems unnecessary and out of place. Its common occurrence, however, allows us to treat it as a motif. In all of the stories above listed, there are characters involved in intensive love relationships. In "Second Best," "Shadow" and "Stocking," there are either married couples, or soon to be. "The Christening" has a family, and "The Prussian Officer" involves a gay officer. There is something dysfunctional about all of these relationships, however, and the anger exposes it. There is no reason for anger if there is not something wrong, so we know that there is underlying unrest in, Ted and Elsie's marriage, for example. The anger is supposed to hint at trouble, then it is up to the reader to discern from clues in the rest of the text the particular irregularity in the story.

In "Shadow" and "Stocking" the anger is among husbands and wives. The two stories are basically equivalent in message and structure: wife has hidden secret from husband, husband finds out, responds with jealous rage. For contrast, however, Elsie does not really hate Ted back, as opposed to the husband and wife in "Shadow" who both hate each other until the end, when they become merely cold. Ted's hate also dissipates, however.

Lawrence uses the anger motif to signal change. In the previous two mentioned stories, while there is anger, change is happening. Anger is an external symptom of not only problem, but also solution. Anger does not happen without friction (in "Stocking" and "Shadow," there is inherent class difference. Elsie is dumber than Ted, and the wife is not over Archie), but during periods of anger, change occurs. The husband and wife realise that their marriage can be fixed - it just will be different, and Elsie and Ted have a new understanding of one another.

Anger as a sign of change is also accurate for "Second Best." Anne realises over the course of the story that she wants to/must marry Tom. Her anger directed at moles demonstrates her wish to move past the engaged Jimmy and on to Tom, to start to get her life in order. She goes from fear of moles to the courage to kill one - through her pent up anger. The mole as a sign of her frustration in love and sex shows change, because she is angry when the mole is alive, but as she kills it in great anger, she becomes happy. She is engaged and going to take part in a normal life.

The anger in "The Christening" and "The Prussian Officer" is different because it is associated with love and resentment. Hilda and Laurie hate Emma because she has brought shame upon the family. As the father indicates, the family is dysfunctional in the first place, partially due to his failings and the lack of mother. This is the "problem" which is indicated by all of the anger and resentment. Hilda and Laurie are also jealous because they are probably virgins, but their sister is not. The anger in this family is a festering bitterness, not a passionate hatred as in the first three stories analysed.

The Orderly in "The Prussian Officer" holds deep anger for the officer and resents his love. It oppresses the desires of the Orderly to be with his girlfriend. There is underlying conflict, just as in the other stories. The orderly and his officer are polarized in social status, attitude, and orientation. This underlying friction leads to strong anger on the part of the orderly in response to love from the Captain. This results in the death of the captain.

In spite of plot differences, Lawrence is fond of using the anger motif to convey multi-leveled relationships. The relationship between Anne and the mole is not merely rodent-human. The Captain and Orderly do not only associate as ordinate/subordinate, much to the orderly's chagrin. The Rowbotham sisters resent Emma for what she has done, not for any immediately apparent reason. After the initial identification, the reader has to find the true meaning of the anger in each story in order to fully understand

A STUDY OF D.H. LAWRENCE'S EARLY POEMS AND SONS AND LOVERS:

The Question of Form

The object of this essay is to study some of D. H. Lawrence's early poems frcm Rhyming Poems and Look! We have come through in relation to Sons and Lovers, an attempt which is, to my mind, worth undertaking. Being drawn from sources of similar experiences, the poems and the novel often illuminate each other.

But what is more important is that taken together, they throw much light on the struggle Lawrence had to go through to develop a true medium of expression for his art, a medium which requires the readers' sympathetic attention and appreciation and which yields very little if approached with the wrong kind of expectations. My plan is to defend Lawrence from certain critics' accusations of "formlessness" or "artlessness" which they find is the dominant fault in his early works by showing that Lawrence does have his own ideas on form. It is hoped that the approach to the question of form will not be a theoretical one but will begin with, and lead back to, the poems and the novel; as Lawrence says in the Foreword to Fantasia of the Unconscious: "This pseudo-philosophy of mine - polly-annalytics as one of my respected critics might say - is deduced from the novels and poems, not the reverse.

The novels and poems come unwatched from one's pen. And then the absolute need one has for some sort of satisfactory mental attitude towards oneself and things in general makes one try to abstract some definite conclusions from one's experiences as a writer and a man. These 'pollyannalytics' are inferences made afterwards from the experiences". "They want me to have form; that means they want me to have their pernicious, ossiferous, skin - and - grief form, and I won't. "I It is from quotations like the above that Lawrence's awareness of his own refusal to submit to conventional demands of farm is proved.

This fact is of importance because it suggests at the outset that Lawrence knew what he was doing. Even critics like R. P. Blackmur and Antony West who see a 'lack' in Lawrence's poems recognize that in his case it is not an incapacity but a deliberate refusal to submit to the formal requirements which seem necessary to these critics. Blackmur for instance remarks: "This absence of the advantages of craft is not particularly due to the inability to use them, but to a lack of interest. Lawrence hardly ever, after the first, saw the use of anything that did not immediately devour his interest, whether in life or in art." Blackmur's criticism is representative of much of the criticism on Lawrence's poetry and it is clearly set out at the beginning o£ his famous essay "D. H. Lawrence and Expressive Form" "This essay proposes to outline an attack upon Lawrence on the grounds just laid out; that the strength of his peculiar insight lacks the protection and support of a rational imagination and that it fails to its own disadvantage to employ the formal devices of the art in which it is couched." West launches a similar charge against Lawrence: "He had all the poet's equipment, but he entirely lacked the discipline that would have allowed him to make use of it.

"His failure to use the 'formal devices of art' or the poet's equipment', or what Blackmur also calls 'the craft and convention of the art of poetry' condemns him and whatever alternative he has to offer. I think A. Alvarez is more sensitive and perceptive of the principles underlying Lawrence's poetics and does Lawrence more justice when he says that Lawrence is not interested in surface polish - close and perfect rhyme being invariably a constriction to him. "For an essential part of Lawrence's genius was his fluency; and I mean something more literal than the ease with which he wrote: rather, the sense of direction in all the flowing change and variation in his work.

This fluency has its own forms without its own conventions." (italics mine) Lawrence himself distinguishes between two kinds of poetry in his Introduction to New Poems: "The poetry of the beginning and the poetry of the end must have that exquisite finality, perfection which belongs to all that is far off.... This completeness, this consummate ness, the finality and the perfection are conveyed in exquisite form: the perfect symmetry, the rhythm which returns upon itself like a dance where the hands link and loosen and link for the supreme moment of the end.... But there is another kind of poetry: the poetry of that which is at hand: the immediate present. In the immediate present, there is no perfection, no consummation, nothing finished." Although "Poetry of the' Present" is meant to refer to the free-verse poems of Look! We have come through, the tendency to escape the "finality" or "perfection" of "exquisite form" can already be detected in Rhyming Poems.

The first poem of Rhyming Poems, The Wild Common, one of the earliest poems Lawrence wrote, begins in a regular pattern with rhymes in alternate lines: "The quick sparks on the gorse bushes are leaping, Little jets of sunlight-texture imitating flame Above them, exultant, the pewits are sweeping: They are lords of the desolate wastes of sadness their screaming proclaim" The first three lines are of approximately the same length, with a pause at the end of each line. The last line of the stanza seems to be deliberately split into two. halves so that 'proclaim' can rhyme with 'flame' and a sort of symmetry or finality is reached. But at the close of the poem, the flux of energ-that fills the living soul of the 'I' of the poem refuses to be contained in a regular pattern: "Oh but the water loves me and folds me, Plays with me, sways me, Lifts me and sinks me as though it were living blood, Blood of a heaving woman who holds me, Owning my supple body a rare glad thing, supremely good."

The second line is broken up into short, breathless utterances and words like "heaving", "supple" convey a sense of active motion. "Blood" and "Good" are no longer perfect rhymes. Any feeling of fixity or contrived symmetry is gone. In the revised version the outbursts of energy are even more remarkable: "But how splendid it is to be substance, here! My shadow is neither here nor there; but I, I am royally here! I am here! screams the pewits; the may-blobs burst out in a lau I am here! they hear! Here! flick the rabbits. Here! pants the gorse. Here! says the insects far and near" These outbursts can hardly be contained in anything of "exquisite finality".

Christopher Hassall sees Lawrence using the black flowers on the Etruscan vases and dishes as an emblem for what he calls poetry of the present.? Lawrence rejects Greek beauty which appears to have a boiled down effect to him (as "it too much cooked in the artistic consciousness") in favour of the subtle beauty of Etruscan paintings - "the wonderfully suggestive edge of the figures. It is not outlined. It is the flowing contour where the body suddenly leaves upon the atmosphere." This is not an incapacity to achieve formal perfection but a deliberate avoidance of it. A study of Lawrence's ideas on the function of art can lead to a better understanding of his ideas on form. In Chaos in Poetry's Lawrence says that poets or artists "reveal the inward desire of mankind. They show the desire for chaos and the fear of chaos.

The desire for chaos is the breath of their poetry. The fear of chaos is in their parade of forms and technique." The true nature of man belongs to chaos - "man, and the animals, and the flowers, all live within the strange and for ever surging chaos." However, man finds this chaos or reality difficult to bear and in his terror, invents a protective cover for himself, "wraps himself in a vision" and "fixes some wonderful erection of his own between himself and the wild chaos." This erection or "cosmic umbrella" is ultimately a harmful substitution, a simulacrum made up of "consciousness, mind and civilization" which makes a man "bleached and stifled" because he is imprisoned within the conventional ideas or values of a particular civilization. The function of art or poetry is to bring man back into contact with chaos.

"Then comes a poet, enemy of convention, and makes a slit in the umbrella; and lo! the glimpse of chaos is a vision, a window to the sun". The importance of art is that it enables man to see beyond the assumptions of the civilization he has built up as a protection, which becomes his prison. In The White Peacock and Study of Thomas Hardy, Lawrence deals with the same idea. Lettie shares the moral cowardice of most people who fear the "genuine draught from chaos" and closes herself to life. Unlike Hardy's heroes and heroines who struggle to "burst suddenly out of bud and take a wild flight into flower", she ceases to live and her plight is beautifully epitomized in the image of the tent. To let in chaos or to open oneself to life as symbolized by the sun means to accept a reality which is not fully known or possessed and controlled. "The business of art is to reveal the relation between man and his circumambient universe, at the living moment" writes Lawrence in Morality and the Novel. If the function of art is to reveal the ever-changing -relations and the never-ceasing living moments, it cannot be expected to perform this function in a form which does not take into consideration the nature of the subject matter.

If the subject matter itself, or the stuff of experience, is changing or even chaotic, an 'orderiy' form with an order imposed from the outside will be a falsification. Lawrence is aware of the dangers that poetry may fall into. In Chaos in Poetry, he says that the new vision of life brought in by the poet can be easily patched up by the "painted patch of the simulacrum", a patch that only looks like the vision in the slit but is a false one. Then poetry degenerates into a mere matter of words, an empty parade of forms and technique.

There is no breath of true poetry in it. "The poetasters can make pretty sFnny bubbles for the Christmas- tree, which never burst, because there is no breath of poetry in them, but they remain till we drop them." Lawrence quarrels with the poems in the American edition of A Second Contemporary Verse Anthology precisely because they are just "bubbles of sound and image", like candy, "sweet nothings, tender trifles and amusing things."l Instead of revealing chaos, art reveals "pot-bound consciousness" and a "solid and ornamental concept of life".

Works of art become "old soup of old bones of life, heated up again for a new consomme". The question of form in Lawrence's novels is also a point for dispute. There has been much adverse criticism on the so-called "formal imperfections" exhibited by Sons and Lovers. A contemporary review writes: "It has no particular shape and no recognizable plot; themes are casually taken up, and then as casually dropped, and there seems no reason why they should have been taken up unless they were to be kept up." Another reviewer complains in Nalion that it is a "difficult" book: "It is `difficult' every way - difficult to read (though not for the usual cause, since no obscurity of phrase disfigures it), difficult to appraise, difficult above all to apprehend".

The absence of a plot is felt to give an air of incompleteness of something unfinished to the novel: "Definite plot there is none... Paul, the unheroic hero, is left still vacillating before his life, and there is no reason why a later book should not continue the record of his aimless way." More recent criticism pursues the same line of attack. Mark Schorer in Technique as Discovery outlines his objection to Sons and Lovers on very similar grounds as Blackmur does to Lawrence's poems - a lack of craft or technique. Schorer sees Sons and Lovers as an example of "meanings confused by an impatience with technical resources".

Lawrence fails to use the technique in fiction in its two respects (language to express the quality of the experience in question and point of view as a mode of dramatic delimitation and thematic definition) or uses it inadequately, thus resulting in a discrepancy between intention and performance. But the attitude Lawrence has towards the question of form in his novels is basically the same as that towards his poems. From his remarks on the novel and novelists we can see that the aesthetics of imperfection he holds proper for his poems applies-also to his novels.

Lawrence is insistent that people should see the form that Sons and Lovers has. In the famous letter to Garnett, he patiently defines the "idea" which the novel follows. Much has been said about how the novel is different from Lawrence's summary of it and that it is wisdom after the event etc.; the important thing to notice is that Lawrence believes there is a controlling idea running through his novel. It may not have a plot like a Jane Austen novel but it is not formless.

As one contemporary critic has sensitively observed, the novel "has little or no pretension to plot-architecture, its incident is not external." There are no external incidents in Sons and Lovers like the elopement of Lydia Bennet in Pride and Prejudice which cause a spectacular and radical change in the feelings of one character towards another. Lawrence is sure that he has worked out his theme and it is important to see in what terms he looks upon his theme: it is like life, and the development is "slow, like growth".

He views his work in organic terms, like life itself, which is different from the perfected finish many people expect a work of art to possess. Lawrence was very anxious to convince others that he had taken great pains over the form of the novel. In his letter to A. W. McLeod (Sept. 1912), he declares that he has been working vigourously at "licking it (then called `Paul Morel' or the 'colliery novel') into form" and he writes to Edward Garnett, saying, "And I want to defend it, quick. I wrote it again, pruning it and shaping it and filling it in. I tell you it has got form - form: haven't I made it patiently, out of sweat as well as blood." Frieda Lawrence is equally vehement in defending Sons and Lovers: "I think the honesty, the vividness of the book suffers if you subject it to form.

I have heard so much about 'form' with Ernest; why are you English so keen on it? Their own form wants smashing in almost any direction, but they can't come out of their snail house". Lawrence's ideas on form in fiction are perhaps best expressed in his criticism on Thomas Mann. which begins: "But Germany is now undergoing that craving for form in fiction, that passionate desire for the mastery of the medium of narrative, that will of the writer to be greater than and undisputed lord over the stuff he writes, which is figured to the world in Gustave Flaubert". Lawrence is against the kind of aestheticism which sees life as having no value except as material for beautiful artistic structure.

This craving for formal artistic perfection is shown by the exertion of the author's will which attempts to force an order on his subject matter (or life). The dichotomy between life as imperfection, impermanence, and art as perfection and permanence which fascinates artists like Keats and Yeats (Ode to the Grecian Urn and Byzantium) does not appear real to Lawrence. He believes that if life is imperfect, it is the business of art to embody this imperfection rather than ignore it in search of formal perfection. The fault of artists like Mann is that they not only allow the values of life and art to be separated, but also exalt the latter. Life becomes corrupt and in turn corrupts art. "He has never given himself to anything but his art.

This is all well and good, if his art absorbs and satisfies him, as it has done some great men, like Corot. But then there are the other artists, the more human, like Shakespeare and Goethe, who must give themselves to life as well as to art. And if they were afraid of, or despised life, then with their surplus they would ferment and become rotten. Which is what ails Thomas Mann. He is physically ailing, no doubt. But his complaint is deeper: it is of the soul". The desire for form comes from a relentless drive of the will, a desire to control and posses the unknown and unknowable reality which can become a great destructive power as in the case of Hermione in Women in love. That is why Lawrence is so much in opposition to novels which show this attitude. He detects this influence in Proust and Joyce and refuses to consider their works of any merit.

The explanation Paul struggles to give Miriam about the special qualities of his paintings is reminiscent of Lawrence's own description of poetry of the present: "There is scarcely any shadow in it; it's more shimmer, as if I'd painted the shimmering protoplasm in the leaves and everywhere, and not the stiffness of the shape. That seems dead to me. Only this shimmer ness is the real living. The shape is a dead crust. The shimmer is inside really." Compare this with: "They do not know that free verse has its own nature, that it is neither star nor pearl, but instantaneous like plasm. It has no goal in either eternity.

It has no finish. It has no satisfying stability, satisfying to those who like the immutable."Z Certain implications have been read into Lawrence's aesthetics of imperfection which are simply results of misunderstanding and faulty judgment. One obvious example is to conclude from his avoidance of formal perfection that his writing is loose, careless and undisciplined. T. S. Eliot said Lawrence wrote only sketches for poems, nothing ever quite finished. W. H. Auden said Lawrence made a mistake in identifying art with life, ignoring the fact that an effect of the unfinished in art can only be achieved by "much thought, labour and care".

But the truth is just that Lawrence has spent much thought, labour and care on his works. This can be seen from the endless revisions he is willing to make of the poems if he feels that they can be improved. As James Reeves says, Lawrence is not afraid to give himself away by writing badly. "What does it matter if half the time the poet fails in his effort at expression! The failures make it real. The act of attention is not easy. It is much easier to write poesy. Failure is part of the living chaos. And the groping reveals the acts of attention, which suddenly passes into pure expression".

He is willing to try as many ways as possible to get closest to what he wants to say. His diligence and sense of responsibility recalls Eliot's commendation of Pound's hard work in the introduction to the Selected Poems of Ezra Pound. Many of the early poems are a great deal re-written. As Lawrence says modestly in the Preface to Collected Poems, these poems "were struggling to say something which it takes a man twenty years to be able to say." If we compare the revised versions with the early versions we can usually see the struggle, and the effort Lawrence puts forward to get rid of those pseudo-archaic and overworked phrases like "sharpen", "enrichen", "troth I trowed", "withouten" etc. Again, The Wild Common can serve as an example to show how the later version is an improvement of the earlier.

The poem in its original form as it appears in Amores sounds laboured and tedious, with forced comparisons from things like "a passionate woman" or "the soul of the wind". In the revised form, it is charged with life and movement. This is the original version of the verse which forms a transition in the poem, when the narrator becomes aware of the possibility of loss: "What if the gorse flowers shriveled and kissing were' lost? Without the pulsing waters, where were the marigolds and the songs of the brook? If my veins and my breasts with love embossed Withered, my insolent soul would be gone like flowers that the hot wind took." The revised form as printed in the Collected Poems is as follows: "What if the gorse flowers shriveled, and I were gone?

What if the waters ceased, where were the marigolds then, and the gudgeon? What is this thing that I look down upon? White on the water wimples my shadow, strains like a dog on a String, to run on" In the later version, there is a movement towards greater particularity, an effort to replace the conventionally lyrical with the carefully observed and dramatically suitable image. The sentimental association between nature and kissing is replaced by the more appropriate idea of the speaker's isolation, as he is suddenly aware of the possibility of loss. "What if the waters ceased" captures in its movement the urgency and abruptness of the speaker's thought, while "without the pulsing waters" is a weak and undistinguished suggestion.

The "songs of the brook" adds nothing to the meaning of the poem except a facile lyricism, but the "gudgeon" is sharp and precise in sound and meaning. Besides conveying the feeling of life and movement of a fish swimming, the word may even suggest its implied meaning of "deception" - the speaker's awareness of the threat of loss in a surrounding full of life. "My insolent soul" does not convey the dramatic contrast between the abundance of nature and the possibility of annihilation. But "my shadow" is dramatic in that it epitomizes nothingness.

The use of words for a decorative purpose in "If my veins and my breasts with love embossed" to hide an inner emptiness of meaning is replaced by the more honest attempt to confront the situation with a direct and effective question: "What is this thing I look down upon?" A conventional image of flowers blowing in the wind to represent loss is changed to the vivid dramatic image of a dog straining to run away from its master.

Throughout the whole poem the reader can see signs of careful revision, which sharpens and refines the experience to be communicated Lawrence is aware of the danger of writing "poesy" or what he calls the "currency of poetry" instead of real poetry. He quarrels with Ralph Hodgson's poem because he thinks it is "banal in utterance": "The feeling is there, right enough - but not in itself, only represented.. Only here and there is the least touch of personality in the poem: it is the currency of poetry, not poetry itsel¬.".

The terms "loose", "careless" or "undisciplined" clearly do not apply to the writing of Sons and Lovers either. Innumerable examples might be quoted from the novel to prove what care Lawrence has taken in the handling of an incident or the description of a scene, investing each minor detail, a casual movement, a small object, with a vividness and a significance which links it with the rest of the book. There is the unforgettable scene in the early part of the novel about Morel and Mrs. Morel's quarrel in which Mrs. Morel is driven out into the garden in the moonlight.

But what strikes me is the care in which Lawrence builds up the tension leading to the quarrel, the irritation and touchiness each has been privately nursing, and their collision at that specific point of time which makes a violent quarrel inevitable. Mrs. Morel had been angry with Morel since early morning for his running off with Jerry, whom she considered despicable because he was an irresponsible husband and father. She was afraid he would be a bad influence on Morel who was irresponsible enough.

All day long she fretted, dragging about, doing the household chores and attending to the children. We can feel her tension mounting as she was waiting for Morel's return, counting the minutes that flew by. "Nine o'clock passed, and ten, and still 'the pair' has not returned" (note the contempt in her tone).

Her anger was increased when she heard some drunken colliers singing hymns. It reminded her of what a state Morel would likely be in." `As if "Genevieve" weren't good enough,' she said. The kitchen was full of the scent of boiled herbs and hops. On the hob a large black saucepan steamed slowly. Mrs. Morel took a, panchion, a great bowl of thick red earth, streamed a heap of white sugar into the bottom, and then, straining herself to the weight, was pouring in the liquor. Just-then Morel came in.

He had been very' jolly in the Nelson, but coming home had grown irritable. He had not quite got over the feeling of irritability and pain, after having slept on the ground when he was so hot; and a bad conscience afflicted him as he neared the house. He did not know he was angry. But when the garden-gate resisted his attempts to open it, he kicked it and broke the latch. He entered just as Mrs. Morel was pouring the infusion of herbs out of the saucepan. Swaying slightly, he lurched against the table.

The boiling liquor pitched. Mrs. Morel started back. 'Good gracious,' she cried, 'coming home in his drunkenness!' 'Comin'home in his what?' he snarled, his hat over his eye. Suddenly her blood rose in a jet. 'Say you're not drunk!' she flashed." The picture of the kitchen is presented vividly before our eyes, with its smell of boiling herbs. The utensils are described in details: the saucepan is large and black, the panchion is a great bowl of thick red earth. What is more remarkable is the description of Mrs. Morel in the act of pouring the liquor.

The word "streamed" conveys the familiarity and ease with which she goes about doing her household duties, and "strained" beautifully describes the physical exertion she has to make, being weary with waiting and suffering discomfort because of her pregnancy. In the second paragraph, Morel's feelings are described as if Lawrence is anxious to give us an honest picture of the situation from both sides. The differences between their two characters can be clearly seen. Morel is more sensitive to physical discomforts and responds to them more easily because-be understands them. He is aware his sleep in the afternoon has caused him pain. But he does not understand or admit the sense of guilt that is plaguing him inside, which is exactly what his wife wants him to feel. We see Mrs. Morel in a tensed-up posture pouring the liquor suddenly disturbed by Morel.

"The boiling liquor pitched." Mrs. Morel is alarmed and out of her alarm, angered further. Her righteousness and insistence on honesty, on nothing but the truth, which mark her so much as an opposite to her husband, are clearly expressed in her angry accusation "Say you're not drunk." Anyone who reads this passage with attention cannot help agreeing to Jessie Chambers' remark on Lawrence's power to "transform the raw material of life into significant form".

Care is not only seen in the handling of individual incidents and scenes, but also in the organization of the whole, novel. I think Lascelles Abercrombie is definitely mistaken when he says the themes of the novel are casually taken up and casually dropped. Seymour Betsky has made a detailed study of how the themes of Sons and Lovers are developed and interwoven, with a wave-like rhythmic movement which is different from the conventional use of climatic development. I only wish to draw attention to the use in Sons and Lovers of a pattern of comparisons and contrasts which is the principal technique Lawrence employs in organizing his later novels like Women in Love and Lady Chatterley's Lover.

The female characters, for example, can be seen to form a pattern of comparisons and contrasts running throughout the novel. Both Paul and William constantly compare their women to their mother. William complains that his 'Gyp' is not like his mother, at all. "She's not like you, mother. She's not serious, and she can't think." Paul finds Mrs. Leivers' and Miriam's manner of exalting everything to a religious intensity so strange, and contrast their behaviour with his mother's sensible and restrained response to things. "His own mother was logical. Here there was something different, something he loved, something that at times he hated." "William gives his sex to a fribble" who proves her shallowness by forgetting him shortly after his death. Miriam is anything but shallow. She lives every situation with a brooding intensity.

"There was no looseness or abandon about her. Everything was gripped stiff with intensity and her effort, overcharged, closed in on itself." Lily Western is interested in the flowers so long as they make her look pretty: "Has he made a sight of me?" She asked, laughing down on her lover... "You look nice enough, if that's what you want to know," he said. And she walked without her hat.o...

But Miriam has to caress and fondle the flowers in her intense love and desire to possess them: "Miriam went on her kness before one cluster, took a wild looking daffodil between her hands, turned up its face of gold to her, and bowed down, caressing it with her mouth and checks and brows," while Paul, coldly recalling his mother, stood aside, and was appalled at her lack of reserve.

Miriam's unnatural intensity and physical inhibition are contrasted to Clara's ease of movement and physical appeal. A simple incident like the jumping off a stile can serve to illustrate the contrast. Miriam is afraid of the stile. "If she were getting over a stile, she gripped his hands in a little hard anguish, and began to lose her.presence of mind. And he could not persuade her to jump from even a small height. Her eyes dilated because exposed and palpitating. "No!" she cried, half laughing in terror - "no!" Clara naturally gives herself away: "She stood on top of the stile, and he held both her hands. Laughing, she look down into his eyes.

Then she leaped. Her breast came against his; he held her, and covered her face with kisses." Both scenes are again contrasted to a much earlier scene in which Mrs. Morel climbs a fence on her way to Willey Farm with Paul for the first time. Her independence and strength of character are clearly seen in her refusal to let Paul help her. The whole scene comes to life with Lawrence's power of description: Paul tenderly chaffing at his mother and Mrs. Morel childishly and touchingly railing against the stiles: "But at the end of the riding was a fence to climb. Paul was over in a second. 'Come,' he said, 'let me help you.' 'No, go away.

I will do it in my own way.' He stood below with his hands up ready to help her. She climbed cautiously. 'What a way, to climb!' be exclaimed scornfully, when she was safely to earth again. 'Hateful stiles!' she cried. 'Duffer of a little woman,' he replied, 'who can't get over 'em'." The reviewer in Nation who complains about the difficulty of Sons and Lovers lists the inclusion of Beatrice as one of the examples that puzzle him. "Mr. Lawrence fails completely in the delineation of this mocking, elfin sort of creature - so completely that her repeated presence in his work is a marvel to us.

Directly she appears, all seems to fly apart, and we know not in what fancied world we are, nor whence can come the beings who surround us there." I think he has failed to see the significance of including Beatrice, who, although a minor figure making few appearances in the novel, acts as a foil to the other characters, especially to Miriam. Beatrice's gaiety and fearlessness and Miriam's embarrassment and self-consciousness bring out the difference in their characters sharply.

There is also a sharp distinction in the tones they use for each other - Miriam speaking kindly but says the wrong thing ("isn't it an awful shame, to turn you off merely because you didn't pass the exam") and Beatrice teasing wittily, deliberately trying to make Miriam uncomfortable, ("Why, let's look at your shoes.") Beatrice can relax and flirt with Paul, something Miriam can never do. Miriam both hates and is attracted by Paul's behaviour with Beatrice which is heavily coloured by a sexual overtone that is so different from the purity in her own relationship with him. "Miriam saw his eyes trembling with mischief, and his full, almost sensual, mouth quivering.

He was not himself and she could not bear it. As he was now, she had no connection with him;" Beatrice's love-affair with Arthur is a straight-forward account of sexual passion, unlike the unnatural tortured development of Miriam and Paul's relationship.

The possibility of their having a normal marriage life contrasts poignantly with Paul's claim that he is unable to marry any woman as long as his mother lives. The inclusion of Beatrice is therefore not carelessness on Lawrence's part; rather, it provides a subtle variation on the main theme. Instead of carelessness or lack of objectivity, I believe Lawrence's aesthetics of imperfection implies a fluidity of form more than anything else. This is in consistence with the stress he lays on "relatedness", as well as his remarks on the use of rhythm in the poems on the one hand, his method of characterization and his use of 'symbolism' in the novels on the other. Lawrence places so much importance on "relatedness" for he believes that moral values cannot be fixed abstractions.

The values have value only if they are living responses to particular situations at particular moments. His attitude to time which reflects his attitude to form is as emphasis on the moment, "the incarnate Now". "Give me nothing fixed, set, static. Don't give me the infinite or the eternal: nothing of infinity, nothing of eternity. Give me the still, white seething, the incandescence and the coldness of the incarnate moment: the moment, the quick of all change and haste and opposition: the moment, the immediate present, the Now."

Free verse, or "poetry of the present" is a form to embody this incarnate moment: "But in free verse we look for the insurgent naked throb of the instant moment". Free verse enjoys a fluidity of form for all laws and restrictions fail to apply to it. The fluidity of form in Lawrence's novels also comes from his emphasis on, relatedness. In Morality and the Novel, Lawrence defines what morality in his novels means: "And morality is that delicate, for ever trembling and changing balance between me and my circumambient universe, which precedes and accompanies a true relatedness." His novels are not constructed on ordinary fixed moral patterns, his characters are not conceived in moral schemes.

His novels are preoccupied with the relationships between men and men, and men and women, and the novelist's task is to deal with these changing relationships, bringing to the readers' awareness of what is alive and meaningful and what is dead and meaningless. The novel "can inform and lead into new places the flow of our sympathetic consciousness, and it can lead our sympathy away in recoil from things gone dead."

The novel therefore should have a fluidity that can follow the flow and recoil, and Lawrence's aesthetics of imperfection enables him to view and use the novel as "one bright book of life" whereas novels possessing an abstract perfection are dead - "his work has none of the rhythm of a living thing." Lawrence's ideas on scansion and his remarks on the use of rhythm as seen mostly from his letters are a reflection of his aesthetics. I am aware of the difficulties involved in a discussion of metre, rhythm and other technicalities, and my purpose is not to go off to any abstract discussion of technical details but merely to show that fluidity of form is he main characteristic Lawrence considers his poems to have.

In a, letter to Edward Marsh, editor of Georgian Anthology, Lawrence defends his use of rhythm: "My rhythms fit my mood pretty well, in the verse. And if the mood is out of joint, the rhythm often is. I have always tried to get an emotion out of its own course, without altering it." Rather than conforming to a metrical pattern, the rhythm is supposed to fit the mood. That is why A. Alvarez finds that Lawrence's poems have a fluency which is not plottable. "Ear-count, finger-count, and what might be called the logic of received form have nothing to do with it." End of Another Home Holiday is a good example to illustrate the change of rhythm as the mood changes in the poem. As Alvarez says, only in the first tensyllabled line will finger-count pay.

The poem goes on its own way and the lines expand and contract as the speaking voice gathers urgency or relaxes in meditation. The opening quartrain is followed by these lines: "Why is it, that the long, slow stroke of the midnight bell (Will it never finish the twelve?) " Falls again and again on my heart with a heavy reproach?" The quick movement of the first three words is suddenly arrested in the latter half of the line, the eagerness and urgency with which the speaker begins to examine his thoughts change to a slow diffusion of sadness as he is caught again in the conflict. The distorted rhyme ("bell / twelve") not only catches the sound of the bell's repeated strokes but conveys the feeling of uncertainty, and the slow, heavy, tortured movement of the last line continues the suggestion of the bell's strokes and matches the sad self-questioning.

The rhythm is capable of conveying the subtle changes in tone and feeling within such a short space. Lawrence has his own method of scanning a poem. 'I think I read my poetry more by length than by stress - as a matter of movements in space than footsteps hitting the earth." It is different from the ordinary way of separating a poem into more or less regular units. "It all depends on the pause - the natural pause, the natural lingering of the voice according to the feeling - it is the hidden emotional pattern that makes poetry, not he obvious form."

In End of Another-Home Holiday the pull between love and guilt, the acceptance of the bondage of love and the desire to be free from it form the underlying emotional pattern of the poem. At one moment the voice lingers over the long lines with heavy syllable like "crouching", "reproachful", "wretched" and "mourn", as if the speaker is examining himself, torturing himself with the sense of guilt: "Forever, ever by my shoulder pitiful love will linger, Crouching as little houses crouch under the mist when I turn. Forever, out of the mist, the church lifts up a reproachful finger, Pointing my eyes in wretched defiance where love hides her face to mourn."

Then as the desire to free himself from the bondage takes over the control, the voice changes to an assertive tone of declaration. The shorter and more balanced lines take on a majestic leisurely movement: "Oh! but the rain creeps down to wet the grain That struggles alone in the dark, And asking nothing, patiently steals back again! The moon sets forth o' nights To walk the lonely, dusky heights serenely, with steps unswerving:" The speed and' stress of the lines vary with the inward pressure. In Lawrence's poems, as Alvarez has observed, inner pressure and disturbance give to each one its inherent form. There is no obvious form. The awkward words Lawrence some times uses in his early poems due to the exigencies of rhyme (e.g. from Dream-confused. "Listen, her shoon Palpitating on the stair" in order to rhyme with "moon") have been much criticized.

I think it is only fair to say some effective use of rhyme is there and Blackmur is too sweeping in his condemnation that the art of Lawrence's early poems is only attested by its badness. Rhyme is often a constraint on Lawrence and at the height of his creative power Lawrence is using blank verse. But Snap-Oragon, for 'example, can illustrate the use of rhyme which Blackmur considers as an important part of the poet's craftsmanship - "the array of rhymes for prediction, contrast, transition and suspense." "It seemed that I and the morning world Were pressed cup-shape to take this reiver Bird who was weary to have furied Her wings in us, As we were weary to receive her."

Here is both "prediction" and "suspense", if by "prediction," it means the use of a word which by its distinctiveness anticipates a rhyme which then occurs, achieving an effect of inevitability; or does not occur, achieving an effect of surprise. The use of rhyme for contrast is effectively carried out in Autumn Rain "the sheaves of dead men that are slain now winnowed soft on the floor of heaven; manna invisible of all the pain here to us given; finely divisible falling as rain." And Lawrence's awareness of the possibility to use rhyme as an instrument of transition can be shown by the rhyme pattern "hover/clover, cover/rover/over" in the verse in Snap-Dragon beginning "Again I saw a brown bird hover". "Tell Arnold Bennet", Lawrence once wrote to his literary agent, "that all rules of construction hold good only for novels that are copies of other novels.

A book which is not a copy of other books has its own construction, and what he calls faults, he being an old imitator, is what I call characteristics." Although Sons and Lovers is written in conformity with the expectations of the novel-readers of the time, much more than, for example Joyce's Ulysses, the novel shows "characteristics" which are outside the conventional use of the novel. These characteristics, which are more remarkable in his later novels, arise out of Lawrence's aesthetics and his belief in the fluidity of form that a novel has.

"The novel is the highest form of human expression so far attained. Why? Because it is so incapable of the absolute." One of these characteristics is Lawrence's method of characterization which has a fluidity that is an innovation in English fiction. Hints of the method Lawrence will use in The Rainbow are already there in Sons and Lovers. "You mustn't look in my novel for the old stable ego of the character... the characters fall into the form of some other rhythmic form". This fluidity may be one of the difficulties Lawrence's contemporary readers have to face.

The reviewer in Nation is puzzled by the incident of the burnt loaves and he sees no use for it except as an example of Lawrence's offering us 'a slice of life' in his 'sincerity'. But it is a good illustration of the fluidity of Lawrence's method of characterization which allows the characters to lose their stable ego and pass into "allotropic states". Mrs. Morel, in her overwhelming jealousy of Miriam, behaves out of character. She makes a fuss over the burnt bread which is, to use Miriam's words, only two-pence ha'penny.

It is not the money wasted that worries her although she is usually so careful about money. It is her fear and hatred of Miriam's power over her son. 'I should have thought,' said Mrs. Morel bitterly, 'that she shouldn't have occupied you so entirely as to burn a whole overfull o£ bread.' 'Beatrice was here as well as she.' 'Very likely. But we know why the bread is spoilt.' 'Why?' he flashed. 'Because you were engrossed with Miriam,' replied Mrs. Morel hotly. This scene reminds us of Miriam burning the potatoes. so Paul has been amazed and resentful that so many angry words and intense feelings should pass around over a small thing as some burnt potatoes.

The unhealthiness in Mrs. Leivers' attitude has been contrasted to Mrs. Morel's common sense and reasonableness. But now Mrs. Morel is seen to behave momentarily like Mrs. Leivers. Her attitude is equally unhealthy, though in a different way. The concern for Paul's health ("But you're never too tired to go if she will come for you.") is just a cover-up for h°-r jealousy. Another characteristic which is a result of Lawrence's belief in the fluidity of form is the use of 'symbolism'. Symbol for Lawrence does not mean making something definite to stand for something else.

There is no splitting a symbol into a thing and a meaning apart from it, with a mental arrow connecting the two. t Lawrence's emphasis on relationship leads him to a deliberate mistrust and avoidance of statements which to him represent fixity and therefore falsification. Dorothy Van Ghent believes Lawrence makes use of imagery as his expressive medium because "he must make us aware - sensitively aware, not merely conceptually aware - of the profound life force" (italics mine.) His use of symbols is an avoidance of abstract conceptual statements.

To say a scene or an incident is symbolic merely means that it has a significance that ties it up with the rest of the book. The swing episode is such an instance: (I am only quoting the important bits) He was swinging through the air, every bit of him swinging, like a bird that swoops for joy of movement. And he looked down at her.

Her crimson cap hung over her dark curls, her beautiful warm face, so still in a kind of brooding, was lifted towards him. It was dark and rather cold in the shed. Suddenly a swallow came down from the high roof and darted out of the door. 'I didn't know a bird was watching,' he called. She felt the accuracy with which he caught her, exactly at the right moment, and the exactly proportionate strength of his thrust, and she was afraid. Down to her bowels want the hot wave of fear. She was in his hands. Again, firm and in evitable came the thrust at the right moment. She gripped the rope, almost swooning.

There was something fascinating to her in him. For the moment he was nothing but a piece of swinging stuff; not a particle of him that did not swing. She could never lose herself, so, nor could her brothers. It roused a warmth in her. It were almost as if he were a flame that had lit a warmth in her whilst he swung in the middle air. "The best in Lawrence carries the authenticity of a faithfully observed, concrete actuality that refuses to be split; its symbolism is a radiation that leaves it intact in itself."

The description of the cow-shed, the swing itself, the weather and the two young people's reactions does give a picture of a faithfully observed, concrete actuality. At the same time, the episode is symbolic of Paul's living response to experience, and Miriam's frigidity and inability to lose herself. The middle paragraph carries a sexual imagery which foreshadows the failure in their sexual relationship. Miriam is afraid of accepting Paul and leaving herself in his hands. She can only force herself to sacrifice to him.

This episode and many others prove Lawrence's imagination is so concrete that he does not "distinguish between the reality and the metaphor or symbol which makes it plain to us." He gives the episodes in Sons and Lovers as much richness in meaning and significance as he does in other "symbolic" episodes in the later novels, like the barge incident in The Rainbow or the rabbit in Women in Love. A comparative study of the early poems and Sons and Lovers exhibits the interesting development Lawrence undergoes to find his true medium of expression. Traditional ideas of form are often inapplicable as criteria for evaluating his achievement, either as a poet or a novelist. His aesthetics contain implications which to demand of the readers an openness of mind and a sensitivity as great as Lawrence's own.

At the End of *The Rainbow*: Reading Lesbian Identities in D.H. Lawrence's Fiction

Justin D. Edwards, University of Copenhagen

Although there is a large body of critical material that reads D.H. Lawrence's various representations of sexuality, the depictions of lesbianism in Lawrence's work have been virtually ignored. Given this oversight, this paper analyses Lawrence's portraits of lesbian characters in the context of an emerging lesbian identity in early twentieth-century England. Lawrence's novels *The Rainbow* and *The Fox*, I argue, reproduce many of the contemporary discourses on lesbianism which were disseminated by sexual theorists such as Edward Carpenter and Havelock Ellis.

I suggest that the development of this identity was partly responsible for Lawrence's movement away from nineteenth-century British represen-tations of romantic female friendship, and his movement toward a more sexualized depiction of the bonds between women. I conclude this paper by suggesting that the rise of a lesbian identity was also responsible for the development of homophobic discourses that disrupted romantic friendship between women.

Upon publication of *The Rainbow* in 1915, D. H. Lawrence and his publisher, Algernon Methuen, were prosecuted under the Obscene Publications Act of 1857. During the trial, the Crown prosecutor, Herbert Muskett, condemned Lawrence's text for what he referred to as its "immoral representations of sexuality." Methuen, fearing that his business would suffer from the bad publicity, made a formal apology and surrendered all remaining copies to the magistrate.

As a result, Lawrence's novel was not banned, but Herbert Muskett was able to lash out against the author's depictions of "sexual perversion." Muskett's moralizing speech focused on the chapter "Shame," stating that it is "a mass of obscenity of thought, idea and action throughout, wrapped up in language that would be regarded in some quarters as an artistic and intellectual effort." What is significant is the fact that although *The Rainbow* includes numerous descriptions of explicit sexual acts, only the "Shame" chapter seemed to provoke and upset the court.

We must therefore assume that the Crown prosecutor conflated "immoral representations of sexuality" with representations of lesbianism, for it is the "Shame" chapter that describes Ursula's affair with Winifred Inger.

The trial of *The Rainbow* is an important moment in British literary and legal history in that it represents the first public forum in which lesbianism was discussed as a moral (and legal) issue. Thus, by identifying "Shame" as the central morally offensive section of Lawrence's novel, Herbert Muskett (and, by extension, the British legal system) was participating in a cultural shift whereby women's sexuality was becoming recognized as independent of male sexuality—a cultural shift that Lawrence attempted to capture in his novel and to which he, in the end, contributed. One could argue, then, that in *The Rainbow* Lawrence responds to the anxieties generated by the newfound articulation of women's sexuality, anxieties that led to the policing of women's sexual desire, as well as an increase in homophobic discourses regarding sexual relationships between women.

During the mid-Victorian period in British history, women began to question the social constructions that forced them to choose between the patriarchal binary of "the wife" or "the spinster." Through the expansion of capitalism and industry, employment opportunities for single middle-class women had increased in the early 1800s to include clerical and secretarial jobs; prior to this, single women had been relegated to positions as schoolmistress or governess. However, this newfound financial independence for women started to change in the 1850s due to a high level of unemployment that resulted in jobs being taken from single middle-class women and given to unemployed men.

These economic circumstances inspired an early feminist movement and caused many women to critique male patriarchal dominance. This "liberation" movement stressed the importance of women's social and economic independence, and became a precursor to the suffrage enterprise and its fights for political equality. Questions of sexuality, "sisterhood," and lesbianism were an inevitable by-product of this movement during the *fin de siècle*; however, many women chose to dissociate themselves from these topics for fear that such controversial issues might impede the political progress which had been made by the early feminist movement.

By the turn of the century, the feminist counter-culture was becoming represented within fictional texts, the most infamous being Grant Allen's novel *The Woman Who Did*. Furthermore, a journal, *The Freewoman*, was organized as a feminist forum for the discussion of issues such as abortion, birth control, prostitution, and homosexuality. In October of 1915, Stella Browne, one of the women who helped develop *The Freewoman*, presented a paper to the British Society for the Study of Sexual Psychology in which Browne rejected the traditional Victorian notion that female sexual desire was subordinate to the male.

In this paper Browne also separated sexuality from procreation by questioning monogamy, marriage, and family. In addition, she adopted Havelock Ellis's apologetic stance on lesbianism, which stated that society must recognize homosexuals as valuable members of society.

Despite the work of Browne and Ellis, in the early decades of the twentieth century, lesbianism was still a largely invisible category that only now started to become understood as an identity. In nineteenth-century England, sexual desire, sexual acts, and intense love between women did not constitute a condition or perversion that categorized the whole individual.

The female friendship of the Victorian era is a perfect example of how relationships between women have drastically changed in Europe and America. During the eighteenth and nineteenth centuries, deeply felt same-sex friendships were the norm, particularly between women. These relationships ranged from love between sisters to sensual expressions of love by adult women. Carroll Smith-Rosenberg's research into the letters exchanged between female friends during the nineteenth century has revealed many telling portraits of the relationships that existed between women at that time. They were intense, loving, and openly avowed, usually began during adolescence, and often lasted until the death of one of the partners. That these relationships frequently endured geographic separation and heterosexual marriages demonstrates that the central ideals of Victorian female friendship were unquestioned devotion and mutual emotional support. In response to Smith-Rosenberg's research, Lillian Faderman notes that "Romantic friends courted each other, flirted, were anxious about the beloved's responses and about reciprocity. They believed their relationships to be eternal, and in fact the faithfulness of one often extended beyond the death of the other."

Here, Faderman confirms Smith-Rosenberg's assertions that Victorian female friendship was built around a generic and unselfconscious pattern of single-sex or homosocial networks, networks that were supportive and institutionalized in social conventions. As a result, pre-twentieth-century homosocial friendships remained virtually unchanged from the 1760s to the 1880s, a period when "continuity, not discontinuity, characterized this female world." Smith-Rosenberg's terms "continuity" and "discontinuity" imply that prior to the twentieth century there existed a continuum of emotional and sexual impulses rather than a dichotomized structure of "normal" and "abnormal." Certainly nineteenth-century female friendships permitted a great deal of freedom of movement between the poles of today's socially constructed continuum that places "uncompromised heterosexuality" at one extreme and "committed homosexuality" at the other.

We must conclude, then, that around the turn of the century England saw a change in what constituted "acceptable" relationships between women. No longer could women be as openly loving, supportive, or tenacious as they had been in previous decades. The Victorian ideal of female friendship disintegrated as its notion of a fluid continuum was transformed into a rigid dichotomy.

Responding to the development of "the lesbian" as a sexual category—a category developed during the 1890s by Richard von Krafft-Ebing and Havelock Ellis—Lawrence turns away from the literary tradition of romantic female friendship.

In its place, Lawrence adopts a pederastic model of homosexuality: Winifred, the mature teacher, takes on Ursula as a young protégé in a form of kinship that echoes Edward Carpenter's assertion that "a strong attachment in boyhood or girlhood ... between the young thing and its teacher" is important "in the educational sense" for personal growth. Lawrence's depiction of Winifred and Ursula's bond seems to draw on Carpenter's unique placement of women within a pederastic model of same-sex sexuality.

Lawrence responds to Carpenter's 1908 assertion in *The Intermediate Sex* that the early twentieth century has witnessed "a marked development of the homogenic passion among the female sex." And Carpenter goes on to claim that "womankind have drawn more closely together ... to cement an alliance of their own." The "comrade-alliances," as Carpenter calls such bonds, echo his comments on male same-sex sexuality, which espouse a Whitmanian "brotherly love" and romantic connections between older and younger men. Carpenter's discussion of women's "homogenic alliances" may be read as a shift toward a conceptualization of lesbianism within a masculine frame.

It is important to note that Carpenter's comments are in reaction to Richard von Krafft-Ebing's claim that sexual desire between women is extremely rare. For example, in 1893 Krafft-Ebing asserted that there were only fifty documented cases of female homosexuality in medical history. Carpenter refutes this misconception, pointing to Havelock Ellis's case studies in his massive *Studies in the Psychology of Sex* as a source of opposition. Here, Ellis documented the details concerning the sexual desire of his female friends, many of whom were lesbians.

These brief biographies acknowledged the existence of lesbianism as an inherent form of female sexual desire and made it visible as such to the world of medicine, the humanities, and the social sciences. Ellis's understanding (or definition) of female same-sex desire as an identity was based on the notion of an independent female sexuality—a sexuality that was divorced from what early feminists such as Stella Browne saw as the "corrupting forces" of patriarchy. On the other hand, in the eyes of the British legal system—as was seen in the 1895 trials of Oscar Wilde—such a dissemination generated "shameful" rhetoric and homophobic ideologies that ruptured "healthy" bonds between women, bonds that were believed to be non-sexual.

Hilary Simpson's claim that "the 'Shame' chapter is Lawrence's only explicit treatment of female homosexuality" ignores the lesbian relationship that is played out in *The Fox*. Simpson's assertion is understandable, however, for the novella version of *The Fox* (1922) includes a vision of lesbianism that differs greatly from the one in *The Rainbow*. Here, the pederastic model has been stripped away; instead, Banford and March are young women who have chosen to throw off a "life of petticoats and corsets" in favour of the breeches and trousers that suit a life of farming.

This relationship thus avoids the asymmetrical power structures of the Ursula-Winifred union. The narrative of *The Fox*, in fact, is concerned with the relations of power as they are defined through gendered categories and transgressions: March is described as a "loose-balanced young man," whose "straight" and "strong" shoulders make it possible for her to do "most of the outdoor work." Banford, on the other hand, is described as a "small, thin, delicate thing," whose greatest asset to the farm is her inheritance. In a portrait that echoes Havelock Ellis's vision of the "female invert" as a "masculine woman," Lawrence has March take on what the narrator considers to be "a masculine role"; March is even said to be "the man about the place". Here the pederastic model carries no currency, and the male model of homosexuality that was grafted onto Ursula and Winifred's relationship is replaced by a mimicking of heterosexual bonds through various gender performances.

A common thread that binds Lawrence's two treatments of lesbianism can be traced to the ruptures that occur when Ursula and March choose heterosexual bonds. But the reasons for their respective repudiations of lesbianism differ. Ursula, for instance, rejects lesbianism when she feels "a heavy, clogged sense of deadness ... from the other woman's contact." The "deadness" that Ursula experiences is akin to Lawrence's discussion of male homosexuality in his essay on Walt Whitman, in which he argues that "woman is inadequate for the last merging. So the next step is the merging of man-for-man love.

And this is on the brink of death. It slides over into death." This sense of "deadness," which reminds us of Lawrence's own panicked sexuality and of Thomas Mann's homosexual imagery in *Death in Venice,* is not present in *The Fox*. Rather, March's rejection of Banford is inspired more by feelings of gender confusion: March's intimacy with Henry gives her "a life as a woman and a female," for "she, being a woman, must be like that".

This adherence to gender and sexual "norms" is partly seen by the narrator as a rejection of her "perverse ... masculine autonomy". Condemnations of March's "masculine" identity have been correctly read as reactions to the rise of women's independence in the wake of World War I. But I would add that these reactionary comments may also be understood as a questioning of lesbian identities that embrace heterosexual gender roles.

Lawrence's grafting of heterosexual roles onto a lesbian relationship, combined with his diverse representations of lesbianism, lead me to ponder a theoretical question. That is, lesbian readings of *The Rainbow* and *The Fox* open up spaces from which to re-view more recent theories about the continuum between homosocial and homosexual desire. For instance, Eve Kosofsky Sedgwick has built upon Smith-Rosenberg's and Faderman's research into the continuum of desire regarding Victorian female friendships. For Sedgwick, "the diacritical opposition between the 'homosocial' and the 'homosexual' seems to be less thorough and dichotomous for women than for men." Here, Sedgwick argues that the disruption on the continuum between homosocial and homosexual desire is restricted to male kinship. Sedgwick's position assumes that homophobia—which she sees as the central cause of homosocial ruptures between men—is a discursive structure that frames male kinship, a framing that does not surround women's bonds. Seeing a unity in the continuum of women-promoting-women and women-loving-women, Sedgwick goes on to claim that homosocial ruptures between women are not essential to maintaining modern patriarchy.

But when Ursula cuts off her love for Winifred from the rest of her life (as a "secret side-show to her life, never to be opened"), and when March and Branford's relationship is threatened by Henry's (or the symbolic fox's) presence, we are confronted with a homosocial disruption that is reminiscent of those described by Sedgwick.

Moreover, we might cast the specter of Sedgwick's asymmetrical gender triangles over the Ursula-Winifred relationship, for Winifred's lesbian desire receives its fullest expression at the end of the "Shame" chapter, when she enters Ursula's bed, embraces her, and says that she will marry Ursula's uncle. Winifred asserts that she "will marry him," but adds, "he's not like you, my dear—ha, he's not as good as you. There's something even objectionable about him".

This comparison of Ursula to Winifred's future husband (re)affirms her love and desire for her student at a time when lesbianism is emerging as a sexual category; that is, because this desire is not possible within the strict confines of sexual "norms," it can only be sublimated through a commitment to Ursula's male relative. Although Winifred finds "something objectionable" in Ursula's uncle, she is willing to marry him as a way of deferring the sexual desire that she feels for his niece: A version of Sedgwick's "gender triangles" thus emerges: Winifred's inability to commit herself to lesbianism causes her to seek out a relationship with a man who is related—physically and emotionally—to the object of her affection. By marrying Tom, Winifred will not only remain in close contact with Ursula, but also be able to maintain an allusive sexual interaction with her through the sexual relationship with Ursula's uncle.

Winifred's sexual deferral, and the "sort a nausea" and "sense of deadness" that come over Ursula as she contemplates her affair with Winifred, signal the cultural shift away from the Romantic ideal of female friendship and the emergence of a lesbian identity. The very title of the chapter, "Shame," sheds light on Lawrence's homophobic attitude toward female same-sex sexuality. This is further supported by his pejorative reference to Winifred's desire for Ursula, to which Lawrence refers as "part of the perverted life of the older woman." Still, we must ask if the "rupture" of the Ursula-Winifred relationship is really an expression of the author's own homophobia or merely a representation of an ideological shift regarding women's sexuality and lesbianism.

In contemplating this question, it seems appropriate to consider the ambiguous conclusion to *The Fox*. Henry's conquest—the killing of Banford by the falling tree, a symbolic gesture that pits nature against the "unnatural" lesbian act—is seen as an insignificant triumph. The narrative works to question Henry's rupture of the homosocial bond between Banford and March: March resists Henry's assertions of male dominance, and the narrator implies that the ultimate heterosexual union leaves March empty and unfulfilled.

The resolution of this problem is doubtful, and the story ends with their suggested flight to Canada; but this self-imposed exile is seen as an external change that will not engender an internal one. The lack of optimism here suggests that Lawrence was uncomfortable with the contemporary serological categories that framed same-sex sexual bonds as clinical, and therefore treatable, conditions.

Henry's affection, in other words, is inadequate for "treating" March's desire for Banford. The novel's conclusion and Lawrence's simultaneous admiration and repudiation of Winifred point to Lawrence's ambiguous understanding of female homosexuality. His lesbian lovers are seen as "shameful," "perverse and corrupt"; at the same time, they are described as "strong," "fearless," "exquisite," and "proud," and as nourishing a life-enhancing, meaningful, and valuable relationship.

Views of Life of D.H. Lawrence

D.H. Lawrence used his novels Sons and Lovers and Women in Love to express his unhappy views toward his family and the world around him. Lawrence expressed himself through his other writings as well as these two novels to explain how he felt. Lawrence's family life, his too close connection with his mother, and the trials he had while growing up may have severely influenced his writings in his conscious and the unconscious mind.

D.H. Lawrence grew up in a family of four children. His Father was illiterate and his mother came from a higher class(Harrison, 1997, p.1). This same situation was portrayed in the beginning of the novel Sons and Lovers when the narrator recalls his mother's family before she was married, " Mrs. Morel came from a good old burgher family, famous independents who had fought with Colonel Hutchinson, and who remained stiff Congregationalists."(Lawrence, 1913, p.8).

Through the semiautobiographical Sons and Lovers we find out that Lawrence lived a very hard life in a house where there was very little love, "Their marriage life had been one carnal, bloody fight. I was born hating my father: as early as ever I can remember, I shivered with horror when he touched me."(Boulton, 1979, p.190) Along with the difficult relationships that Lawrence had in his own household Lawrence had a difficult relationship with his hometown. Lawrence was considered a strange child because he was very intellectual like his mother.

He enjoyed reading, writing and being academic rather than the idea of hard labour and work. He was a quiet child who kept to himself. (Harrison, 1997, p.1). This idea was portrayed by the narrator, " So Paul was towed round at the heals of Annie, sharing her game. She raced around wildly at larky with the other young wild-cats of the Bottoms. And always Paul flew beside her, living her share of the game, having as yet no part his own. He was quiet and not noticeable."(Lawrence, 1913, p.52).

His home town, Nottingham, affected Lawrence very deeply because of the way he was treated and much of his writings used Nottingham as the backdrop. In most of his novels the life and culture he grew up with in the mining town and in his own house were very apparent(Harrison, 1997, p.1). "Lawrence certainly suffered his whole life from the essential solitude to which his gift condemned him."(1999,) In life Lawrence being the fourth child was loved by his mother but in his novel Sons and Lovers the role that is seen as Lawrence's was not his at first. The older brother named William was the mother's favoured child. See had a very intimate and close relationship with her older son.

Lawrence's character only took over the role as the favoured child after his older brother died(Salgado, 1970, p.130). In Real life Lawrence did have an older brother who similarly was the favoured child his name was Earnest. He, as the same as in the book, moved away and became a clerk. He made 120 pounds a year and was loved the most by his mother. As in the novel William died a sudden death and Paul took the place of the dearly loved son. Mrs. Lawrence from then on made sure her son had everything that would get him out of the coal mining society(Worthen, 1997).

Lawrence wrote the final version of his novel Sons and Lovers in 1913 after his mother died of a long and time consuming death(Lawrence, 1915, p.5(forward)) Even as a child Lawrence was deeply devoted to his mother who was refined but domineering. She cared deeply for her son and insisted that he get a good education(Columbia Encyclopedia, 6th Edition, p.2). In a letter that Lawrence wrote he explained just how close he was to his mother, "This had been a kind of bond between me and my mother.

We have loved each other, almost with a husband and wife love, as well as final and maternal. We knew each other by instinct... We have been like one, so sensitive to each other that we never needed words. It has been rather terrible, and has made me, in some respects, abnormal."(Lawrence, 1913, p.10(Introduction)). In the novel Sons and Lovers He repeated this idea, "Paul loved to sleep with his mother. Sleep is still the most perfect, in spite of hygienists, when it is shared with a beloved."(Lawrence, 1913, p.60) "His relationship with his mother begins to account for his attitude toward sex.

His particular experiences as being a son and a lover may have intensified his preoccupation with the subject; but they certainly did not make it. Whatever his experiences, Lawrence must have been preoccupied with sex."(Lawrence, 1915, (Commentary), p.39). In the novel Women in Love he speaks about relationships as being near to evil. Some critics saw Women in love as to be an obscene novel but are now looked upon as an "intense psychological probing into human relationships. Some few critiques hailed his books as brilliant, others condemned them as neurotic and indecent."(World Book, D.H. Lawrence, 1998). Other works by Lawrence that spoke about his opinion of the world around were also seen as wrong.

The Rainbow was seized in 1915 by police after it had been outlawed for being indecent, and the novel Women in Love was not published because its content was viewed as being not to the best interests of the public. It was not until six years later that he could find a publisher that was willing to publish it(Lawrence, 1915, (Forward), p.6). In November of 1914 after Great Britain had entered the war Lawrence wrote and published a collection of stories called The Prussian Officer which was considered politically and morally offensive but represented his views of the country entering the war(Lawrence, 1915, (Forward), p.6).

"Some see these novels as a disease of modern life in all its manifestations. The life patterns that Lawrence reflects in Sons and Lovers and may have happened in his life are that of which have transgresses against the natural direction of life and the conditions in which humans normally live. His novels follow a very conventional and basic organizational way of writing that some critics see as naïve and that of an amateur"(Salgado, 1970, P.112). This may have been a real factor in Lawrence's real life causing him to have such difficult relationships with women, including his wife.

Lawrence has a talent for imagery some see as a direct cause of his upbringing. His use of repetition becomes apparent and nagging in both novels Sons and Lovers and Women in Love(Salgado, 1970, P.130). Lawrence may have used repetition because of the way his own life flowed as a child and as an adult. After he married, Lawrence traveled back and forth between Europe, Australia and the United States. In his novels his repetition is in the feelings he has. He goes back and forth between hate and love for people. "They experience more than classical satiety. Mad with love in one hour, in the next they are no less mad with hate."(Lawrence, 1915, (Commentary), p.35).

In the novel Women in Love Rupert and Ursula are walking down a road to Beldover. Rupert goes on about how he never wants to be in love and he thinks that Ursula should feel the same way. After a few more sentences he stops and kisses her, "he kissed he face and brow, slowly, gently, with a sort of delicate happiness which surprised her extremely, and to which she could not respond."(Lawrence, 1915, p.192). Rupert is not sure of what he wants and throughout the entire novel he repeatedly goes back and forth between his love for her and his feelings that he doesn't want to love.

Lawrence in his own life mimicked this novel by the way he treated his wife. Lawrence wavered back and forth between love and the lack of need for his wife's love. While writing The Rainbow and Women in Love Lawrence bordered on mental instability, sexual confusion and experimentation. These his outrageous actions had many times challenged his marriage, caused endless health reversals and caused him and his wife to start living in different countries for a period of time as well(Lawrence, 1915 (Forward), p.6). He ended his life with his wife, living together again, but not until after they had a very turbulent filled life(Lawrence, 1915, (Introduction), p.2). He recorded all of these trails and tribulations in a poem cycle named Look! We Have Come Through(Lawrence, 1915, (opening)p. 6). Lawrence left no part of his life untouched.

People now feel that he wrote to discover what he thought, what was thinking in him on an unconscious level and why he thought it(Lawrence, 1915, (Introduction), p.14). Even Lawrence himself realised that "my novels pretend only to be a record of the writer's own desires, aspirations, struggles; in a word, a record of the profoundest experiences in the self."(Lawrence, 1915, (Forward), p.30). With these statements made there are no arguments that even though his writings were controversial. They reflected his own opinions of the world and his family.

On Sons and Lovers Dorothy Van Ghent

Novels, like other dramatic art, deal with conflicts of one kind or another—conflicts that are, in the work of the major novelists, drawn from life in the sense that they are representative of real problems in life; and the usual urgency in the novelist is to find the technical means which will afford an ideal resolution of the conflict and solution of the living problem—still "ideal" even if tragic. Technique is his art itself, in its procedural aspect; and the validity of his solution of a problem is dependent upon the adequacy of his technique. The more complex and intransigent the problem, the more subtle his technical strategies will evidently need to be, if they are to be effective.

The decade of World War I brought into full and terrible view the collapse of values that had prophetically haunted the minds of novelists as far back as Dostoevsky and Flaubert and Dickens, or even farther back, to Balzac and Stendhal. With that decade, and increasingly since, the problems of modern life have appeared intransigent indeed; and, in general, the growth of that intransigence has been reflected in an increasing concern with technique on the part of the artist. D. H. Lawrence's sensitivity to twentieth-century chaos was peculiarly intense, and his passion for order was similarly intense; but this sensitivity and this passion did not lead him to concentrate on refinements and subtleties of novelistic technique in the direction laid out, for instance, by James and Conrad. Hence, as readers first approaching his work, almost inevitably we feel disappointment and even perhaps shock, that writing so often "loose" and repetitious and such unrestrained emotionalism over glandular matters should appear in the work of a novelist who is assumed to have an important place in the literary canon. "There is no use," Francis Fergusson says, "trying to appreciate [Lawrence] solely as an artist; he was himself too often impatient of the demands of art, which seemed to him trivial compared with the quest he followed." And Stephen Spender phrases the problem of Lawrence in this way: what interested him "was the tension between art and life, not the complete resolution of the problems of life within the illusion of art....

For him literature is a kind of pointer to what is outside literature.... This outside ness of reality is for Lawrence the waters of baptism in which man can be reborn." We need to approach Lawrence with a good deal of humility about "art" and a good deal of patience for the disappointments he frequently offers as an artist, for it is only thus that we shall be able to appreciate the innovations he actually made in the novel as well as the importance and profundity of his vision of modern life.

Sons *and* Lovers appears to have the most conventional chronological organization—the extreme reverse of Conrad's intricate cross-chronology; it is the kind of organization that a naive autobiographical novelist would tend to use, with only the thinnest pretense at disguising the personally retrospective nature of the material. We start with the marriage of the parents and the birth of the children. We learn of the daily life of the family while the children are growing up, the work, the small joys, the parental strife. Certain well-defined emotional pressures become apparent: the children are alienated from their father, whose personality degenerates gradually as he feels his exclusion; the mother more and more completely dominates her sons' affections, aspirations, mental habits. Urged by her toward middle-class refinements, they enter white-collar jobs, thus making one more dissociation between themselves and their proletarian father. As they attempt to orient themselves toward biological adulthood, the old split in the family is manifested in a new form, as an internal schism in the characters of the sons; they cannot reconcile sexual choice with the idealism their mother has inculcated.

This inner strain leads to the older son's death. The same motif is repeated in the case of Paul, the younger one. Paul's first girl, Miriam, is a cerebral type, and the mother senses in her an obvious rivalry for domination of Paul's sensibility. The mother is the stronger influence, and Paul withdraws from Miriam; but with her own victory Mrs. Morel begins to realise the discord she has produced in his character, and tries to release her hold on him by unconsciously seeking her own death. Paul finds another girl, Clara, but the damage is already too deeply designed, and at the time of his mother's death, he voluntarily gives up Clara, knowing that there is but one direction he can take, and that is to go with his mother. At the end he is left emotionally derelict, with only the "drift toward death."

From this slight sketch, it is clear that the book is organized not merely on a chronological plan showing the habits and vicissitudes of a Nottinghamshire miner's family, but that it has a structure rigorously controlled by an idea: an idea of an organic disturbance in the relationships of men and women—a disturbance of sexual polarities that is first seen in the disaffection of mother and father, then in the mother's attempt to substitute her sons for her husband, finally in the sons' unsuccessful struggle to establish natural manhood. Lawrence's development of the idea has certain major implications: it implies that his characters have transgressed against the natural life directed condition of the human animal—against the elementary biological rhythms he shares with the rest of biological nature; and it implies that this offense against life has been brought about by a failure to respect the complete and terminal individuality of persons—by a twisted desire to "possess" other persons, as the mother tries to "possess" her husband, then her sons, and as Miriam tries to "possess" Paul. Lawrence saw this offense as a disease of modern life in all its manifestations, from sexual relationships to those broad social and political relationships that have changed people from individuals to anonymous economic properties or to military units or to ideological automatons.

The controlling idea is expressed in the various episodes—the narrative logic of the book. It is also expressed in imagery—the book's poetic logic. In previous studies we have discussed, from a number of points of view, the function of imagery in novels, but nowhere else do we find the image so largely replacing episode and discursive analysis and taking over the expressive functions of these, as it does in Lawrence. The chief reason for the extraordinary predominance of the image, as an absolute expressive medium, in Lawrence, lies in the character of the idea which is his subject. He must make us aware—sensitively aware, not merely conceptually aware—of the profound life force whose rhythms the natural creature obeys; and he must make us aware of the terminal individuality—the absolute "otherness" or "outside ness"—that is the natural form of things and of the uncorrupted person.

We must be made aware of these through the *feelings* of his people, for only in feeling have the biological life force and the sense of identity, either the identity of self or of others, any immediacy of reality. He seeks the objective equivalent of feeling in the image. As Francis Fergusson says, Lawrence's imagination was so concrete that he seems not "to distinguish between the reality and the metaphor or symbol which makes it plain to us." But the most valid symbols are the most concrete realities. Lawrence's great gift for the symbolic image was a function of his sensitivity to and passion for the meaning of real things—for the individual expression that real forms have. In other words, his gift for the image arose directly from his vision of life as infinitely creative of individual identities, each whole and separate and to be reverenced as such.

Let us examine the passage with which the first chapter of *Sons and Lovers* ends-where Mrs. Morel, pregnant with Paul, wanders deliriously in the garden, shut out of the house by Morel in his drunkenness. Mrs. Morel is literally a vessel of the life force that seems to thrust itself at her in nature from all sides, but she is also in rebellion against it and the perfume of the pollen-filled lilies makes her gasp with fear.

The moon was high and magnificent in the August night. Mrs. Morel, seared with passion, shivered to find herself out there in a great white light, that fell cold on her, and gave a shock to her inflamed soul. She stood for a few moments helplessly staring at the glistening great rhubarb leaves near the door. Then she got the air into her breast. She walked down the garden path, trembling in every limb, while the child boiled within her....

She hurried out of the side garden to the front, where she could stand as if in an immense gulf of white light, the moon streaming high in face of her, the moonlight standing up from the hills in front, and filling the valley where the Bottoms crouched, almost blindingly. There, panting and half weeping in reaction from the stress, she murmured to herself over and over again: "The nuisance! the nuisance!"

She became aware of something about her. With an effort she roused herself to see what it was that penetrated her consciousness. The tall white lilies were reeling in the moonlight, and the air was charged with their perfume, as with a presence. Mrs. Morel gasped slightly in fear. She touched the big, pallid flowers on their petals, then shivered. They seemed to be stretching in the moonlight. She put her hand into one white bin: the gold scarcely showed on her fingers by moonlight. She bent down to look at the binful of yellow pollen; but it only appeared dusky. Then she drank a deep draught of the scent. It almost made her dizzy.

Mrs. Morel leaned on the garden gate, looking out, and she lost herself awhile. She did not know what she thought. Except for a slight feeling of sickness, and her consciousness in the child, herself melted out like a scent into the shiny, pale air.

She finally arouses Morel from his drunken sleep and he lets her in. Unfastening her brooch at the bedroom mirror, she sees that her face is smeared with the yellow dust of the lilies.

The imagery of the streaming moonlight is that of a vast torrential force, "magnificent" and inhuman, and it equates not only with that phallic power of which Mrs. Morel is the rebellious vessel but with the greater and universal demiurge that was anciently called Eros—the power springing in plants and hurling the planets, giving the "glistening great rhubarb leaves" their fierce identity, fecundating and stretching the lilies. The smear of yellow pollen on Mrs. Morel's face is a grossly humourous irony. This passage is a typifying instance of the spontaneous identification Lawrence constantly found between image and meaning, between real things and what they symbolize.

Our particular culture has evolved deep prohibitions against the expression, or even the subjective acknowledgment of the kind of phallic reality with which Lawrence was concerned—and with which ancient religions were also concerned. Certainly one factor in the uneasiness that Lawrence frequently causes us is the factor of those cultural prohibitions. But these prohibitions themselves Lawrence saw as disease symptoms, though the disease was far more extensive and radical than a taboo on the phallus. It was a spiritual disease that broke down the sense of identity, of "separate selfhood," while at the same time it broke down the sense of rhythm with universal nature. Paul Morel, working his fairly unconscious, adolescent, sexual way toward Miriam, finds that rhythm and that selfhood in the spatial proportions of a wren's nest in a hedge.

He crouched down and carefully put his finger through the thorns into the round door of the nest.

"It's almost as if you were feeling inside the live body of the bird," he said, "it's so warm. They say a bird makes its nest round like a cup with pressing its breast on it. Then how did it make the ceiling round, I wonder?"

When Paul takes his first country walk with Clara and Miriam, the appearance of a red stallion in the woods vividly realises in unforced symbolic dimension the power which will drive Paul from Miriam to Clara, while the image also realises the great horse itself in its unique and mysterious identity.

As they were going beside the brook, on the Willey Water side, looking through the brake at the edge of the wood, where pink champions glowed under a few sunbeams, they saw, beyond the tree-trunks and the thin hazel bushes, a man leading a great bay horse through the gullies. The big red beast seemed to dance romantically through that dimness of green hazel drift, away there where the air was shadowy, as if it were in the past, among the fading blue bells that might have bloomed for Deirdre....

The great horse breathed heavily, shifting round its red flanks, and looking suspiciously with its wonderful big eyes upwards from under its lowered head and falling mane.

A simple descriptive passage like the following, showing a hen pecking at a girl's hand, conveys the animal dynamics that is the urgent phase of the phallic power working in the boy and the girl, but its spontaneous symbolism of a larger reality is due to its faithfulness to the way a hen does peck and the feeling of the pecking—due, that is, to the actuality or "identity" of the small, homely circumstance itself.

As he went round the back, he saw Miriam kneeling in front of the hen-coop, some maize in her hand, biting her

lip, and crouching in an intense attitude. The hen was eyeing her wickedly. Very gingerly she put forward her hand. The hen bobbed for her. She drew back quickly with a cry, half of fear, half of chagrin.

"It won't hurt you," said Paul.

She flushed crimson and started up.

"I only wanted to try," she said in a low voice.

"See, it doesn't hurt," he said, and, putting only two corns in his palm, he let the hen peck, peck, peck at his bare hand. "It only makes you laugh," he said.

She put her hand forward, and dragged it away, tried again, and started back with a cry. He frowned.

"Why, I'd let her take corn from my face," said Paul, "only she bumps a bit. She's ever so neat. If she wasn't, look how much ground she'd peck up every day."

He waited grimly, and watched. At last Miriam let the bird peck from her hand. She gave a little cry—fear, and pain because of fear—rather pathetic. But she had done it, and she did it again.

"There, you see," said the boy. "It doesn't hurt, does it?"

There is more terse and obvious symbolism, of the typical kind in Lawrence, in that sequence where Clara's red carnations splatter their petals over her clothes and on the ground where she and Paul first make love, but we acquire the best and the controlling sense of Lawrence's gift for the image, as dramatic and thematic expression, in those passages where his urgency is to see *things* and to see them clearly and completely in their most individualizing traits, for the character of his vision is such that, in truly seeing them as they are, he sees through them to what they mean.

We have fairly frequently noticed in these studies the differentiating significance of a writer's treatment of nature—that is, of that part of "nature" which is constituted by earth and air and water and the nonhuman creatures; and we have found that attitudes toward nature were deeply associated with attitudes toward human "good," human destiny, human happiness, human salvation, the characteristic problems of being human. One might cite, for instance, in Tom *Jones,* Fielding's highly stylized treatment of outdoor nature (as in the passage in which Tom dreams of Sophia beside the brook, and Mollie Seagrim approaches): here nature has only generalized attributes for whose description and understanding certain epithets in common educated currency are completely adequate—brooks murmur, breezes whisper, birds trill; nature is really a linguistic construction, and this rationalization of nature is appropriate in Fielding's universe since everything there exists ideally as an object of *ratio,* of reasoning intelligence.

We have noticed in Jane Austen's Pride *and Prejudice* (in the description of Darcy's estate, for example) that outdoor nature again has importance only as it serves to express rational and social character—wherefore again the generalized epithet that represents nature as either the servant of intelligence or the space where intelligence operates. In George Eliot's *Adam Bede,* where there is relatively a great deal of "outdoors," nature is man's plow field, the acre in which he finds social and ethical expression through work; this is only a different variety of the conception of nature as significant by virtue of what man's intelligential and social character makes of it for his ends.

With Emily Bronte, we come nearer to Lawrence, though not very near. In *Wuthering Heights,* nature's importance is due not to its yielding itself up to domestication in man's reason, or offering itself as an instrument by which he expresses his conscience before God or society, but to its fiercely unregenerate difference from all that civilized man is—a difference that it constantly forces on perception by animal-like attacks on and disruptions of human order.

In Hardy, nature is also a daemonic entity in its own right, and not only un rationalizable but specifically hostile to the human reason. It is worth noting that, among all English novelists, Hardy and Lawrence have the most faithful touch for the things of nature and the greatest evocative genius in bringing them before the imagination. But there are certain definitive differences of attitude.

Both Emily Bronte's and Hardy's worlds are dual, and there is no way of bringing the oppositions of the dualism together: on the one side of the cleavage are those attributes of man that we call "human," his reason, his ethical sensibility; and on the other side is "nature"—the elements and the creatures and man's own instinctive life that he shares with the nonhuman creatures. The opposition is resolved only by destruction of the "human": a destruction that is in Emily Bronte profoundly attractive, in Hardy tragic. But Lawrence's world is multiple rather than dual.

Everything in it is a separate and individual "other," every person, every creature, every object (like the Madonna lilies, the rhubarb plants, the wren's nest, the stallion); and there is a creative relationship between people and between people and things so long as this "otherness" is acknowledged. When it is denied—and it is denied when man tries to rationalize nature and society, or when he presumptuously assumes the things of nature to be merely instruments for the expression of himself, or when he attempts to exercise personal possessor ship over people—then he destroys his own selfhood and exerts a destructive influence all about him.

In *Sons and Lovers,* only in Morel himself, brutalized and spiritually maimed as he is, does the germ of selfhood remain intact; and—this is the correlative proposition in Lawrence—in him only does the biological life force have simple, unequivocal assertion. Morel wants to live, by hook or crook, while his sons want to die. To live is to obey a rhythm involving more than conscious attitudes and involving more than human beings—involving all nature; a rhythm indifferent to the greediness of reason, indifferent to idiosyncrasies of culture and idealism.

The image associated with Morel is that of the coal pits, where he descends daily and from which he ascends at night blackened and tired. It is a symbol of rhythmic descent and ascent, like a sexual rhythm, or like the rhythm of sleep and awaking or of death and life. True, the work in the coal pits reverses the natural use of the hours of light and dark and is an economic distortion of that rhythm in nature—and Morel and the other colliers bear the spiritual traumata of that distortion; for Lawrence is dealing with the real environment of modern men, in its complexity and injuriousness. Nevertheless, the work at the pits is still symbolic of the greater rhythm governing life and obedience to which is salvation. Throughout the book, the coal pits are always at the horizon.

On the fallow land the young wheat shone silkily. Minton pit waved its plumes of white steam, coughed, and rattled hoarsely.

"Now look at that!" said Mrs. Morel. Mother and son stood on the road to watch. Along the ridge of the great pit-hill crawled a little group in silhouette against the sky, a horse, a small truck, and a man. They climbed the incline against the heavens. At the end the man tipped the wagon. There was an undue rattle as the waste fell down the sheer slope of the enormous bank....

"Look how it heaps together," [Paul says of the pit] "like something alive almost—a big creature that you don't know.... And all the trucks standing waiting, like a string of beasts to be fed.... I like the feel of men on things, while they're alive. There's a feel of men about trucks, because they've been handled with men's hands, all of them."

Paul associates the pits not only with virility but with being alive. The trucks themselves become alive because they have been handled by men. The symbolism of the pits is identical with that of Morel, the father, the irrational life principle that is unequally embattled against the death principle in the mother, the rational and idealizing principle working rhythmlessly, greedily, presumptuously, and possessively.

The sons' attitude toward the father is ambivalent, weighted toward hate because the superior cultural equipment of the mother shows his crudeness in relief; but again and again bits of homely characterization of Morel show that the children—and even the mother herself—sense, however uncomfortably, the attractiveness of his simple masculine integrity. He has, uninjurable, what the mother's possessiveness has injured in the sons.

"Shut that doo-er!" bawled Morel furiously.

Annie banged it behind her, and was gone.

"If tha opens it again while I'm weshin' me, I'll ma'e thy jaw rattle," he threatened from the midst of his soapsuds. Paul and the mother frowned to hear him.

Presently he came running out of the scullery, with the soapy water dripping from him, dithering with cold.

"Oh, my sirs!" he said. "Wheer's my towel?"

It was hung on a chair to warm before the fire, otherwise he would have bullied and blustered. He squatted on his heels before the hot baking-fire to dry himself.

"F-ff-f!" he went, pretending to shudder with cold.

"Goodness, man, don't be such a kid!" said Mrs. Morel. "It's *not* cold."

"Thee strip thysen stark nak'd to wesh thy flesh i' that scullery," said the miner, as he rubbed his hair; "nowt b'r a ice-'ouse!"

"And I shouldn't make that fuss," replied his wife.

"No, tha'd drop down stiff, as dead as a door-knob, wi' thy nesh sides."

"Why is a door-knob deader than anything else?" asked Paul, curious.

"Eh, I dunno; that's what they say," replied his father. "But there's that much draught i' yon scullery, as it blows through your ribs like through a five-barred gate."

"It would have some difficulty in blowing through yours," said Mrs. Morel.

Morel looked down ruefully at his sides.

"Me!" he exclaimed. "I'm nowt b'r a skinned rabbit. My bones fair juts out on me."

"I should like to know where," retorted his wife.

"Iv'ry-wheer! I'm nobbut a sack o' faggots."

Mrs. Morel laughed. He had still a wonderfully young body, muscular, without any fat. His skin was smooth and clear. It might have been the body of a man of twenty eight, except that there were, perhaps, too many blue scars, like tattoo-marks, where the coal-dust remained under the skin, and that his chest was too hairy. But he put his hands on his sides ruefully. It was his fixed belief that, because he did not get fat, he was as thin as a starved rat.

Paul looked at his father's thick, brownish hands all scarred, with broken nails, rubbing the fine smoothness of his sides, and the incongruity struck him. It seemed strange they were the same flesh.

Morel talks the dialect that is the speech of physical tenderness in Lawrence's books. It is to the dialect of his father that Paul reverts when he is tussling with Beatrice in adolescent erotic play (letting the mother's bread burn, that he should have been watching), and that Arthur, the only one of the sons whom the mother has not corrupted, uses in his lovemaking, and that Paul uses again when he makes love to Clara, the uncomplex woman who is able for a while to give him his sexual manhood and his "separate selfhood." The sons never use the dialect with their mother, and Paul never uses it with Miriam. It is the speech used by Mellors in *Lady Chatterley's Lover;* and, significantly perhaps, Mellors's name is an anagram on the name Morel.

Some of the best moments in the children's life are associated with the father, when Morel has his "good" periods and enters again into the intimate activity of the family—and some of the best, most simply objective writing in the book communicates these moments, as for instance the passage in chapter 4 where Morel is engaged in making fuses.

Morel fetched a sheaf of long sound wheat-straws from the attic. These he cleaned with his hand, till each one gleamed like a stalk of gold, after which he cut the straws into lengths of about six inches, leaving, if he could, a notch at the bottom of each piece. He always had a beautifully sharp knife that could cut a straw clean without hurting it. Then he set in the middle of the table a heap of gun-powder, a little pile of black grains upon the white scrubbed board. He made and trimmed the straws while Paul and Annie filled and plugged them. Paul loved to see the black grains trickle down a crack in his palm into the mouth of the straw, peppering jollily downwards till the straw was full. Then he bunged up the mouth with a bit of soap—which he got on his thumb-nail from a pat in a saucer—and the straw was finished.

There is a purity of realization in this very simple kind of exposition that, on the face of it, resists associating itself with any symbolic function—if we tend to think of a "symbol" as splitting itself apart into a thing and a meaning, with a mental arrow connecting the two. The best in Lawrence carries the authenticity of a faithfully observed, concrete actuality that refuses to be so split; its symbolism is a radiation that leaves it intact in itself. So, in the passage above, the scene is intact as homely realism, but it radiates Lawrence's controlling sense of the character integrity of objects—the clean wheat straws, the whitely scrubbed table, the black grains peppering down a crack in the child's palm, the bung of soap on a thumbnail—and that integrity is here associated with the man Morel and his own integrity of warm and absolute maleness. Thus it is another representation of the creative life force witnessed in the independent objectivity of things that are wholly concrete and wholly themselves.

The Vital Self

Nineteenth-century English novelists submitted, on the whole, to the dry world shrinkage of positivism. Their Christianity, where it obtained, was likely to be the echo, not the genuine cry, of faith. Jane Austen, Thackeray, Dickens, George Eliot, Meredith, Hardy—all relinquished the eternal in an attempt to take hold of the temporal; all were empiricists of human life. By mid-century the metaphysical hunger and ferment of the Romantics had all but disappeared. No wonder G. K. Chesterton found it necessary to complain, in 1905, that "everything matters—except everything." "The modern idea," Chesterton wrote in *Heretics*, "is that cosmic truth is so unimportant that it cannot matter what anyone says." By 1905, however, Shaw's *Man and Superman* had already been written, and Forster's explorations into a "terrible" and "mysterious" reality were under way: the Romantic appetite for the infiniteness of the cosmos was at that very moment being reborn. In Lawrence, Forster, and Virginia Woolf, in Yeats and Shaw, British literature was once again to open itself to wonder, to let in the stars.

It was in Lawrence's work above all that the eternal made inroads into the temporal, tearing up nineteenth-century skepticism and nearly tearing up the novels as well. No one else could approach Lawrence, in those early, metaphysically anarchic decades of the century, in the vigour and drama and urgency of his belief. Here was a prophet, not out of the pages of history, but, of all things, in the Café Royal, in Taos, in Oaxaca—a prophet very much in the flesh. He did not belong, and he was not understood. Yet nothing could shake his certainty and his mission. Almost alone in this century, Lawrence enjoyed the forgotten luxury, and laboured under the responsibility, of a metaphysical conviction.

It is curious how Lawrence's critics have held back from granting him his great fundamental certainty. Bewildered, perhaps, by the secondary inconsistencies so rife in his work, by the absolute tone of each partial statement—perhaps driven, too, by the notion that they are "saving" Lawrence's art from ideas—they tend to see him as lacking, in William Troy's words, "some cohesive view of the universe wholly absorbed in the personality" and to regard his works as "records of the successive steps taken by his mind in the effort to discover for himself some such view."

The truth, however, is that there was nothing but coherence for Lawrence. When Lawrence said, for example, that "everything lies in *being*," he spoke sincerely, religiously, categorically. It was intuition, however, not intellectual argument, that told him this was so. And, cohesive in itself, his intuition cast a philosophical shadow that was also to prove cohesive, for all the broken appearance it took on from the changing planes of Lawrence's mind. What sets Lawrence's work apart from that of his great contemporaries, what makes it so strange and yet so compelling, is precisely its anachronistic passion and certitude, the way Lawrence was immersed in it, breathing it like an atmosphere. If there is anything "successive" in his work, it is his effort to unfold an intuitive assurance already known, to lay it *finally* bare, and to capture the satisfactions that seemed to be inherent in it.

What has yet to be noted is how Lawrence's metaphysic sprang from and, indeed, was his experience—and also how it answered to poignant psychological needs. Here was a man who believed—unaccountably, it seemed—that there is in the universe a "principle towards which man turns religiously—a *life* of the universe itself." And yet instead of appearing to be toying with metaphysics, he seemed, on the contrary, to be burning with faith.

His world-uniting and world-revering belief glowed in everything he wrote, and constituted his mission. He spoke, not at a venture, but from the pulpit of a certitude. How does a man come upon so much conviction? Surely not at the behest of intellect. We must, I think, discount Troy's opinion that it was "undoubtedly" in reaction "against the scientific rationalism of the later nineteenth century" that Lawrence "plunged himself into the most abject nature-mysticism." The mind cannot do so much. Lawrence reacted, certainly, against scientific rationalism; but he reacted because of his mysticism, not into it. Lawrence's mysticism was a natural—or, as one prefers, an unnatural—involuntary growth. "It is not really helpful," Troy writes, "to be told by psychoanalysts that he suffered from one or another malady."

On the contrary, Lawrence cannot be understood apart from his maladies. "Physical belief" of the kind that drove him can spring, like a geyser, only from subterranean pressures. And in Lawrence "physical belief" was, it would seem, the same as mystical belief. It is safe to guess—and, as we shall see, the records confirm—that something in Lawrence's notoriously strained filial experience, in combination with his exquisitely fluid sensibility, gave rise in him to a propensity to mysticism—to that whole world of "marvelous" feeling that would later crystallize into his rainbow-sensuous yet profoundly metaphysical world view. And thus it happens that to find the union of the man and his faith we would do well to look, not to his intellectual history, but to the point where his emotion finally bursts into the fire of his thought.

It is in *Sons and Lovers,* as I read it, that this conflagration first occurs. The book affords the rare opportunity of observing the genesis of an aesthetic metaphysical vision. And this genesis is not only of keen psychological interest in itself; it also provides a key to Lawrence's later development.

Alfred Kazin nearly puts his hand on this key when—in his fine introduction to the Modern Library edition of the novel—he notes that Lawrence's motive as a writer was his attempt to re-create "the mutual sympathy he had experienced with his mother." Kazin, however, goes awry when he adds that this "ecstasy... never congealed into a single... idol or belief." In fact, it congealed into a metaphysic that was to become the mainstay of Lawrence's fiction. After *Sons and Lovers,* especially, the universe Lawrence lived in, and wrote in so beautifully, was but the glowing flesh or, at worst, the eternally renewed promise of the mystical self-dispersal that Lawrence had known with his mother. Both belief and idol, it was a universe of apotheosized feeling.

This burgeoning of psychology into metaphysics is the hidden drama of *Sons and Lovers.* If it is easy to miss, the reason is that the oedipal drama, with its crackling tensions and dilemmas, is the fore ground in a novel that is, after all, almost entirely foreground. Consisting, as it does, of a few scattered paragraphs, the metaphysic of *Sons and Lovers* might seem merely incidental—musings in the intervals of the oedipal conflict. Indeed, Lawrence presents it as scarcely more than incidental. In reality, however, it constitutes, not a digression from the psychological dilemma, but precisely its solution—insofar, that is, as it was to admit of one.

On the oedipal plane itself we find an impasse, a crippling relationship too powerful to overcome. Paul Morel cannot desire where he loves; and he cannot love where he desires. Body and soul will not conjoin. His soul is bonded to his mother's, irrevocably; his body, however, "mad with restlessness," urges him "towards something else." Yet with neither the refined and thoughtful Miriam nor the robust and sensual Clara does Paul manage to free himself from his mother. He only appears to travel from her, as a man in a snow storm, wandering in a circle, only supposes he is leaving the scene of his despair.

Sensing Paul's misery, Mrs. Morel grows tired and takes ill; and both Paul and his mother hope, even as they fear, that her death will free him at last to "really love another woman." His life has been "like a circle where life turned back on itself"—his mother "bore him, loved him, kept him, and his love turned back into her." But Mrs. Morel's death fails to break the circle: "His soul could not leave her, wherever she was. Now she was gone abroad into the night, and he was with her still." So we learn from the last page of the book.

Even though dead, Mrs. Morel holds Paul "up, himself." His identity, then, is somehow one with hers. She, however, has gone "abroad in the night"; hence it is with the vast night, much as it terrifies him, that Paul must now begin to feel connected. His mother has passed into the world; will not the world now "be" his mother? "So instead of a release and a deliverance from bondage, the bondage was glorified and made absolute": thus, shrewdly, Jessie Chambers, the original of the Miriam of the novel. "Lawrence handed his mother the laurels of victory," she added. Indeed he did; but it was on the "living" universe that he placed the laurels. His bond with his mother came to be his bond with time and space and with whatever might lie "beyond."

As Daniel Weiss, Frank O'Connor, and others have shown, Freudian theory accounts for a good deal of Paul's story. Indeed, Freud's "The Most Prevalent Form of Degradation in Erotic Life" reads almost like a direct comment on Lawrence's brave and stunning book. And doubtless Lawrence's own connection with his mother, like Paul's, could not easily have been more "oedipal" than it was; it was a classic case. Yet Freudian theory does not explain enough. It leaves untouched the strength of Paul's connection with his mother, the iron in it, and the ease with which it passes, at her death, and indeed (as we shall see) before it, into a mystical worship of the world.

Lawrence's bond with his mother was—no other word—mystical. And it was this, I believe, that made it the unalterable and magically strengthening bond that it was. It was this that made it the seed of a mystical vitalism. Lawrence described this aspect of the relationship in a letter sent to Rachel Annand Taylor in December 1910:

> We knew each other by instinct. She said to my aunt—about me:
>
> "But it has been different with him. He has seemed to be part of me."—And that is the real case. We have been like one, so sensitive to each other that we never needed words. It has been rather terrible and has made me, in some respects, abnormal.
>
> I think this *peculiar fusion of soul*... never comes twice in a life-time—*it doesn't seem natural*. When it comes it seems to distribute one's consciousness far abroad from oneself, and one understands! I think no one has got "Understanding" except through love [my italics].

Lawrence concluded: "Nobody can have the soul of me. My mother has had it, and nobody can have it again. Nobody can come into my very self again, and breathe me like an atmosphere."

This letter, so bleak and absolute, has the uncompromising accents of truth. And surely what it reveals is that, whatever else it may have been, Lawrence's bond with his mother was mystical: a shaft into revelation, a numinous enlargement of self. So absolute was it that, Lawrence believed, there could be no going beyond it. Nor could merely personal or, for that matter, sexual relationships seem anything but desolation by comparison. No wonder Paul cannot be satisfied with Miriam or Clara, that he is always wanting "something else." And no wonder his mother seems to him the "pivot" of everything: the "one place in the world that... did not melt into unreality." There in the past, so Lawrence must always have felt, was the farthest reach that his soul could go. Why should he then try to break out of the "circle"?

The true problem, rather, was to bring his body into it. This he could not do, of course, so long as his mother was the obvious "pivot" of his soul. And hence Paul is right to try to free himself through sexual intercourse with other women. But it is not other women who then seem to be the new "reality" with which his soul is fused. It is the world. "The highest of all was to melt out into the darkness and sway there, identified with the great Being," Paul feels after intercourse with Miriam. And as for intercourse with Clara: "They had met and included in their meeting the thrust of the manifold grass stems, the cry of the peewit, the wheel of the stars." Together they "know the tremendous living food which carried them always, gave them rest within themselves." So Clara has reason to complain that she is not really there for Paul. None of Lawrence's heroes ever "really loves a woman." Though all passionate lovers, it is the Infinite that they love, "the great Being." They go to a woman as metal goes into a furnace, for a "melting out."

So it was that, seeking to escape his "circle" with his mother through sexual relations, Lawrence found himself in a still greater circle, a circle as large as the world. Trying to leave the filial circle through eroticism, he only expanded and eroticized it. Sex with its tendency to dissolve the ego, to merge the mind with the blood, freed him from any limited personal attachment and, in the words of his letter to Mrs. Taylor, distributed his "consciousness far abroad." In sexual intercourse Lawrence seems to have found himself, not really free from his mother, but precisely where his relation with her had always put him—at the heart of "Understanding." As if by a homing instinct, his body found its way at last, without conscious guilt, into that "peculiar fusion" that his soul had so long enjoyed. And so it was that Lawrence became the messiah of sexual intercourse, of a "wholeness" known only in the blood.

What sexual congress brought into view for Lawrence was not a bodiless realm of the soul but precisely the world as the body of the soul: the world as the tremendous living flood that gives the soul rest within itself. In such a *founded* carnal creation, where matter is so necessary to spirit, the body became as real to Lawrence as the soul—as centreed and as luminously radiant. And not only did the expanded circle of the soul make room for the body; it was dependent upon the body, which served as its eye or, better, as the hand that felt it. So it was that the long-estranged sensual and spiritual currents in Lawrence finally flowed together.

In sexual intercourse, he became whole. At the same instant, he merged with the Whole. Hence the apparent contradiction in Lawrence's later insistence on being "single" and "integral" and, on the other hand, on "melting out." For Lawrence, at least in sexual congress, these two states were one.

Why does Lawrence not make more of this "solution" to his problem in *Sons and Lovers?* The reason, I think, is that he is not yet conscious of it as one. When he was to become conscious of it, he would make more of it than it could easily bear. He would generalize it as a solution for the miseries of all men. And he would pretend or hope that it would yield a more lasting satisfaction than it could, dependent as it was upon passing physical sensation.

But meanwhile he merely accepts it as a datum of his experience; he "makes" nothing of it. He enjoys it as a solution before he recognizes it as one. Hence the total absence of surprise in his hero Paul, who suddenly finds himself, in sexual congress, in the midst of a "great Being" without the least sign of astonishment. It is as if he were simply entering his own living room. And, indeed, with Lawrence was this not in a sense the case? The large circle of the great Being is, after all, identical in essence with the filial one; however far the first reaches out to the stars, a Nottinghamshire parlor once accommodated it. The attributes that (according to Mircea Eliade) distinguish the sacred—namely power, reality, being, the founded, and permanence—were, for Lawrence, common to both his mother and the great Being. Lawrence was to be "born" from each, loved by each, kept by each, and his soul was to turn back to find its source in each. Sexual intercourse thus awakened in him only a familiar intuition. So it is that the bud of the Absolute opens in *Sons and Lovers* without surprise or remark.

If Lawrence's bond with his mother was in one sense inescapable, in another it merely prepared the way for what was to become the great bond of his life and the great theme of his work: his sympathy with the world. The metaphysic so casually cast up in *Sons and* Lovers will be elaborated and become all-pervading in the books to follow. On the other hand, the oedipal dilemma as such will simply disappear, a "solution" to it having been found.

Perhaps only in one way did Lawrence's memory of his mother colour the concept of being that otherwise became detached from her. Whenever her death, his own isolation, struck him afresh, his sense of Being was invaded by shadow: the "night" then became more an invitation to death than an assurance that his mother held him up even from there. His notion of Being was thus to oscillate between activity and stillness, flaming life and shadowy death. Now it was a "tremendous living flood"; now the place to enter a "death sleep." As Lawrence said in his poem "At a Loose End," his mother's death threw "a shadow inviolate" into his own "flame of living." When the flame was low, the shadow loomed forth and became the night.

Even apart from this morbid element, Lawrence's erotic experience of Being was never to prove a true redemption. His intuition of a universal life perhaps stitched and sustained him but, as was suggested, could not satisfy him. If it afforded deep security and peace, it did so only on occasion; there was always the need to begin the quest again. Hence the restlessness, the repeated "rebirths," in Lawrence's heroes and heroines.

"Being," after all, does not make a satisfactory lover; hard to find, it is still harder to hold on to. Lawrence liked to believe that mysticism could be a permanent state of the soul; but judging from his protagonists, Lawrence must often have found himself waiting, like an empty vessel, to be filled.

Regardless of this, Lawrence's feeling that a "great Being" supported his body and soul was one of the strongest ever to give birth to art. And what rich observation, what passionate conceptions, it sponsored. It is impossible altogether to regret the controlling role of mystical intuition in Lawrence's books. And all the more is this so when one realises that, far from being an intellectual construction, it was the mainspring of his being: the one thing that gave him the mission to write and the one thing besides that permitted him to be whole.

D.H. Lawrence's Narrators, sources of knowledge, and the Problem of Coherence

Readers of D. H. Lawrence have long been intrigued by the quality and texture of his prose. Its complex fragmentation has elicited widespread comment; its linguistic challenges are critical commonplaces. As part of what remains to be done, I want to examine Lawrence's use of fictional narrators and to focus on two related problems that it creates: the problem of coherence and, below that, the problem of the text's sources of knowledge. Analysis of Lawrence's narrators reveals that problems of coherence can be traced to his use of various narrative voices, and that these various voices depend on assumptions about his sources of knowledge which require careful scrutiny.

My aim is to look across the wide span of Lawrence's fiction; to identify a line of technical development; to situate that line within the context of published criticism, both theoretical and practical, occasionally challenging received critical views; and, finally, as I reconsider some central passages in the Lawrence canon, to reach fresh conclusions about narrative coherence, sources of knowledge, and Lawrence's narrators.

This cluster of concepts has attracted extensive commentary, most of it designed to help readers understand Lawrence's characters and themes. Such understanding is not my purpose. Whereas Keith Sagar, Mark Spilka, and Stephen Miko regard Lawrence's narrators as vehicles of information or interpretation rather than as difficult constructs in the text, contemporary critics have located the sources of Lawrence's imaginative power in his highly developed intuitive and sensory equipment, in his adaptation of the carnivalesque, or in his ability to "transcended" experience, and they have derived his conception of knowledge from biblical typology, from Romantic poetry, or from Aestheticism.

Diane Bonds understands this cluster of concepts as a narratological problem: but her deconstructive insights, though penetrating, are confined to the subversive features of Lawrence's texts. The philosophical and narratological connections between narrators, knowledge, and coherence remain therefore to be defined. I anticipate that some of my distinctions may help to refine a critical method—rhetorical in origin, comparative in application—for negotiating the vexingly difficult bond between narrator and character.

Two related issues require at least preliminary comment. First, the notion of coherence as an aesthetic aim was beginning to be challenged by many early-Modernist writers. Marcel Proust, for example, analyzing Ruskin's criticism, wrote: "Apparently he moves at random from one idea to the next. But in truth the imagination which guides him follows his deepest inclinations, which impose on him a superior logic in spite of himself—so much so that, at the end, he finds he has obeyed a hidden plan which, when it is finally unveiled, imposes in retrospect a kind of order on the whole." Such deeper patterns of coherence, lying below the level of conscious planning or structuring, reveal the structural components of intuition as they manifest themselves in narrative choices.

Second, the concept of knowledge needs to be defined in a philosophical context. Whereas Conrad despairs at the loss of an underlying unity that would illuminate daily life, and whereas Woolf relies heavily on immediate sensory experience, Lawrence glimpses something beyond the mind that knowledge cannot reveal but that intuition-residing in the blood, "where we have our strongest self-knowledge" can. Whereas Kant views experience as already created "by the 'intuitions' of time and space... and known by no other means than those it names," Patrick Whiteley writes: "Lawrence rejoices that the lens [of unity] is shattered; he embraces the chaos that Western civilization wants to bring under its idea of order. For Lawrence, to be one with this darkness that grounds human existence is to turn the mind away from itself and back toward the body from which the mind arose before it became conscious of itself."

For Lawrence mind and body ought ideally to form a monistic whole. "But why do you persist in separating soul and body?" he demanded of Rachel Annand Taylor (26 October 1910). "I can't tell... one from the other." Yet that condition of wholeness can occur only when the mind can no longer inspect itself, and can no longer distinguish between imagination and knowledge.

That this condition is rarely achieved generates a kind of narrative shock. Lawrence's narrators, inveighing more and more against their society, "voice the conscience of the individual trapped in a morally corrupt society," thereby defining the implied relationship between a narrator and the characters about whom he writes. But the notion of giving conscience a "voice" begs the question of how a particular narrator discovers this moral-political content within each character-and of how the mode of discovery changes in successive literary works.

In Lawrence's early fiction the lack of coherence among sources of knowledge within the text fosters narrative instability. The White Peacock, published in 1911 when Lawrence was only twenty five, and Sons and Lovers, published two years later, illustrate his early difficulties with narrative control. In The White Peacock the narrator Cyril wavers between involvement and distance, between sensuousness and physical restraint. Notice the final sentence of the following passage from chapter five, where I have clarified the narrator's focalization by employing italics to indicate what Lawrence might have written: We moved across to the standing corn. The sun being mild, [I noticed that] George had thrown off his hat, and [that] his Black hair was moist and twisted into confused half-curls.

Firmly planted, he swung with a beautiful rhythm from the Waist. On the hip of his belted breeches hung the scythestone; his shirt, faded almost white, was torn just above the belt, and showed the muscles of his back playing like lights upon the white sand of a brook. There was something exceedingly attractive in the rhythmic body [To me his rhythmic body seemed exceedingly attractive].

Delight in the rhythmic sensuousness of work jostles against the narrator's attempt to efface his own pleasure. Like the tear in George's faded shirt, the passage opens inward toward discovery and visual stimulation. In the text knowledge enters through the eyes until the last sentence. There the narrator's indirection muffles the lure of male musculature, which is displaced from observation to meditation. A comparison of Connie Chatterley's visual apprehension of Mellor's, half naked at his wash-basin, nicely distinguishes her visual and emotional "shock" from Cyril's shift in perspective.

Later, when George and Lettie sit down in the forest, the narrator records the hum of bees and concludes: "The sight of their clinging, clambering riot gave satisfaction to the soul". Whose soul? Two perspectives-that of the characters and that of the narrator-appeal for attention. The narrator does not yet know where to position himself so that he can plumb and then record depths of emotional experience. That skill will come as Lawrence develops a more expressive authorial voice.

In the meantime the loss of his mother, who was "strong and steadfast" but also "rather scornful" affected Lawrence profoundly. Seeking to recover her presence vicariously, he introduced into his prose a fresh voice of judgment which had not been present in The Trespasser, the novel he drafted shortly before she died in 1910. The effect is curious. Lawrence introduced into Sons and Lovers the fresh technical problem of unifying judgment with narrative flow. To clarify the change, I compare two passages, one that I have recast in order to eliminate disruption, the other Lawrence's original, which reveals several fractures worth observing: first, the tenses would tee feeling and would reach out shift incoherently to felt and was; second, the incoherent time signal soon, which reflects a continuing action, requires a modal verb; and third, in the words "Both felt," the focalization of the final sentences shifts to Walter and Gertrude Morel as a couple. Here are the two versions, their differences italicized:

Recast

And Morel sitting there, quite alone, having nothing to think about, felt vaguely uncomfortable. At such times his soul reached out in its blind way to her and found her gone. Then he felt a sort of emptiness, almost like a vacuum in his soul. He appeared unsettled and restless, and, feeling oppressed in that atmosphere, he affected his wife. Both felt an oppression on their breathing, when they were left together for some time.

Then he went to bed, and she settled down to enjoy herself alone, working, thinking, and living. And Morel sitting there, quite alone, having nothing to think about, would be feeling vaguely uncomfortable. His soul would reach out in its blind way to her, and find her gone. He felt a sort of emptiness, almost like a vacuum in his soul. He was unsettled and restless. Soon he could not live in that atmosphere, and he affected her. Both felt an oppression on their breathing, when they were left together for some time. But once he had gone to bed, she could settle down to enjoy her alone, working, thinking, and living.

Apart from the way Lawrence perfectly frames the passage within the word "alone," the instability of perception (tenses, focalization) suggests that in 1913 Lawrence's sources of knowledge were diffuse or unreliable. Struggling to represent the soul's knowledge, Lawrence encounters a series of disruptions. The most interesting is the subtle way the narrator slants the words "having nothing to think about" and "His soul would reach out in its blind way" (my emphasis); the narrator's words reflect not his own voice but embody Mrs. Morel's criticism of her husband. This confirms Carol Sklenicka's point that "the perspective of Gertrude Morel governs much of the novel."

Later, when Paul and Miriam are alone, reeling in the moonlight, Lawrence writes a passage in which two forms of disruption appear:

He turned and looked at her. She stood beside him, for ever in shadow. Her face, covered with the darkness of her hat, was watching him unseen. But she was brooding. She was slightly afraid—deeply moved and religious. That was her best state. He was impotent against it. His blood was concentrated like a flame in his chest. But he could not get across to her. There were flashes in his blood. But somehow she ignored them. She was expecting some religious state in him.

Still yearning, she was half aware of his passion, and gazed at him, troubled.

This is characteristic Lawrentian writing, the flow of emotional responses initiated by a verbal stimulus; but its fractured focalization is notable. First, the choice of linking verbs—was or were occurs nine times—shows that the passage's perspective is disrupted from inner revelation to outer observation, as in the choice of "There were flashes in his blood" over the more interior "Flashes stirred his blood."

The passage, sometimes angled unexpectedly toward objective rather than subjective forms of experience and knowledge, wavers. Second, the exterior judgment at the centre—"That was her best state"—derives from an omniscient external voice that disrupts the passage's flow, so that the passage seems to stutter. The unit of blood-and-blockage created by "His blood was concentrated like a flame in his chest. But he could not get across to her" has immediately to be repeated (in paraphrase) as "There were flashes in his blood. But somehow she ignored them" (my italics). Such disruptions can be interestingly linked to similar disruptions of narrative presentation in E. M. Forster's A Passage to India, but in 1913 Lawrence was still experimenting with narrative perspectives, not yet having found a voice that, when mastered, was uniquely his.

Early in The Rainbow (1915), when Tom and Lydia Brangwen attempt to reestablish their emotional connection, the narrator confronts the problem of depicting Tom metamorphosed into a new self while showing how awareness of change is thrust upon him, beyond his own power. I want to illustrate Lawrence's new control of language and coherence by examining a brief passage—first in my recast form—in order to separate my "active" from Lawrence's necessarily "passive" appraisal of Tom's change. (Italics distinguish the two forms.)

Recast

He felt as if a daze had come over his mind, as if he had another centre of consciousness. Another activity had started somewhere in his body-in his breast or in his bowels. He felt as if a strong light were burning there, as if he was blind within it, unable to know anything, except that this t transfiguration burned between him and her, connecting them, like a secret power.

Since she had come to the house he had gone about in a daze....

D. H. Lawrence

A daze had come over his mind; he had another centre of consciousness. In his breast, or in his bowels, somewhere in his body, there had started another activity. It was as if a strong light were burning there, and he was blind within it, unable to know anything, except that this transfiguration burned between him and her, connecting them, like a secret power.

Since she had come to the house he went about in a daze, scarcely seeing even the things he handled, drifting, quiescent, in a state of metamorphosis. He submitted to that which was happening to him, letting go of his will, suffering the loss of himself, dormant always on the brink of ecstasy, like a creature evolving to a new birth.

Two points are worth making about this pair of passages. First, the kind of disruption evident in Lawrence's earlier work has largely disappeared. His technical grasp is more exact and mature: narrative knowledge (i.e., what is knowable for the reader) is restricted to Tom's emotions as understood by the narrator and as expressed in the narrator's lyrical phrases. Second, the implicit moral system of the novel has been transferred from omniscient statements in Sons and Lovers like "That was her best state" to images and analogies that encode the implied author's views.

For instance, in the sentence that begins, "It was as if a strong light were burning there," the strong light represents less clearly Tom's analogy than the narrator's and beyond it a reader can infer that feelings converted into analogies are implicitly admired and, for the narrator, are also a kind of "letting go of his will" and a waiting "on the brink"—not of emotional "ecstasy" (as for Tom) but of artistic ecstasy. That ecstasy leads the narrator to discover an interpretive system that only appears to be within Tom's focalization. It is of course outside, used often to explore the psyches of other characters. And as these analogies and images gradually acquire an evaluative function in each text, they also require us, in consequence, to distinguish the central ways in which critics like me can talk about the bond between narrator and character.

Here, Tom and the narrator share what I call a second-degree bond, in which both character and narrator draw from similar sources of knowledge but use different linguistic idioms. The "as if" structure is a doorway to a complementary idiom: what Paul Hernadi calls "substitution narration"—by which he means "the narrator's sympathetic substitution of his own words for [his character's] thoughts and feelings"—and what Roy Pascal calls "dual voice."

A more pointed example of this kind of narratorial bonding occurs in the novel's second generation, when Anna and Will resist each other, she crying, he accusing:

> "What are you crying for?" came the question again, in just the same tone. And still there was silence, with only the sniff of her tears.
>
> His eyes glittered, and as if with malignant desire. She shrank and became blind. She was like a bird being beaten down. A sort of swoon of helplessness came over her. She was of another order than he, she had no defence against him. Against such an influence, she was only vulnerable, she was given up.

The sentence about Will's eyes holds special critical interest. Recast within Anna's focalization (as Lawrence might readily have done), the sentence would read: "To her his eyes glittered with malignant desire." The result? The rewritten sentence improves the passage's coherence since, as originally written, the words are the narrator's: it is he, not Anna, who interprets the glitter of Will's eyes, which is viewed from outside Will's consciousness (hence as if with malignant desire).

Since at this juncture the narrator does not offer certainty, he only records his own intuitive impression. Yet that impression, because it is followed by "She shrank and became blind," becomes implicitly part of Anna's focalization. Hence the incoherence. Gerald Prince says that "incoherent commentaries expressed by the narrating voice... cast doubt on the interpretive powers of the narrator." A more useful way to view what Lawrence achieves is to see incoherence as part of the interpretation of the text—to see incoherence as a reflection of the idea that a character's conscience is trapped within a morally corrupt society. Ideologically, incoherence becomes the technical counterpart of entrapment.

Moreover, it is worth saying that the "as if" structure, by now a Lawrentian heuristic, becomes a central functioning unit of his imagination. It is a rhetorical device for regauging and reformulating what a character like Will expresses or what a character like Anna feels—not just more vividly, but in ways that offer clarification and illumination for the novel's readers. In passages of Free Indirect Style, each "as if" structure, simile, or metaphor generates a fresh layer of interpretive understanding—always at an angle to the character's focalization, forming usually a second-degree bond.

For example, after Paul Morel looks into Miriam's eyes, these words follow: "He turned aside, as if pained", where the "as if" changes the focalization from Paul to the narrator. And the sentence above, "She was like a bird being beaten down," which uses the narrator's simile, helps to form an interpretive layer that eventually opens a window onto the implied author's value system, which in Lawrence's fiction has often been difficult to assess. It is therefore too reductive to say about Lawrence's fiction that "the character and narrator together struggle for a language-in which to express their realizations." Rarely do they struggle for, or in, the same language. A more precise and discriminating critical vocabulary are needed.

To move in that direction invites a pointed question about Lawrence's work: what happens when he approaches the borders of language function? What happens when he transcends the old language that, as Virginia Woolf put it reveals "gig-lamps symmetrically arranged" and, instead, discovers the "luminous halo" of subjective experience. Scott Sanders is surely right to say that Lawrence "forced his characters through the medium of words to the boundaries of language, beyond which they could sense powers and orders of being which neither he nor they could name."

In The Rainbow Lawrence, apart from experimenting with the angle of bonding between narrator and character, has—like Woolf or Proust—determined to reveal fresh layers of the dark unknown of intuition and instinct. That much is widely agreed. What is not is Lawrence's peculiar use of heuristics—conceptual heuristics—to explore a topos of darkness that exists beyond and beneath the light of nineteenth-century rationalism.

In the splendid passage that follows, Lawrence responds to the problem of coherence by using binary form as the heuristic to explore dialectical forces. As he experiments with angles of bonding, he accumulates increments caught in a widening narrative net. Ursula's knowledge and idiom yield gradually to the narrator's without, however, reaching full separation.

The two opening paragraphs reveal the narrator's presence (angle) in what Stefan Oltean calls a "highly articulated rendering of the [girl's] internal states." The third paragraph modulates to the narrator's record—so assured as to be quoted—of the alien group's defensive certainty, not as Ursula might imagine it but as the narrator does: yet that record still falls, because of the narrator's extreme empathy, within the range of Ursula's intuitive awareness. The final paragraph, in which opposed forces join, is articulated entirely in the narrator's distinct idiom and barely sustains Ursula's awareness.

That which she was, positively, was dark and unrevealed, it could not come forth. It was like a seed buried in dry ash [of disiilusion and falsity]. This world in which she [Ursula Brangwen] lived was like a circle lighted by a lamp. This lighted area, lit up by man's completes consciousness, she thought was the entire world: that here all was disclosed for ever.

Yet all the time, within the darkness, she had been aware of points of light, like the eyes of wild beasts, gleaming, penetrating, vanishing. And her soul had acknowledged in a great heave of terror only the outer darkness. This inner circle of light in which she lived and moved, wherein the trains rushed and the factories ground out their machine-produce and the plants and the animals worked by the light of science and knowledge, suddenly it seemed like the area under an arc-lamp, wherein the moths and children played in the security of blinding light, not even knowing there was any darkness, because they stayed in the light.

> But she could see the glimmer of dark movement just out of range, she saw the eyes of the wild beast gleaming from the darkness, watching the vanity of the camp fire and the sleepers; she felt the strange, foolish vanity of the camp, which said "Beyond our light and our order there is nothing?"

> turning their faces always inward towards the sinking fire of illuminating consciousness, which comprised sun and stars, and the Creator, and the System of Righteousness, ignoring always the vast darkness that wheeled round about, with half-revealed shapes lurking on the edge.

The dialectic between character and narrator, darkness and light, angel and beast culminates in a synthesis where opposed forces finally impinge on each other. The opening "Yea" signals an ironic register beyond Ursula's idiom:

> Yea, and no man dared even throw a firebrand into the darkness. For if he did, he was jeered to death by the others, who cried "Fool, anti-social knave, why would you disturb us? with bogeys? There is no darkness. We move and live and have our being within the light, and unto us is given the eternal light of knowledge, we comprise and comprehend the innermost core and issue of knowledge. Fool and knave, how dare you belittle us with the darkness?"

> Nevertheless the darkness wheeled round about, with grey shadow-shapes of wild beasts, and also with dark shadow-shapes of the angels, whom the light fenced out, as it fenced out the more familiar beasts of darkness. And some [in the camp], having for a moment seen the darkness, saw it bristling with the tufts of the hyena and the wolf; and some, having given up their vanity of the light, having died in their own conceit, saw the gleam in the eyes of the wolf and the hyena, that it was the flash of the sword of angels, flashing at the door to come in, that the angels in the darkness were lordly and terrible and not to be denied, like the flash of fangs.

About this passage—a favourite of critics—two matters require comment. First, the focalization is again curious, modulating outward in circles. It progresses from the narrator's description of Ursula acknowledging "the outer darkness" in paragraph 1; to Ursula's consciousness as it is increasingly revealed in the narrator's idiom (e.g., "System of Righteousness"); to the narrator's commentary, in biblical style, quoting the smug creatures who assume that "the eternal light of knowledge" shines on them alone; and finally to a focalization in which the narrator continues to limit himself to the symbols of the unconscious that populate Ursula's consciousness but emphatically uses his own language.

In a motion circling outward, the narrator strives to extend Ursula's perception, privileging his extension rhetorically, empowering it with the weight of authority, and, most important, participating vitally in her discovery of the depths of darkness. The narrator goes well beyond his normal function, in earlier works, of supplying metaphors; he is now a fresh source of knowledge about the subconscious and its mysterious connections, through the gleaming eyes of light, to the conscious sphere.

It is insufficient to say that "Ursula must get to know the familiar beasts of darkness better." Ursula intuits, but the narrator contextualizes. She responds to sensory and paresensory data; he penetrates it critically. She ascends, but he illuminates. This distance between internal and external focalization is wider than usually assumed—closer to Conrad than to Joyce.

It seems very likely that in composing The Trespasser (1912) and Sons and Lovers (1913) Lawrence found a niche of new perception when he discovered first that Sigmund and Helena, lying on the beach, comprise "two grains of life in the vast movement" of oceans, clouds, and circling spheres and then, with rapidly developing insight, that Paul and Clara, after making love, had pierced the known in order to discover "life wild at the source" where, dwarfed by a "magnificent power," they comprise "only grains in the tremendous heave". The known prefigures the light of the campfire, the darkness plumbing an order below language, below perception, below even consciousness. This order is articulated with great difficulty, it may invite disruption, and it may require the narrator's direct intervention. The "vastness" and "tremendousness" are overwhelming—to the characters, whose instinctual response is awe, and to the narrator, who must struggle both to open categories of perception and to negotiate rhetorical modes of expression.

Second—apart from the passage's focalization—its impressive coherence is, after all, disturbed in paragraphs three and four by the biblical voice, with its lordly repetitions and its "unto us is given." That voice, although it arguably extends Ursula's critique of the "Sunday" system of thought in chapter ten, nevertheless substitutes a rhetorical mode for the discovery of new knowledge which the passage centrally explores. The difficulty is real. Instead of discovering the function of the vital animal eyes as they connect light/consciousness and dark/unconsciousness, the narrator's heuristic of a three-part spatial model (i.e. light and dark, with eyes between) is skewed: it "discovers" rhetoric of revelation and apocalypse in "the flash of fangs" and "the flash of the sword of angels." One cannot deny the grandeur of such language, nor the differences between it and the categorical absolutes of the Sunday system; but one can say that Lawrence, by drawing on a known rather than a partially unknown language system, compromises the deeper search for conduits of exchange between conscious and unconscious regions.

That deeper search, however, is only delayed. Near the end of The Rainbow—while the horses thunder near Ursula, impinging on her psyche—the gleaming points of animal eyes emerge, activated now, given clearer shape and sharper function, successfully mediating between Ursula's conscious and unconscious minds. In such writing Lawrence brilliantly captures the space between the two minds: it is a space full of dynamic activity, like atoms leaping in a chemical transaction. In the horses scene Ursula's new knowledge of herself derives not from the chafing of one rhetorical code against another but from the interplay of her conscious and her unconscious selves. Here, Lawrence fully controls his sources of knowledge, making them function both technically and thematically.

There is another approach to the conjunction of sources of knowledge and narrative coherence in Lawrence's work. In a later passage from The Rainbow, which follows Ursula and her lover Anton Skrebensky to the ocean's edge, I differentiate between the passage I have recast and the passage Lawrence wrote in order to show both the divided focalization and the problem it entails within this mixed perspective:

Then there, in the great flare of light, she clinched hold of him, hard, as if suddenly her had the strength of destruction, she fastened her arms round him and tightened him in her grip, whilst her mouth sought his in a hard, rending, ever-increasing kiss, till she felt that his body was powerless in her grip; his heart seemed to melt in fear from her fierce, beaked, harpy's kiss. She pressed in her mouth as if it were a beak, till she seemed to have the heart of him. She took no notice as the water washed again over their feet; she seemed unaware.

D. H. Lawrence

Then there, in the great flare of light, she clinched hold of him, hard, as if suddenly she had the strength of destruction, she fastened her arms round him and tightened him in her grip, whilst her mouth sought his in a hard, rending, ever-increasing kiss, kill his body was powerless in her grip, his heart melted in fear from the fierce, beaked, harpy's kiss. The water washed again over their feet, but she took no notice. She seemed unaware, she seemed to be pressing in her beaked mouth, kill she had the heart of him.

Accounting critically for the differences between these two passages will illuminate Lawrence's narrative method, whose complexity can be daunting. A comparison yields several things. By positioning last the sentence beginning "She took no notice," the recast passage improves coherence because Ursula's distant awareness now follows her instinctual destruction of Skrebensky's spirit: but what one loses is Lawrence's odd rhythm that places a pause before the thrust of Ursula's beaked mouth. It is not an issue of "stylistic failure," as Graham Hough asserts. That pause, really a shift in perspective, is a useful reminder of the disruptive force that helps to map Lawrence's earlier work. In Lawrence's text the perspective modulates from the certainty of "his body was powerless" and "his heart melted," to the focally uncommitted "The water washed again over their feet," then to the narrator's impression of a gouging beak which is recorded by a narrator who watches Ursula but also understands the significance of her act. The area between the dietetic and mimetic poles of discourse, between "narrator" and "reflector," is especially striking.

Of broader concern, a comparison of passages shows Lawrence's narrator employing (as before) both his own language and Ursula's as conduits for impressions sent from her subconscious realm. That sort of discovery, typical of Modernism, is an immense narrative resource. Already the narrator knows that Skrebensky's "heart melted," that the water "washed again over their feet," that Ursula's mouth was "beaked": whereas these perceptions, recast wholly within Ursula's focalization, become subjective, known only to Ursula—as in "his heart seemed to melt," "She took no notice as the water washed again over their feet," her mouth seemed like a beak. As rewritten, Ursula's psychic rape of Skrebensky is imagined rather than witnessed; it is communicated to the reader unmediated rather than documented by the narrator. When Lawrence's narrator, like Forster's, assumes multiple locations within a single paragraph, the reader learns to accept the oscillation as part of the technical liquidity that Modernist writing invents.

Most of the critical commentary on this well-known passage grapples with Ursula's aggression and Skrebensky's victimization, as if the lovers, inverted, were Tess and Alec d'Urberville, his aggressive coarseness violating her "feminine tissue, sensitive as gossamer." But what an interesting difference between the couples. Hardy's judging, moralizing voice ("the coarse appropriates the finer") is muted. Lawrence's narrator never asks, What is the moral scheme toward which a reader can be led? but rather, What does this character experience, deep inside, in a region of darkness or chaos, that can be communicated to a reader? And at what angle of bonding? Knowledge depends on narrative position. If the narrator shifts his location—steps outside the region of darkness to look at the characters and their physical surroundings, tries to watch and to feel with them—then incoherence may result, as in "The water washed again over their feet, but she took no notice."

For Lawrence the problem of focalization is always the problem of when to shift from inside to outside. It is as if the narrator's sources of knowledge recurrently dry up—or are shut off, or blocked—so that a visual default quickly fills in the space. Intuition is unstable, like the flash of fangs. Without inspiration or strict control, intuition—lapsing—allows a small narrative fissure to open. This is not a criticism of Lawrence's genius but an attempt to define the distinction of his technical resources and the uniqueness of his imagination.

As Lawrence's imagination operates more capaciously and begins more subtly to integrate forms of disruption, a major realignment takes place. The angle of bonding between narrator and character gradually shifts from a similarity of perspective to a dissimilarity of perspective. This central shift characterizes Lawrence's work of the Twenties, but has its source in the later parts of Women in Love (1920), where the realignment of the narrator's sympathy is especially marked. I want to conclude my discussion of knowledge and coherence—and Lawrence's increasingly complex uses of them—by examining passages from his final decade that probe the minds of Gurdon Brangwen and then Oliver Mellor's. Both passages illustrate how, he sense of profound disruption remains but are now increasingly mastered, so that disruption is masked by the poise and authority of an assured narrative voice.

Readers of Women in Love always notice the subtle evolution of Gurdon's character from the narrator's cautious appreciation to his cold skepticism. But critical junctures along this path have been harder to isolate. A passage about Gurdon, which is both artistically accomplished and puzzlingly focalized, holds particular interest because of its subtle "rupture." Charles Ross seconds F. R. Leavis's notion that the organization of Women in Love "is so rich and close" that there is "not a scene, episode, image or touch but forwards the organized development of the themes."

In a sweeping sense surely that is true. But in individual passages one is often surprised to find not lapses or flaws, nor even contradictions, but curious shifts (even dissonances) that reveal a counterforce through which some deeper structure can emerge. It is as if what Lawrence wrote about Etruscan art were also true of his own prose, with "one thing springing from another, things mentally contradictory fusing together emotionally." These shifts need analysis.

In the passage below, the differences are instructive between what Lawrence wrote and what he might have written if he had focalized the passage to separate more fully Gurdon's mind from the narrator's. As Gurdon, awake and "destroyed into perfect consciousness," lay motionless, her "wide eyes staring... into the darkness," Gerald lay asleep with his arms encircling her. The recast passage transfers the brooding depths of revelation to Gurdon but cannot accommodate the narrator's central question:

Recast

As she lay, she seemed to hear waves breaking on a hidden shore, long, slow, gloomy waves breaking with the rhythm of fate, so monotonously that to her it seemed eternal. This endless breaking of slow, sullen waves of fate held her like a possession, whilst she lay with dark, wide eyes looking into the darkness. It seemed she could see so far, as far as eternity—yet it was as if she saw nothing. She was suspended in perfect consciousness.

D. H. Lawrence

She seemed to lie hearing waves break on a hidden shore, long, slow, gloomy waves breaking with the rhythm of fate, so monotonously that it seemed eternal. This endless breaking of slow, sullen waves of fate held her like a possession, whilst she lay with dark, wide eyes looking into the darkness. She could see so far, as far as eternity—yet she saw nothing. She was suspended in perfect consciousness and of what was she conscious.

In Lawrence's final clause the narrator queries the reader but delays his answer (she was at last "conscious of everything") until the sentence that follows: "This mood of extremity, when she lay staring into eternity, utterly suspended, and conscious of everything, to the last limits, passed, and left her uneasy".

This is an immensely interesting passage. Its repetitions of wide eyes penetrating darkness—each repetition building on the previous one, extending it and enlarging it toward the extreme of "eternity"—illustrate Lawrence's rhetorical mastery. The passage is also interesting for the way the sequential motion across Gurdon's consciousness is interrupted. The reader, entering the dark recesses of Gurdon's subconscious mind, is given an impression ("She seemed to lie hearing waves") which is then glossed by the narrator (the waves break "with the rhythm of fate").

Then the sequential motion itself is broken—not by words like "yet it was as if she sawyer nothing" (which would sustain her seeming to hear waves breaking) but by the more forceful clause "yet she saw nothing." This clause offers a categorical judgment that the narrator infers from his own separate sources of knowledge. As if to increase the accumulating distance between character and reader, this clause is followed by a question aimed not at the character but at the reader: "and of what was she conscious?"

This is not a matter of self-interrogation. The question forces the reader out of Gurdon's focalization and into the narrator's, inviting an intimacy between reader and narrator that supplants the bond between character and narrator. The final summary sentence invites us to think critically about a character who earns our grudging interest and our uneasy respect. It is the kind of narrative stance that Thomas Mann adopts in Death in Venice.

This shift from character to reader constitutes a core feature of Lawrence's imagination. What he learned early—to transfer experience from mother to son in Sons and Lovers, from female to male in The Trespasser, and from male to female in The Rainbow's third generation—he continued to refine: valences shift according to his unstable focalization. The narrator's knowledge often depends on the distance between narrator and character, disruption signifying that the narrator's access to the character's psyche has been blocked, as the next passage demonstrates.

Once Oliver Mellor's finds himself involuntarily mated to Connie Chatterley, he ponders in chapter 10 the implications of their union, searching for ways to connect their personal and social spheres. To clarify the point I will make, I have repositioned three contiguous paragraphs from Lady Chatterley's Lover (1928), taking them up individually.

The opening paragraph offers a series of recognitions, all of them focalized within Mellor's mind and in his idiom, opening outward, lily-like, from understanding to wisdom. Notice that the middle sentences could all be prefaced by the words "He knew."

He went down again, into the darkness and seclusion of the wood. But he knew that the seclusion of the wood was illusory. The industrial noises broke the solitude, the sharp lights, though unseen, mocked it. A man could no longer be private and withdrawn. The world allows no hermits. And now he had taken the woman, and brought on himself a new cycle of pain and doom. For he knew by experience what it meant.

What Mellor's knows is extracted in his own sobre idiom: Dorrit Cohn calls this narrated monologue—"a character's mental discourse in the guise of the narrator's discourse." The burden of Mellor's experience cuts a "vertical" incision into the narrator's wider experience and superior ability to generalize, as in "The world allows no hermits," with its gnomic present tense and its assurance. This kind of narrated monologue Lawrence has practiced since about 1920, when his conception of audience began to change, and is refined in transitional works like Mr. Noon (completed 1921) and St. Mawr (1925), where the narrator's presence is pointedly visible.

Sustaining the outward progression of paragraph one, the next paragraph is shaped into a dialogue between Mellor's voice and the narrator's—but so subtly that a reader almost misses Lawrence's fused perspectives. Here, with annotations in capitals, is the paragraph:

He thought with infinite tenderness of the woman. Poor forlorn thing, she was nicer than she knew, and [Now the Narrator Adopts Briefly his Own Idiom] oh, so much too nice for the tough lot she was in-contact with! Poor thing, she too had some of the vulnerability of the wild hyacinths, she wasn't all tough rubber-goods-and-platinum, like the modern girl. And they would do her in! As sure as life, they would do her in, as they do in all naturally tender life.

Tender! Somewhere [The Narrator Reminds Mellors] she was tender, tender with a tenderness of the growing hyacinths, something that has gone out of the celluloid women of today. But [Again the Narrator's Idiom] he would protect her with his heart for a little while. For a little while, before the insentient iron world and the Mammon of mechanized greed did them both in, her as well as him.

This is richer than it appears. Dickensian in its rhetorical motion, the paragraph oscillates between soft and hard, heart and greed, flowers and iron—oppositions that nonetheless mirror the much more subtle dialogue between character and narrator. Take phrasing. Throughout the novel, Mellor's laconic speech, like March's in The Fox (1923), masks his sensitivity and warmth: but the phrases "oh, so much too nice" and "he would protect her with his heart" is part of the narrator's idiom, typically more colloquial and sentimental than Mellor's. In their dialogue of sensibilities Mellor's reaches inward, the narrator's reaches outward, enriching the keyboard registers of the character "inside" with darker and deeper tones.

This is the essence of Lawrence's later style—not juxtaposition, not a counterpoint, but a fusion of lighter and darker voices: horizontal and vertical textures at last merged coherently—"the upright through the horizontal," in the narrator's happy phrase. It is worth saying, with Graham Holderness, that Lawrence "has kept the rhetoric of his people," though certainly Lawrence transforms it by embracing banality as a dominant ironic tone.

The final paragraph (it is Lawrence's second) demands a special kind of attention, even tolerance, as the narrator first summarizes—then extracts a conclusion from—the two paragraphs that (in my rearrangement) preceded:

It was not woman's fault, nor even love's fault, nor the fault of sex.

The fault lay there, out there, in those evil electric lights and diabolical rattling of engines. There, in the world of the mechanical greedy, greedy mechanism and mechanized greed' sparkling with lights and gushing hot metal and roaring with traffic, there lay the vast evil thing, ready to destroy whatever did not conform. Soon it would destroy the wood, and the bluebells would spring no more. All vulnerable things must perish under the rolling and running of iron.

This paragraph, a climax to the sequence, edges outward from Mellor's voice into the narrator's. Repetition is more evident, and the language is more poetic than Mellor's, the diction crisper, the repugnance sharper, and the moral fervor more urgent. To call the passage's effect "horrifying," only exaggerates. The rhetoric of authority reflects a narrowing of moral purpose while the novel's depth of understanding widens. Critics who argue that Lawrence has lost control of his narrative, who for instance chastise his "uncritical identification with Mellor's," misunderstand the role that the narrator assumes.

The narrator chooses not to include what the narrator of version two (called John Thomas and Lady Jane) had included—namely, the direct series of Mellor's impressions introduced by the verb "seemed," as in: "The lights at Stacks Gate and at Tevershall seemed wickedly sparkling, and the blush of the furnaces, faint and rosy since the night was cloudless, seemed somehow aware.

A curious dread possessed him, a sense of defencelessness. Out there, beyond, there were all those white lights and the indefinable quick malevolence that lay in them." This is language that seeks what Lawrence, writing to Dorothy Brett, called "bottomless pools" (19 December 1926) —that which mines his character's psyche, penetrating vertically, "going way down into yourself, down till you really feel [what] would be right" (V, 632; letter to Gertrude Cooper, 23 January 1927).

The narrator takes the phrase "Out there"—common to both versions—and reconfigures the double exchange of sights "out there" and their effect on Mellor's, to a quite different exchange of sights within the narrator's horizontally encompassing sweep ("vast evil thing," "All vulnerable things"), which suppresses Mellor's feelings in order to display the narrator's. As Cohn remarks, "the more conspicuous and idiosyncratic the narrator, the less apt he is to reveal the depth of his characters' psyches".

This edging outward of narratorial discourse extends the larger ethic of masculine control that hides the voices of dissonance; yet this dissonance inheres in all of the structural irregularities of the late work.

Earlier, in the case of Ursula, the narrator allows a visual default to help him shape a scene; in the case of Gurdon, two perspectives join to form an assessment; in the case of Mellor's, the narrator's poetry of anger draws on neither Mellor's idiom nor his sources of knowledge but in narrated monologue deliberately returns to the apocalyptic mode of The Rainbow, divested now of biblical rhetoric.

When one stops to consider in what other "interior" forms-Lawrence might have expressed this final paragraph—psycho-narration (the narrator's discourse about a character's consciousness) or quoted interior monologue—these alternative forms prohibit the drive toward certainty that the narrator's own voice must project in order for the balance of voices coherently to reflect—and to reinscribe—the novel's confident architectural oppositions of Wragby and wood, Clifford and Mellor's, insentience and sentience.

The search for knowledge in Lady Chatterley's Lover is not so much inward, into the psyche (as it was in Lawrence's middle works), but outward, into the culture that defines and constrains a character. What is especially worth saying is that the narrator participates in that constraint. In Lady Chatterley's Lover he does so by pushing the characters toward forms of knowledge that find closure, that chafe against the open forms toward which the characters, thinking about themselves, are regularly drawn-as, for instance, in Connie's awakening to her pregnancy (chapter 10), in the night of sensual passion (chapter 15), and in Mellor's final, embracing letter (chapter 19).

At the end of Lawrence's career the lack of connection that exists between a character and his culture (as that culture is defined by the narrator) shows up masked in passages like the one that begins, "It was not woman's fault." The disharmony passes almost unnoticed, yet it signals a conflict between a mode of discovery and a mode of certainty.

The problem is real at another level, too. Lawrence did not place the final paragraph last, but second. Such disruptions of coherence can be illustrated frequently in his later work. They subtly manifest Lawrence's well-known resistance to any form of social entrapment.

But at the end, coherence and knowledge are unexpectedly linked in Lawrence's work: the narrator's early judging voice runs like a vein through the rest of the prose; but at the heart of his later fiction, judgment impedes patient development, and rhetorical modes, although yielding brilliant explorations, suffer some incompatibility in purpose and effect. Psychic disruption remains an enduring feature of Lawrence's imagination; its implications for his art, which help to explain the change in quality after Women in Love, are only now being analysed.

If one may now generalize: recasting passages of a text to reveal their masked assumptions yields a sort of X-ray of an author's artistic motives. Recasting clarifies his choices, facilitates a fuller understanding of the narrator's complex stance, and allows readers more keenly to observe perceptual, conceptual, and artistic changes across the span of an author's work.

By locating the intersection of psychic disruption, sources of knowledge, and aesthetic coherence in the work of D. H. Lawrence, this critical method does two things more: it demonstrates the need for a conceptual terminology that will differentiate degrees of bonding between character and narrator, and it points to the study of Lawrence's contemporaries, where similar interpretive problems emerge as cultural values change.

Lawrence is poised to reveal this cultural moment, when assumptions about art and knowledge were undergoing ferment and revision, because his art, more clearly than that of his contemporaries, exhibits features that are both familiar from the Victorian novel and yet innovatively fresh. To study the properties of Lawrence's imagination is to index the cultural crisis of Modernism. I conclude, finally, that as these varied ruptures in focalization and coherence reflect the way the narrator's sources of knowledge "dry up" or shift or become striated with rhetorical excess, so also do they reflect the fragmentation endemic to Modernist culture. Indeed, this fragmentation is rein scribed into Lawrence's technical choices so seamlessly that readers have often missed seeing it.

Bibliography

Bloom, Harold, ed. Sons and Lovers. Modern Critical Interpretations. New York & Philadelphia: Chelsea House Publishers, 1988.

Bonds, Diane S. Language and the Self in D. H. Lawrence. Studies in Modern Literature, No. 68. Ann Arbor, MI: UMI Research Press, 1978; 1987.

Callow, Philip. Son and Lover: The Young D. H. Lawrence. New York: Stein and Day, 1975.

Chambers, Jessie. D. H. Lawrence: A Personal Record. Cambridge: Cambridge U. Press, 1935; 1980.

Clarke, Colin, ed. D. H. Lawrence: The Rainbow and Women in Love. London: Macmillan, 1969; 1978.

D. H. Lawrence: Sons and Lovers. A Casebook. London: Macmillan, 1969;1979.

Draper, R. P., ed. The Critical Heritage: D. H. Lawrence. London & New York: Routledge, 1970; 1977.

Ebbatson, Roger. Lawrence and the Nature Tradition: A Theme in English Fiction 1859-1914. Sussex: Harvester Press, 1980.

Farr, Judith, ed. Twentieth-century Interpretations of Sons and Lovers: A Collection of Critical Essays. Englewood Cliffs: NJ: Prentice-Hall, Inc., 1970.

Finney, Brian. Penguin Critical Studies: D. H. Lawrence: Sons and Lovers. London: Penguin Books, 1990.

Harvey, Geoffrey. Sons and Lovers: The Critics Debate Series. London: Macmillan, 1987.

Holderness, Graham. D. H. Lawrence: History, Ideology and Fiction . Dublin: Gill and Macmillan, 1982.

Ingram, Allan. The Language of D. H. Lawrence . London: Macmillan, 1990.

Kalnins, Mara, ed. D. H. Lawrence: Centenary Essays . Bristol: Bristol Classical Press, 1986.

Kelsey, Nigel. D. H. Lawrence: Sexual Crisis . London: Macmillan, 1991.

Lawrence, D. H. Mornings in Mexico. With an Introduction by Ross Parmenter. Salt Lake City: Gibbs M. Smith, Inc., 1982.

MacLeod, Sheila. Lawrence's Men and Women . London: Heinemann, 1985.

Messenger, Nigel. How to Study a D. H. Lawrence Novel. London: Macmillan, 1989.

Meyers, Jeffrey. D. H. Lawrence and Tradition. London: The Athlone Press, 1985.

Moore, Harry T. The Priest of Love: Celebrated Life of D. H. Lawrence. Rev. ed. Harmondsworth : Penguin Books, 1974, 1982.

Moynahan, Julian, ed. D. H. Lawrence: Sons and Lovers - Text, Background and Criticism. Harmondsworth & New York: Penguin, 1968; 1977.

Murfin, Ross C. Sons and Lovers: A Novel of Division and Desire. Twayne's Masterwork Studies No. 7. Boston: Twayne Publishers, 1987.

Niven, Alstair. D. H. Lawrence: The Novels . Cambridge: Cambridge U. Press, 1978.

Pinkney, Tony. D. H. Lawrence and Modernism. Iowa City: U of Iowa P, 1990.

Sagar, Keith, ed. A D. H. Lawrence Handbook Manchester : Manchester U. Press, 1982.

Saldago, Gamini. A Preface to Lawrence, Preface Books. London: Longman, 1982.